LEGENDARY LOCALS

OF

FOREST HILLS AND REGO PARK

NEW YORK

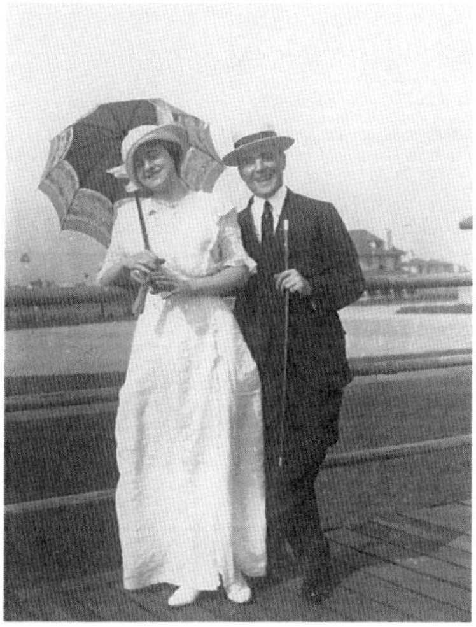

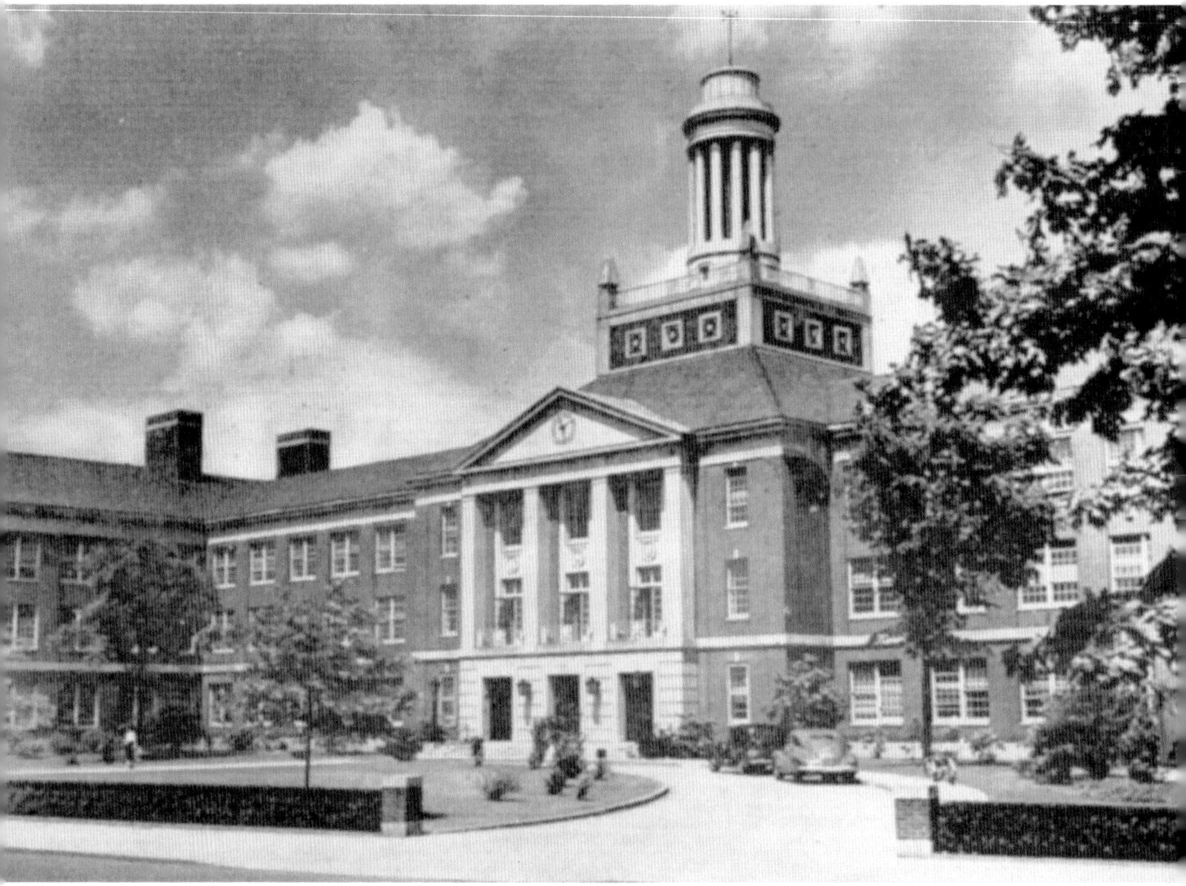

Forest Hills High School
Underneath its storied cupola, Forest Hills High School has shaped the careers of notables with its curriculum and extracurricular activities since 1941. (Author's collection.)

Page 1: Theobald Henry Engelhardt and his Wife, Louise, August 10, 1913
In the largely undeveloped Forest Hills of the 1930s, architect Theobald Henry Engelhardt designed some of the most elegant apartment houses in the Colonial style, situated on pristine landscapes. (Courtesy of Trudy and Bernie Smith.)

LEGENDARY LOCALS

OF

FOREST HILLS AND REGO PARK

NEW YORK

MICHAEL H. PERLMAN

FOREWORD BY JERRY SPRINGER

LEGENDARY LOCALS

ISBN 978-1-4671-0188-2

Legendary Locals is an imprint of Arcadia Publishing
Charleston, South Carolina

Printed in the United States of America

Library of Congress Control Number: 2014944107

For all general information, please contact Arcadia Publishing:
Telephone 843-853-2070
Fax 843-853-0044
E-mail sales@arcadiapublishing.com
For customer service and orders:
Toll-Free 1-888-313-2665

Visit us on the Internet at www.arcadiapublishing.com

Dedication
To my family, friends, and past, current, and future generations of the unique communities of Forest Hills and Rego Park, which I proudly call home.

On the Front Cover: Clockwise from top left:
Carol Channing, Broadway performer, singer, and actress (courtesy of Carol Channing Productions; see page 53), Alfred Kaskel and Philip Birnbaum, influential builder and architect duo (courtesy of Daniel Kaskel; see page 27), Bob Keeshan, children's television personality, known as Captain Kangaroo (author's collection; see page 67), Grosvenor Atterbury, principal architect of the Forest Hills Gardens (courtesy of Church-in-the-Gardens Community House; see page 17), Stevie Wonder, iconic soulful singer, songwriter, and multi-instrumentalist (courtesy of Tom Beetz; see page 60), Carroll O'Connor, actor known as Archie Bunker in *All In The Family* (courtesy of Queens Community Board 6; see page 78), Geraldine Anne Ferraro, triple-term Queens congresswoman (courtesy of Queens Community Board 6; see page 31), Burt Bacharach, legendary composer, singer, and pianist (courtesy of Olaf Heine; see page 52), Helen Keller, courageous lecturer, activist, and author who was blind and deaf (courtesy of the Hof family; see page 108).

On the Back Cover: From left to right:
Rego Construction Company, founders of Rego Park in 1923 (courtesy of Bruce Powell; see page 20), Cord Meyer Development Company, founders of Forest Hills in 1906 (courtesy of Cord Meyer Development Company; see page 15).

CONTENTS

FOREWORD

Forest Hills—It was an idyllic place to grow up. The 1950s: A sense of neighborhood and the American Dream. Friends lived in the same apartment building or on the same block. We went to school together, played in the school yard together, and rooted for the same teams together. We were all going to college, and my first job was working as a ball boy at the West Side Tennis Club for the US Tennis Championships. What was not to like? And Simon and Garfunkel were a year ahead of me at Forest Hills High School.

—Jerry Springer

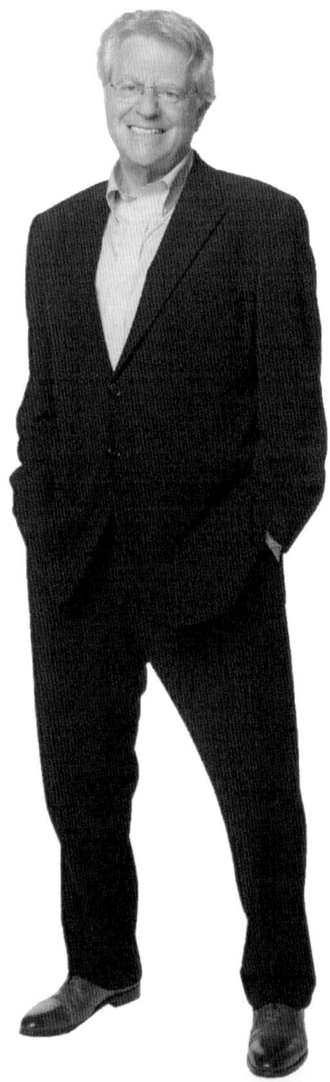

The Face behind *The Jerry Springer Show*
Legendary local Jerry Springer's career is marked with diverse achievements that span from television and radio personality, Broadway performer, movie actor, and country artist to Emmy Award–winning newscaster, lawyer, international emcee, and game show host. To uncover additional intriguing facts, visit page 50. (Photograph by Virginia Sherwood for NBC, courtesy of Jerry Springer.)

ACKNOWLEDGMENTS

I dedicate this book to my supportive parents, Linda and Sol Perlman of Forest Hills; to my relatives and friends; to past, current, and future generations of Forest Hills and Rego Park; to curious individuals who wish to explore both historic neighborhoods; to those who embrace the fine achievements that human nature can cultivate with dreams, willpower, and originality, which are complemented by my neighborhood's architecturally and culturally diverse breeding grounds; and most certainly my readers and the notables contained herein, among many more.

I would like to extend much gratitude to my late grandparents and great-grandparents, who once called Forest Hills home and contributed to my appreciation for culture and history, partially due to their European influences.

This book is dedicated in memory of a dear friend, Mildred "Millie" Press of Forest Hills, who I consider "adopted family" and who has been an inspiration since my childhood with her soulful and giving personality traits. She said she would be first in line to purchase my book, but passed away prior to its publication.

Additional parties I wish to thank are as follows: Arcadia Publishing and a most dedicated editor, Erin Vosgien; my Marymount Manhattan College writing professor, Elisabetta di Cagno; my LaGuardia High School of Music & Art and Performing Arts writing teacher, the late Karyn Kay; historian and president Jeff Gottlieb of the Central Queens Historical Association; president Mitchell Grubler of the Queens Preservation Council; the Four Borough Neighborhood Preservation Alliance; Rego-Forest Preservation Council; Rego Park Jewish Center; archivists Rachael Boone and Loretta Campbell of the Church-in-the-Gardens (CITG); the CITG Community House; district manager Frank Gulluscio of Queens Community Board 6; archives committee chair Eugenia S. Frangos and vice president Beatrice E. Hunt of the West Side Tennis Club; chief executive officers Susanna and Robert Hof of Terrace Sotheby's International Realty; chief operating officer Anthony Colletti and vice president of leasing Mary K. Hughes of Cord Meyer Development Company; the Queens Chamber of Commerce; historian Marjorie Melikian; architect and historian George Bryant; and some notables and their families who I had the privilege of corresponding with.

INTRODUCTION

Achieving success does not unfold after the sun has set or while you are having dreams, but as the sun rises, comes a day of promise. Then it is up to you to cultivate your dreams with a dedicated and passionate heart; but first, be grateful for the bonds that could be established, the knowledge that can be grasped, the wonders achievable by the mind's innermost chambers, and the natural and built environment that harbors stepping stones. A fulfilling day mounts to accomplishments, success stories, and perhaps recognition on a community or societal level. If you are able to impact one being, including yourself, that is a notable's achievement. While you may question your arrival, first embrace the light, the fresh air, and your worth in the moment and throughout your journey.

Come upon the historically, architecturally, and culturally unique neighborhoods of Forest Hills and Rego Park, which share the same soil and are cultivated by the footsteps of generations past, current, and future. Being raised in, inhabiting for the short or long term, working in, or visiting these two distinct yet harmonious communities—which are blessed to be steeped with history, art, architecture, landscapes, and parks among natural wonders, recreational opportunities, commercial novelties, and educational, civic, or religious institutions in connection with diverse personalities—can shape an individual, a group, and its demographics.

Forest Hills and Rego Park are a breeding ground for knowledge and creativity, and the relationship is reciprocal. Some Forest Hills and Rego Park notables have directly shaped the community, but the community also helped give birth to their achievements, further influencing its sense of place and society.

The once rural area of Forest Hills was named by Cord Meyer Development Company in 1906. Its westernmost section was renamed Rego Park in 1923 by president Henry L. Schloh and secretary and treasurer Charles I. Hausmann of the Rego Construction Company, often referred to as the Real Good Construction Company. Cord Meyer Jr. acquired 600 acres in Whitepot, which was developed from six farms. The Russell Sage Foundation then acquired 142 acres from Cord Meyer, south of today's Long Island Railroad, paving the way for the Forest Hills Gardens in 1909. Today, it is internationally recognized as America's earliest planned garden community.

The firms sensed opportunity and had faith and commitment, enabling them to become visionaries for future generations. They appointed architects who became household names and were far from a product of mass production. Some were Grosvenor Atterbury, Frederick Law Olmsted Jr., Benjamin Dreisler, Benjamin Braunstein, Theobald Henry Engelhardt, Robert Tappan, and Philip Birnbaum.

Some of the community's spirited sections are the outstandingly preserved Forest Hills Gardens, comprised of Tudor and Arts-and-Crafts mansions and accompanied by lush landscapes around winding paths and parks; the Tudor and Colonial commercial and residential district of Austin Street in Forest Hills, once nicknamed "The Village;" the Georgian Colonial and Art Moderne garden-style apartment houses in the Cord Meyer section north of Queens Boulevard; and the Rego Park Crescents south of the Long Island Railroad off 63rd Drive, which consists of concentric semicircular roads, alphabetical street names, and Old English row houses built by the Rodman & English firm.

Forest Hills and Rego Park have been impacted by pivotal historic events from a local to an international level. In Station Square in the Forest Hills Gardens, patriotic celebrations were common, and on July 4, 1917, Colonel Roosevelt stood atop the Long Island Railroad Station steps and recited his landmark "One Hundred Percent American" speech. In 1923, the Forest Hills Tennis Stadium, America's first concrete tennis stadium, was developed at the West Side Tennis Club. On its historic field, players ranged from Don Budge to Bill Tilden to Arthur Ashe to Billie Jean King.

Generations came to witness the birth of the US Open. The Forest Hills Music Festival, featuring legends such as Frank Sinatra, The Beatles, and Barbra Streisand, made summers throughout the 1960s and 1970s memorable.

The community benefited by advances in transportation and infrastructure, which increased its population. In 1913, a trolley line was inaugurated from 59th Street in Manhattan to Queens Boulevard in Forest Hills. Construction was underway to widen the thoroughfare to its 200-foot width in 1914, and was completed in 1935. By 1936, Independent Subway System (IND) stations opened on Woodhaven Boulevard, 63rd Drive, 67th Avenue, Continental Avenue, and on Union Turnpike. Mayor John Francis Hylan's wishes for the creation of a publicly owned and operated subway were fulfilled.

The 1939 World's Fair in Flushing Meadows Corona Park contributed to a residential boom, with apartments such as the Old English–style Queens Gardens complex on Queens Boulevard in Rego Park, and buildings named after presidents, such as The James Madison in the Cord Meyer area of Forest Hills. The 1964 World's Fair ushered in additional developments, such as the Kennedy House and Birchwood Towers in Forest Hills.

Around the period of both World's Fairs, commerce increased along thoroughfares such as Queens Boulevard, 63rd Drive, Continental Avenue, Austin Street, Woodhaven Boulevard, 108th Street, and Metropolitan Avenue. Some popular eateries were the Ham N' Eggery coffee shop, Henry's vegetarian restaurant, Knish Nosh, Ben's Best Delicatessen, T-Bone Diner, Shalimar Diner, and Howard Johnson's. Shopping at Alexander's, Woolworth's, and Buster Brown Shoes; bowling at Hollywood Lanes; seeking entertainment at the Forest Hills, Midway, Trylon, Continental, Cinemart, and Drake movie theaters; and spending a day at Fairyland Amusement Park became the norm.

Forest Hills High School opened in 1941 and helped foster the careers of numerous notables. Some of the many religious institutions that have thrived are Forest Hills Jewish Center, Church-in-the-Gardens, Rego Park Jewish Center, Our Lady Queen of Martyrs, Queens Jewish Center, Our Lady of Mercy, Saint Luke's Episcopal Church, First Presbyterian Church of Forest Hills, Our Lady of the Angelus, and Our Saviour Lutheran Church.

As a result of the sense of place that Forest Hills and Rego Park have long offered, some past and current residents have taken pride in calling it home. Your next-door neighbor can be considered a notable, and at some point may be referred to as a celebrity.

Forest Hills is known for talk show personality Jerry Springer, composer Burt Bacharach, the Ramones, Simon & Garfunkel, children's show host Bob Keeshan who portrayed Captain Kangaroo, actor and comedian Rick Overton, musician Chieli Minucci of Special EFX, the courageous author and lecturer Helen Keller, and *The New York Times* best-selling artist for Marvel and DC Comics, John Stanisci. Austin Street is where the "Queen of Pop" Madonna performed back in 1983.

Legends who called Rego Park home include actor Eddie Bracken, comic actor Sid Caesar, actress June Havoc, dancer Gypsy Rose Lee, Miss America 1945 Bess Myerson, television comedian Marty Ingels, and television producer Fred Silverman.

The Forest Hills Gardens is home to some longtime residents such as Floyd Hasselriis, who was born in 1922. He is the son of the internationally recognized miniaturist Malthe M. Hasselriis, who painted Eleanor Roosevelt and Pres. John F. Kennedy. Floyd was a State Assembly candidate in 1948 who opposed development on what later became Yellowstone Park in Forest Hills. On the board of directors of the Forest Hills Gardens Corporation, he helped maintain the community's sidewalks and parks.

Public School 101's brick building opened in 1927, and today, Hasselriis is recognized as the oldest living member of the first kindergarten class. "Our teacher sang 'Marching Along Together,' a song on how we would work our way out of the Depression. When my father didn't have a job, my mother went into the business of making crabapple jelly from the crabapple tree in front of our house. I went up to Metropolitan Avenue to the 5 cent and 10 cent store, and carried jars for our crabapple jelly, and we traded them in at the grocery for food."

Floyd continued, "Forest Hills was wild. We would roast marshmallows in empty lots, mark up sidewalks for hopscotch, and play ring-a-levio. Parents never worried where their kids were, but we just had to be home by six. We built platforms in our tree, and could climb up to the top and see the Woolworth Building."

Modern day Forest Hills and Rego Park continue to host creative visionaries. As a case in point, few theaters across New York City have achieved the record of Cinemart Cinemas at 106-03 Metropolitan Avenue, which opened in 1927 as the Metropolis Theatre. Owner Nicolas Nicolaou, a four-decade employee, and manager Sal Parete, a seven-decade employee, take pride in the longest continuously operated independent movie theater in Queens. It offers five screens and digital and film projection, along with the popular Theater Café next door. "Forest Hills deserves the respect of its history, and to allow its residents to bring younger generations to the Cinemart, as their parents and grandparents have for nearly nine decades," said Nicolaou.

Among the greatest of notables are local volunteers who collaborated with Friends of the QueensWay and the Trust For Public Land, and are determined to introduce their rendition of Manhattan's High Line to Queens. The "QueensWay" project would repurpose central Queens's abandoned Long Island Railroad Rockaway Beach Branch tracks into a 3.5-mile elevated park with incentives for the environment, recreation, education, the arts, culture, and the borough's economy. Queens is the most ethnically diverse area worldwide, and the QueensWay has the potential to become a major destination that would connect residents and visitors to opportunities along a symbolic representation of 21st century urban design.

In the pages that follow, may you feel inspired by the accomplishments of some of the numerous notables who are linked to Forest Hills and Rego Park history. Furthermore, may you engage in a productive life and serve as an inspiration to yourself, your family, friends, neighborhood, society, and future generations.

CHAPTER ONE

Community and Development

In 1652, Newtown was settled by Englishmen from New England and consisted of Whitepot, named after the purchase of land from the Indians in exchange for three white clay pots. Whitepot consisted of six family-operated farms, named after Ascan Backus, Casper-Joost Springsteen, Horatio N. Squire, Abram V.S. Lott, Sarah V. Bolmer, and James Van Siclen.

The oldest living member of one of the native families was Frederick D. Backus, who told historian Lucy Allen Smart about Whitepot's residents: "The neighbors were few when I was a boy, and some that lived a mile away we called neighbors. The farmers raised hay, grain, and vegetables to supply the New York markets. Fruit and nuts were in abundance, and every farmer would take his apples to a cider mill, which was located on the Hempstead Swamp Road; now Yellowstone Avenue. The children attended the Whitepot School, but we all had to go to Newtown to church." The sole remnant of Whitepot is the 18th-century Remsen Cemetery.

In 1900, Whitepot's population consisted of 30 German residents who planted potatoes and celery. In 1906, Cord Meyer Development Company purchased 600 acres and renamed it Forest Hills after its high elevation and proximity to Forest Park. Roman Avenue between Queens Boulevard and Austin Street was the first street to be cut through, and 10 two-family brick homes were erected.

The Russell Sage Foundation purchased 142 acres south of the Long Island Railroad from Cord Meyer, and appointed principal architect Grosvenor Atterbury and landscape architect Frederick Law Olmsted Jr. to design the Forest Hills Gardens, modeled on an English garden suburb in 1909.

By 1923, president Henry L. Schloh and treasurer Charles I. Hausmann of the Rego Construction Company discovered 17th-century farmland in Forest Hills West owned by Chinese farmers. They named Rego Park after their advertising slogan, "REal GOod Homes," and began developing 525 eight-room one-family frame houses.

After a trolley line was extended from Manhattan to Forest Hills in 1914 and Queens Boulevard was widened to 200 feet in 1935, Forest Hills's population numbered 23,300. The IND subway line opened in 1936. Then the 1939 and 1964 World's Fairs arrived, which further modified the landscape with Georgian Colonial and Art Moderne apartments related to household names such as architect Philip Birnbaum and developer Alfred Kaskel.

Shop owners knew patrons on a first-name basis. Residents sat on stools, enjoying the soda fountains at Woolworth's, McCrory's, and Addie Vallins. Today, longtime surviving businesses include Ben's Best Delicatessen, owned by Jay Parker, and the world-famous Knish Nosh, once owned by Sam Heller, "The Godfather of Queens Boulevard." Alberto Restaurant, owned by siblings Roberto and Silvana Chiappelloni, has been a Forest Hills institution for four decades.

In a 2013 interview, Ruth Mueller, who was born in 1922, stated that she has witnessed Rego Park's transformation. She lived in a frame house, which was elevated to make the land level. She reminisced, "I would swing on Weeping Willow trees, see movies at the Trylon Theater, and walk five minutes to the new subway."

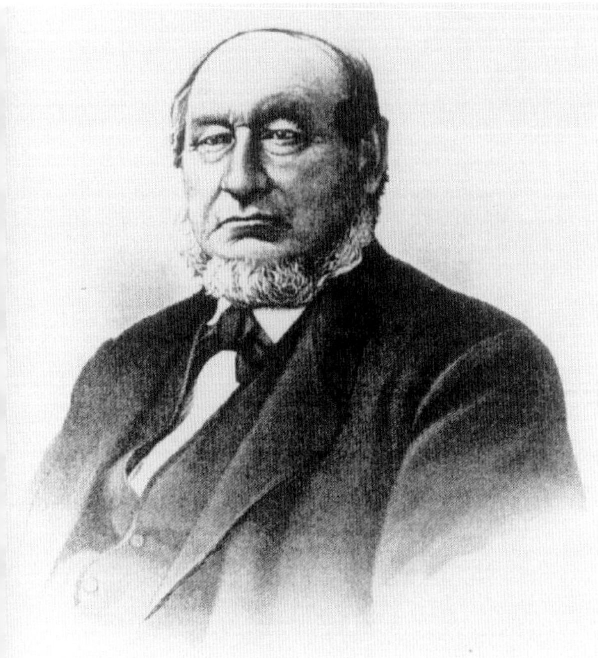

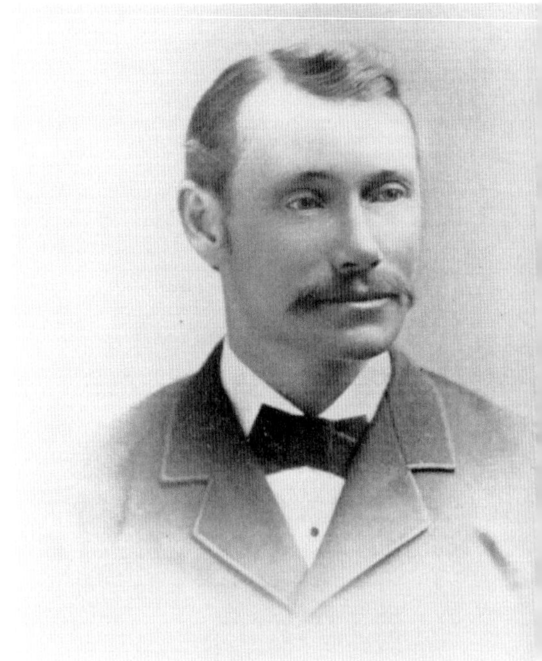

Ascan Backus Family

Forest Hills was known as Whitepot prior to 1906, and consisted of six farms named after Ascan Backus, Casper-Joost Springsteen, Horatio N. Squire, Abram V.S. Lott, Sarah V. Bolmer, and James Van Siclen. Ascan William Christian Backus (1814–1880), a native of Saxe-Gotha, Germany, arrived in America in 1829 without a dollar, but in 1849, purchased 40 acres in what was known as the Remsen estate, which had Revolutionary War ties. His acquisitions grew to 800 acres, and with four wagons, he supplied the New York market with crops including wheat, rye, Timothy grass, cabbages, peas, beets, and horseradish. His farm benefited Army purchases during the Civil War. Nicknamed "The King Farmer of Long Island," he was also the largest commercial farmer in America.

Ascan's children were John E. Backus (1846–1911), Frederick D. Backus (1850–1937), Charles Ludwig, Cornelius, George A., Emma A., Mary Eliza, and Pauline W. Frederick's son was named Ascan Backus II (1879–1948) and his daughter was Wilhelmina Backus (1877–1940). As deputy bridge commissioner of Queens, John was integral in the Queensboro Bridge's construction. Frederick was president of Cord Meyer Development Company, which offered stock in exchange for Whitepot's farms, contributing to Forest Hills's early development. Frederick developed a road between Queens Boulevard and Metropolitan Avenue, and in collaboration with Cord Meyer Development Company in 1909, named it Ascan Avenue to commemorate the Ascan Backus legacy.

In 1951, one of the last direct descendants to live in Forest Hills, Pearl K. Backus, a resident of The Lexington House at 68-10 108th Street, passed away. The wood-framed Ascan Backus homestead once stood on the northeast corner of Queens Boulevard at 69th Road.

Julie Backus Stout, the great-great granddaughter of Ascan Backus, said, "He was a hard-working, respected businessman, a beloved parent, and a good farmer and individual with a terrific sense of humor, which he passed down to his son, grandson, great-grandson, great-great-grandson, and his great-great-great grandsons. It is possible that many wonderful comedians lived in Forest Hills, since they could feel the vibes of Ascan Backus, who lived, loved, laughed, and farmed there."

Ascan Avenue remains a most attractive thoroughfare. Standouts are the Tudor-style Sutton Hall apartments, designed by the award-winning architect Benjamin Braunstein, and the Tudor Neo-Gothic style Our Lady Queen of Martyrs Church, designed by Maginnis & Walsh and modeled after England's Durham Cathedral. Pictured are Ascan Backus (left) and John E. Backus. (Both courtesy of Julie Backus Stout.)

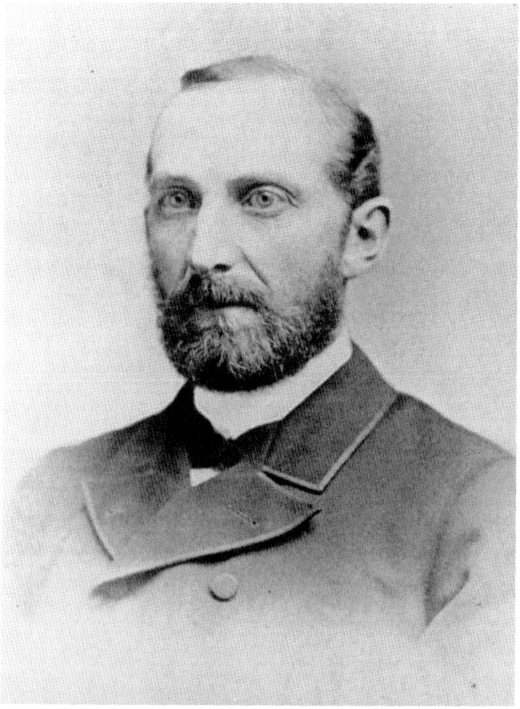

Springsteen Family
The Springsteen family consisted of influential Dutch farmers who owned a significant parcel of land in Whitepot, the boundaries of which would now encompass the south side of Queens Boulevard between Ascan Avenue and 77th Avenue in Forest Hills. The porch-fronted Springsteen homestead, erected in 1898, stood at 112 Queens Boulevard (renumbered 108-36 Queens Boulevard) through the late 1940s. Farmer David Springsteen (1849–1911, pictured at left), who was also a director of Cord Meyer Development Company, represented the ninth Springsteen generation to settle locally and was among one of the first families of Queens. Under the authorization of a Dutch king in the mid-1600s, the family acquired the land. David had six children named Azariah, David, Harry, George, Nelson, and Ella, some of whom remained in Forest Hills until their death. (Left, courtesy of Queens Community Board 6; below, author's collection.)

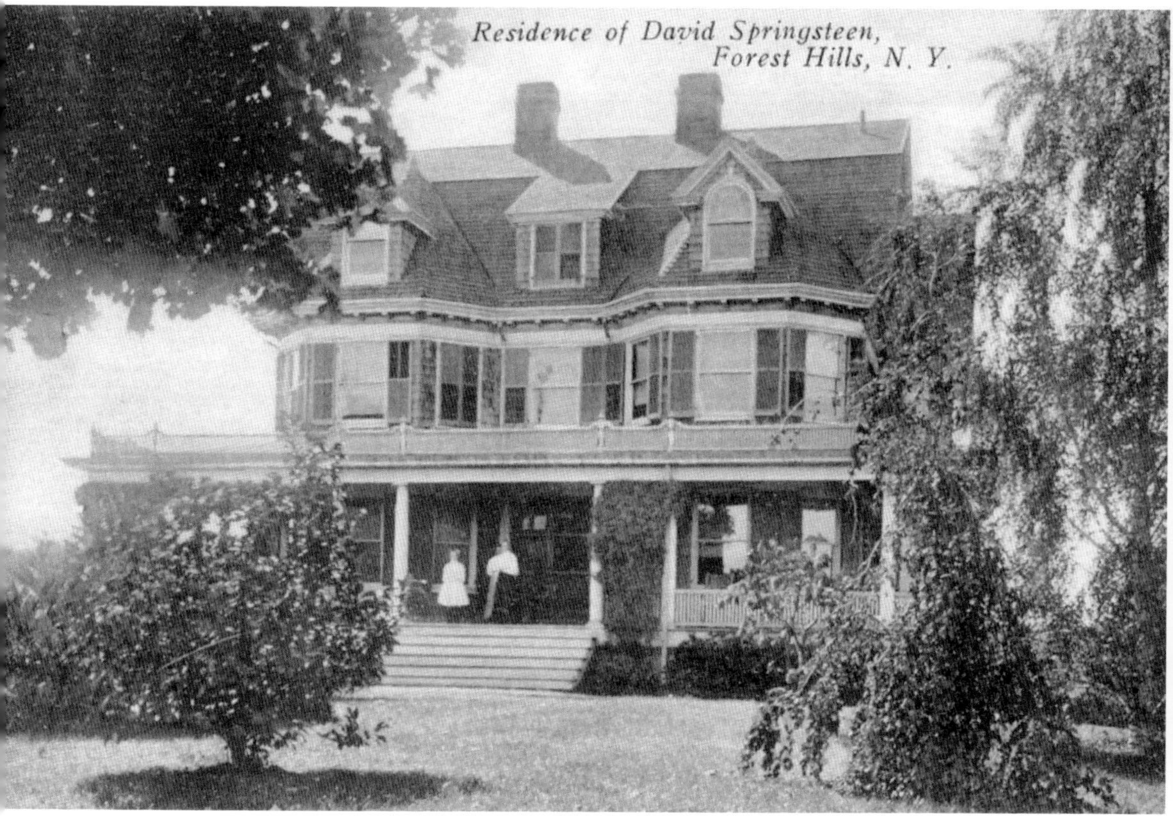

Remsen Family

Designated a New York City Landmark in 1981, the Remsen Cemetery, situated between Trotting Course Lane and Alderton Street in Forest Hills, is a remnant of the area's colonial past, when small private cemeteries were preferred. The Remsen family immigrated in the 17th century from northern Germany.

Jeromus Remsen Sr. (1735–1790) fought in the French and Indian War, and as a colonel of the Kings and Queens County Militia in the Battle of Long Island, he commanded the 7th New York Regiment in the American Revolutionary War. In 1699, the Remsen family erected a homestead on their farm, which was located adjacent to the cemetery until 1925. Today, only the cemetery survives, with tombstones dating from 1790 to 1819. Rego Park had a single road known as Remsen's Lane, which is now 63rd Drive, Fleet Court, and 64th Road.

The 1981 Remsen Park Coalition plaque reads, "Within this park lies the remains of Revolutionary War Veteran Colonel Jeromus Remsen. Buried in the confines of this site were his cousins Major Abraham Remsen, Captain Luke Remsen, Lieutenant Aurt Remsen and their families. The Remsen family was amongst the first settlers of this area, originally known as White Pot."

A 1925 survey revealed brownstone inscriptions of Jeromus, Anna, Jerome (two), Cornelius, Ann Elizabeth, Bridget, and Major Abraham Remsen. The Veterans Administration erected non-brownstone graves commemorating Colonel Remsen, Maj. Abraham Remsen, and brothers Aurt and Garrett Remsen, who were also Revolutionary War officers. Remsen Cemetery has a World War I memorial, with two doughboy statues flanking a flagpole and honoring Forest Hills's service. Nearby is Public School 144, which is named the Col. Jeromus Remsen School. (Courtesy of Jeff Gottlieb.)

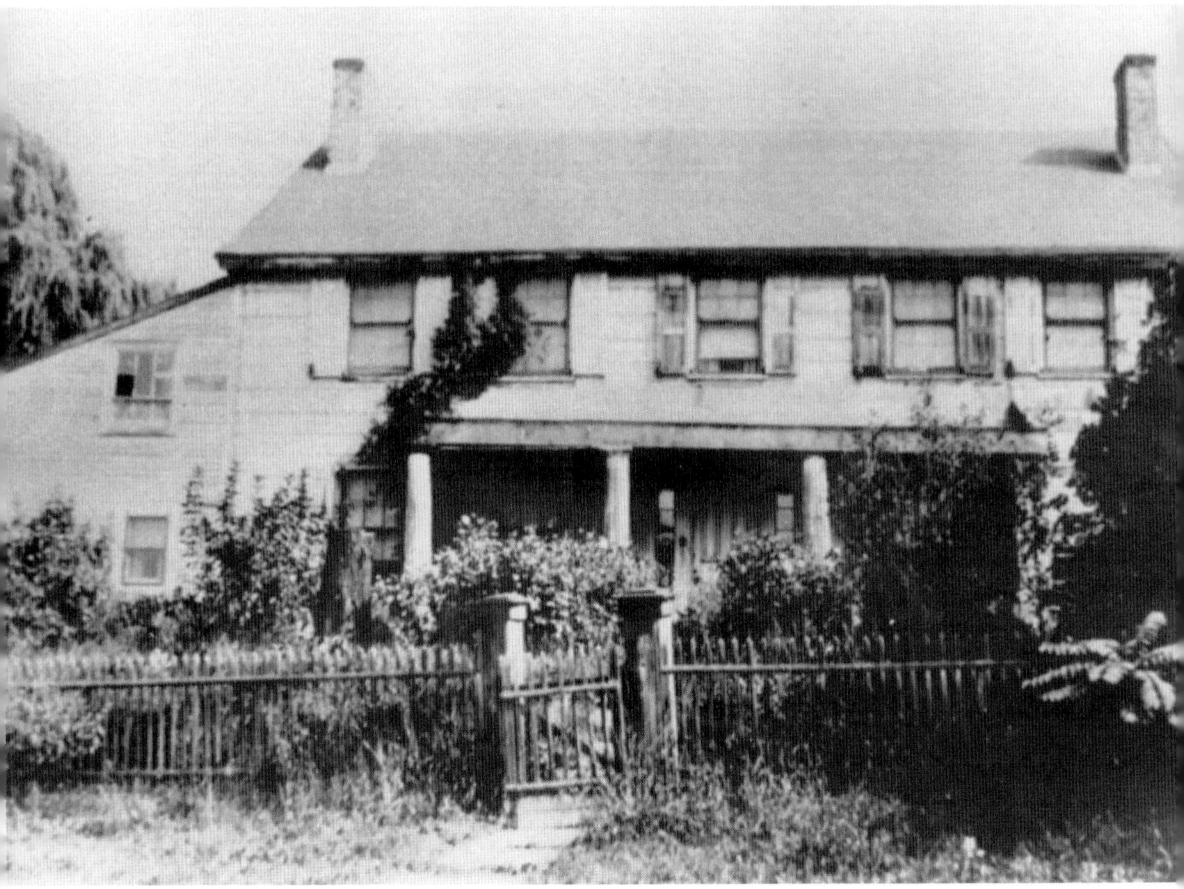

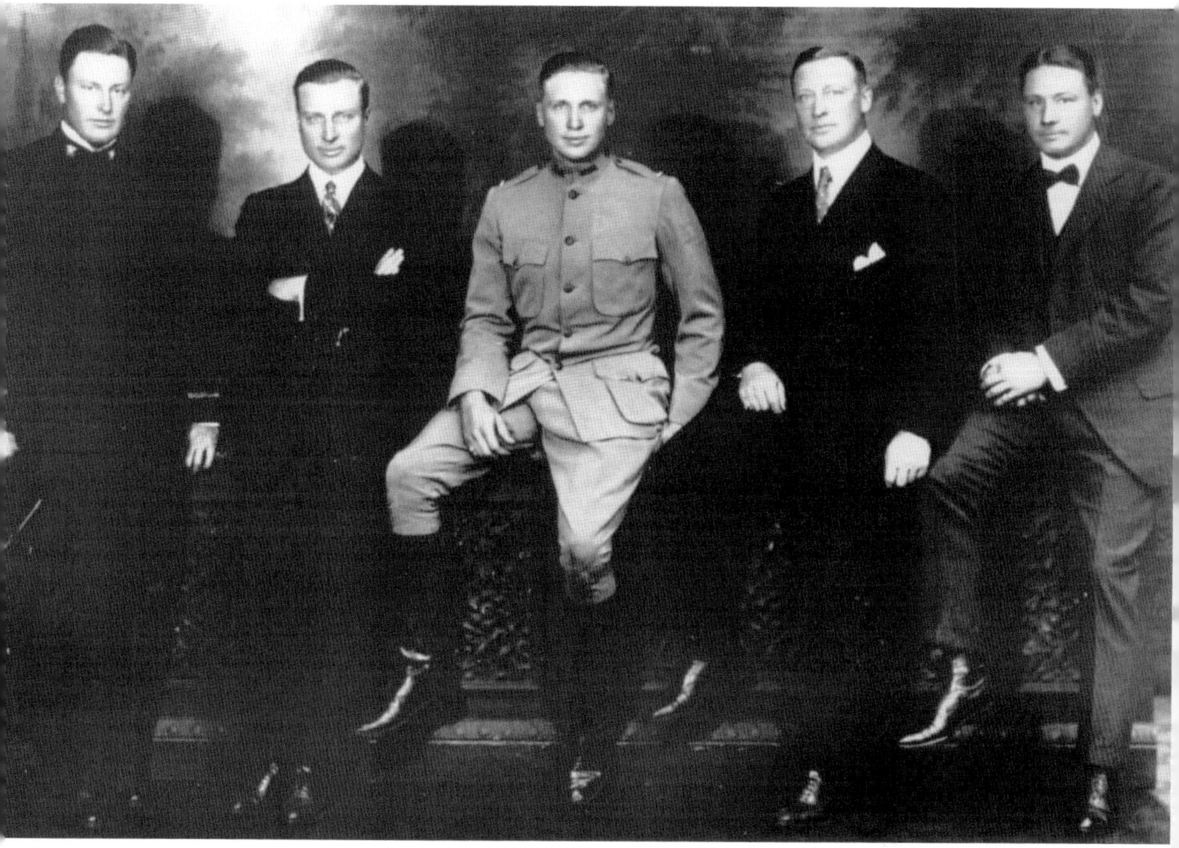

Cord Meyer Development Company

In 1906, the Cord Meyer Development Company, headed by Cord Meyer Jr. (1854–1910), purchased 600 acres in the Hopedale section of Whitepot from farmer Frederick Backus and renamed it Forest Hills after its high elevation and proximity to Forest Park. That year, the company developed 10 Neo-Renaissance row houses on Roman Avenue (now 72nd Avenue) between Austin Street and Queens Boulevard, which housed the area's first carpenter, plumber, and electrician. Cord Meyer laid out, named, and improved streets with public utilities north of the Long Island Railroad and developed 340 houses. George C. Meyer later acquired his father's position.

In the 1920s, the firm developed the award-winning Forest Close and Arbor Close assemblages, comprised of Old English row houses with central communal gardens. Other award winners were the Colonial-style garden apartment houses the Lexington, Livingston, and Kelvin in the Cord Meyer section of Forest Hills, north of Queens Boulevard. One of Austin Street's earliest residences was known as the Portsmouth Apartments. In the 1950s, the Seminole and Balfour Apartments were developed, followed by the Continental in the early 1960s. Today, the firm largely focuses on condo development. Pictured here from left to right are Robert, George, Cord, Charles, and J. Edward Meyer. (Courtesy of Cord Meyer Development Company.)

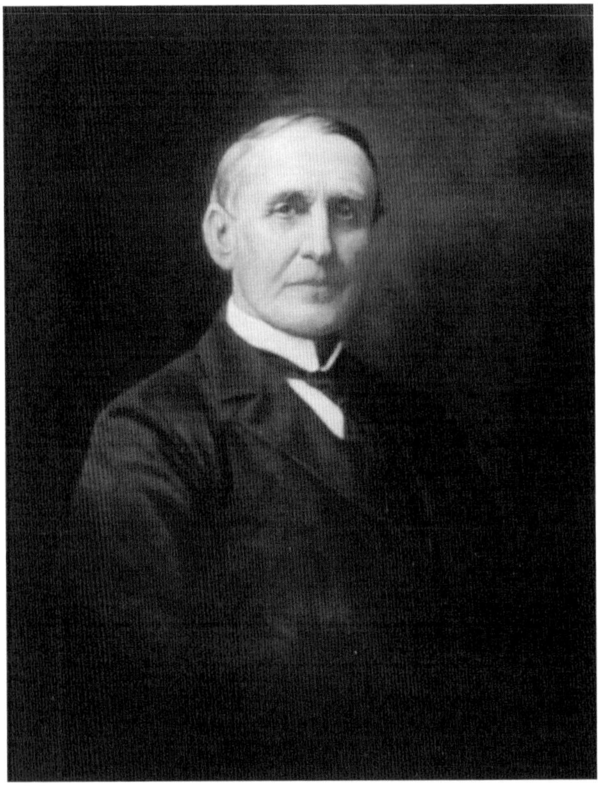

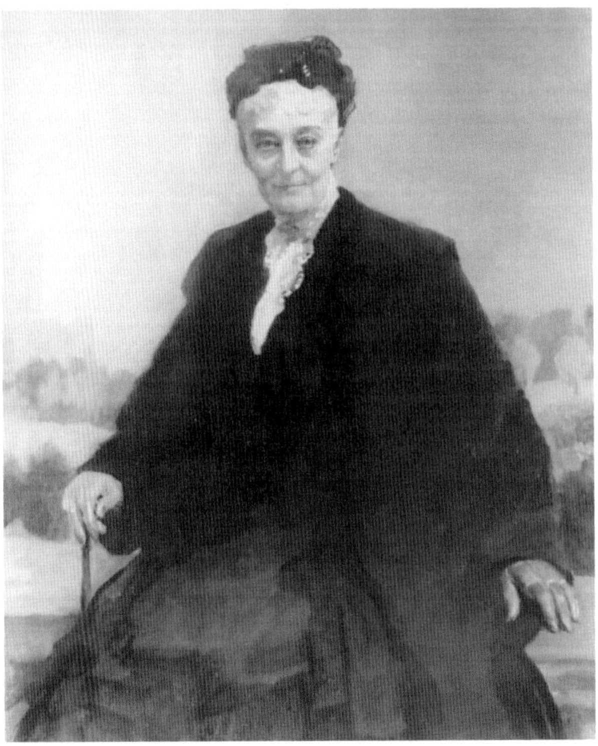

Russell Sage and Margaret Olivia Slocum Sage

Raised in poverty, Margaret Olivia Slocum Sage (1828–1918, pictured at bottom) became a teacher and wed capitalist Russell Sage (1815–1906, top), who amassed his fortune in the telegraph, railroad, and lumber industries. She acquired his estate of $65 million after his death. Established in April 1907 with a $10 million endowment by Margaret Sage, the Russell Sage Foundation had a mission of advocating "for the improvement of social and living conditions in the United States." Today, the foundation is one of America's oldest private philanthropies and publishes and funds research in the social sciences.

Beginning in 1909, the foundation purchased land south of the Long Island Railroad for the development of the Forest Hills Gardens. It would total 142 acres and be governed by its subsidiary, the Sage Foundation Homes Company. The foundation appointed architect Grosvenor Atterbury and landscape architect Frederick Law Olmsted Jr. The Church-in-the-Gardens, whose covenant was adopted in 1912, benefited by Margaret Sage's gift, which led to the development of a permanent Gothic-style edifice at 50 Ascan Avenue, dedicated in October 1915. Russell Sage Junior High School 190 at 68-17 Austin Street, which opened in 1954, bears tribute to Margaret's husband, Russell Sage. (Top, courtesy of Russell Sage Foundation; bottom, courtesy of Church-in-the-Gardens.)

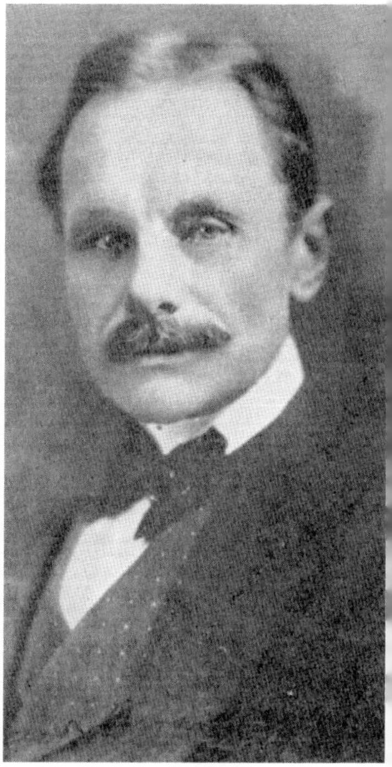

Grosvenor Atterbury and Frederick Law Olmsted Jr.
Step under the Long Island Railroad trestle and discover America's earliest planned garden community. Established in 1909, the 142-acre Forest Hills Gardens is reminiscent of an English suburb with Tudor and Arts-and-Crafts mansions, Station Square with its towering Forest Hills Inn and Tea Garden, Public School 101, churches, and winding streets with majestic trees and parks. This internationally recognized model of urban planning, influenced by Sir Ebenezer Howard's Garden City Movement, was designed by principal architect Grosvenor Atterbury (1869–1956, pictured at right) and landscape architect and conservationist Frederick Law Olmsted Jr. (1870–1957, below).

When prefabrication was largely unexplored, Atterbury developed eight-by-four-foot hollow concrete blocks for his homes, which helped curb costs and labor while promoting beautiful design.

Atterbury was president of the Architectural League of New York. Olmsted Jr., a principal of the Olmsted Brothers, envisioned American garden suburbs where residents could live harmoniously with nature. The National Park Service Organic Act (1916) featured his quote: "To conserve the scenery and the natural and historic objects and the wildlife therein, and to provide for the enjoyment of the same in such manner, and by such means as will leave them unimpaired for the enjoyment of future generations."

Today, the Forest Hills Gardens Corporation preserves their vision through restrictive covenants. (Right, courtesy of Church-in-the-Gardens; below, courtesy of Library of Congress.)

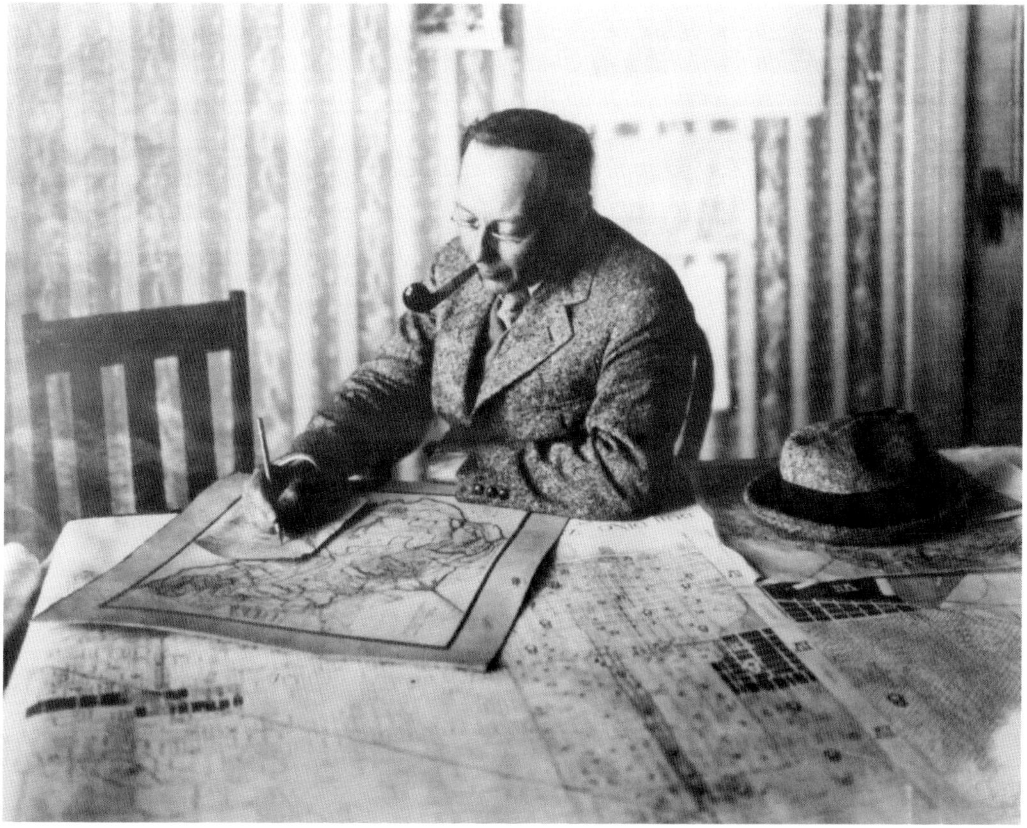

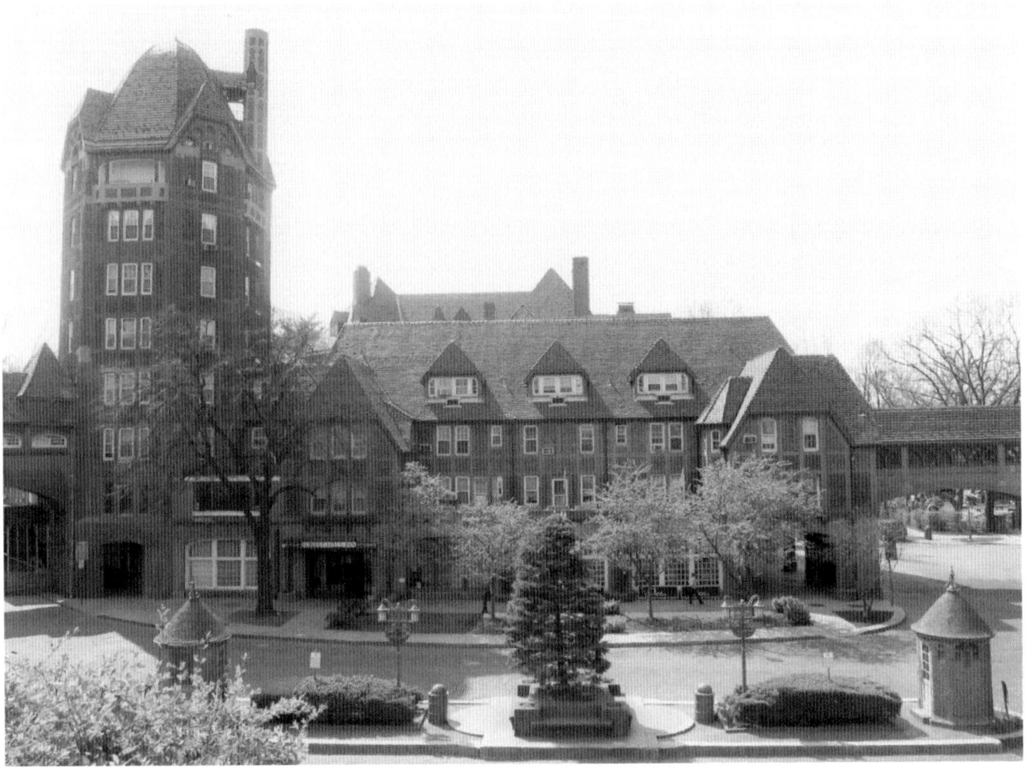

Forest Hills Inn and the Tea Garden

The Forest Hills Inn and the Tea Garden at 1 Station Square opened in 1912, and was designed by architect Grosvenor Atterbury and landscape architect Frederick Law Olmsted Jr. Station Square was conceived as a town center with the inn, adjoining shops, and the train station, which took commuters to Penn Station in 13 minutes. The 150-room inn's rates were $14–$18 per week, including meals, and references were required.

The inn was once the center of a classy social life. When tennis championships and music festivals took place at the Forest Hills Tennis Stadium, notable figures would stay at the inn. Roger Williams would perform. The Windsor Room hosted ballroom dancing on weekends and dinner music evenings. The Unicorn Lounge was a pleasant place to relax with friends. Overlooking Station Square was The Sidewalk Café. The Tournament Grille hosted luncheons, dinners, and cocktails, and private functions would take place at The Terrace Room. Much preceded the inn's residential conversion in 1967.

The July 12, 1924, edition of *The Forest Hills Bulletin* read, "The Tea Garden of the Forest Hills Inn is a veritable fairyland, when lighted with Japanese lanterns, with the trickling fountain heard in the background, and a new moon shining overhead. There is no more delightful place in Greater New York for one to spend the dinner hour."

In addition to afternoon teas and weddings, guests would dine to the sounds of the Inn Trio during the warmer months. Program numbers were Dvorak's "Humoresque," Albeniz's "A Night in Seville," Nevin's "A Day in Venice," and Godard's "Canzonetta." The Tea Garden also became the stage set of some early performances by The Gardens Players, such as *Prunella* in 1922, which prioritized on the Tea Garden's natural setting and followed the path of their production *Pomander Walk*.

Serenity, romance, and artistic achievements echo from yesteryear, but today the Tea Garden is a shell of its former glorious self. The Tea Garden is slated for restoration, but in the interim, was adapted as a film set in 2013. (Photograph by Michael H. Perlman.)

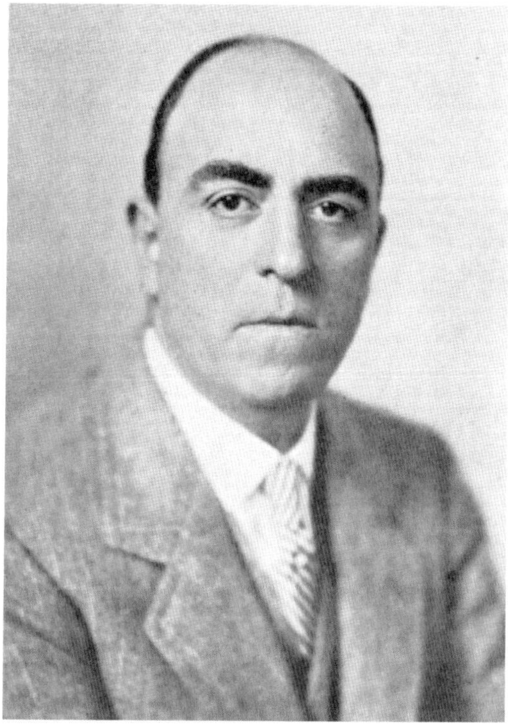

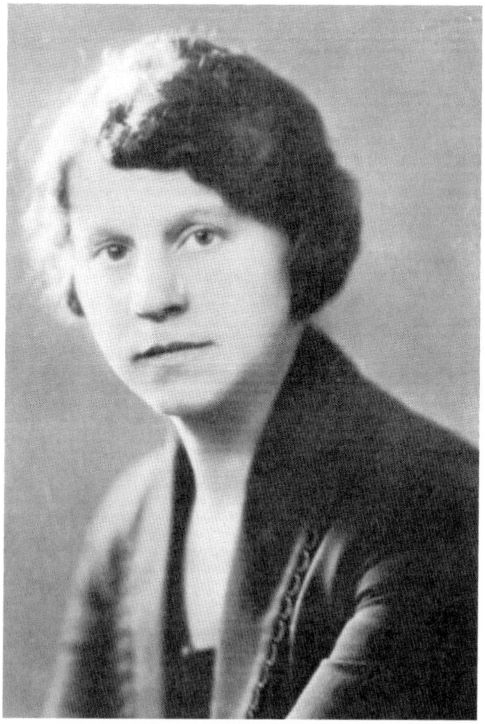

Hof Family

For over a century, the Hof family has called Forest Hills home. Realtor Henry Hof Sr. (1883–1948, pictured above at left) and his wife, Lillian Barning Hof (above at right), settled in the Forest Hills Gardens in 1917. He became a Church-in-the-Gardens trustee and the Forest Hills Taxpayers Association president. As chairman of the building committee of the Community House, he raised needed funds, seeing it to fruition in 1926. Its auditorium, Hof Hall, bears a plaque designed by famed sculptor Adolph Weinman of Forest Hills. Today, paternal grandson Robert Marsh Hof and his wife, Susanna (pictured at left), are chief executive officers of Terrace Sotheby's International Realty in Station Square. "We have our roots and our fruits in the community," said Susanna, referring to their family's six generations that includes their children and grandchildren. Robert Hof stated, "We've probably been in every house in the Forest Hills Gardens, and our office accomplishes at least 90 percent of brokered sales in Forest Hills and adjacent communities since 1968."

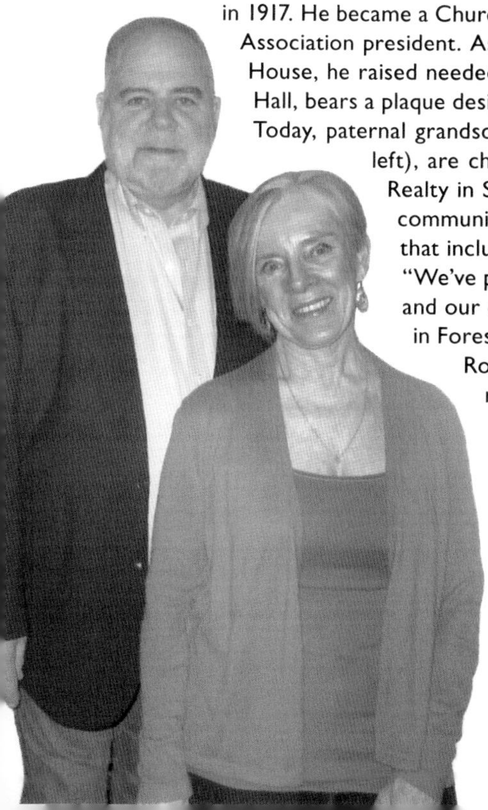

Robert's maternal grandfather, Robert E. Marsh, who resided in the 72nd Avenue row houses off the south side of Queens Boulevard, was vice president of Cord Meyer Development Company, which named Forest Hills in 1906. Past generations were friends of Helen Keller and First Lady Edith Roosevelt, who visited the Hof residence at 254 Greenway North. (Above, courtesy of Church-in-the-Gardens; left, photograph by Michael H. Perlman.)

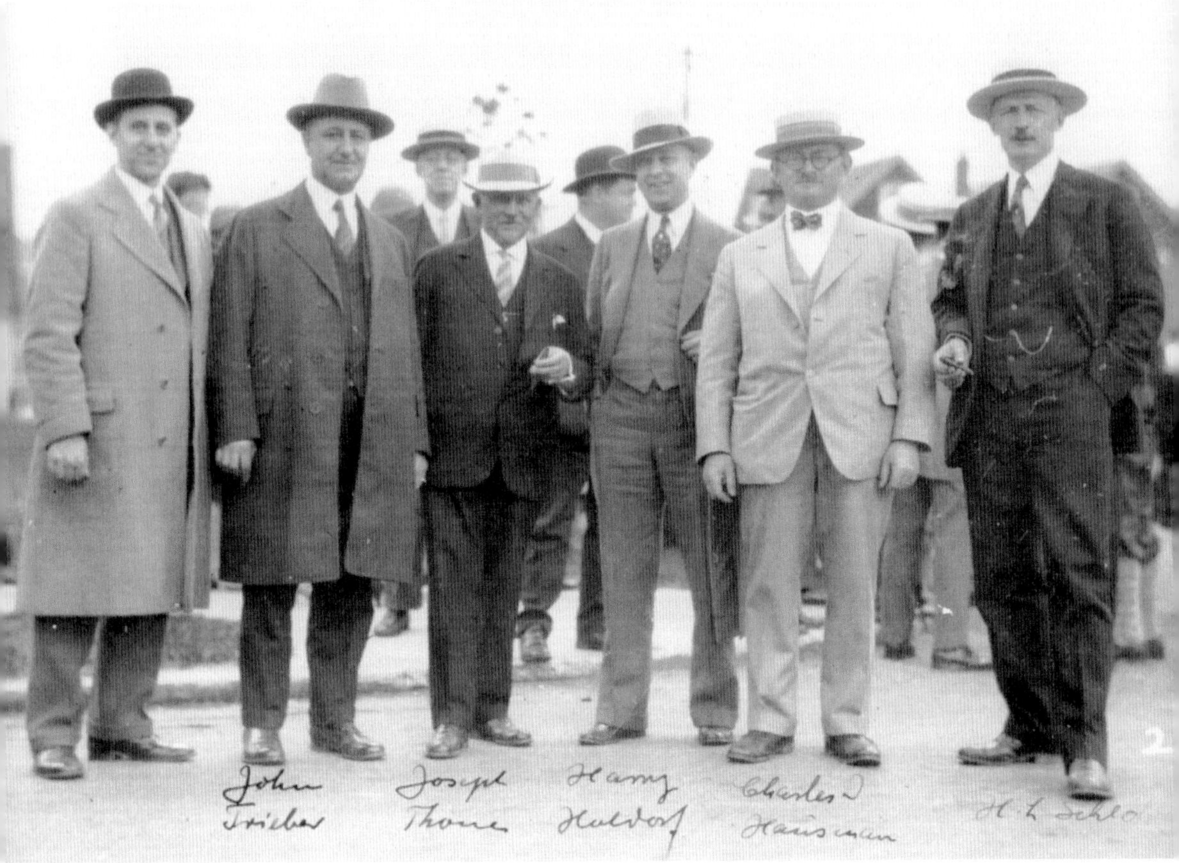

Rego Construction Company

In 1923, the Rego Construction Company, also known as the Real Good Construction Company, acquired land in Forest Hills West and named the area Rego Park after its advertising slogan, "REal GOod Homes." The firm consisted of president Henry L. Schloh and secretary and treasurer Charles I. Hausmann, both of whom immigrated from Germany.

Schloh and Hausmann came upon farmland settled in the 17th century by Dutch and English farmers, followed by German and then Chinese farmers who sold produce to Chinatown. The Rego Construction Company began developing 525 eight-room, one-family Colonial frame houses between 63rd Drive and Elliot Avenue and south of Queens Boulevard, which sold for approximately $7,500.

To complement the houses, the firm developed three apartment houses, which 70 families each called home. They were the Tudor-style Remo Hall at 61-40 Saunders Street (1927), followed by the Spanish Mission–style Jupiter Court at 62-64 Saunders Street (1927), and the Spanish Mission-style Marion Court at 62-98 Saunders Street (1929). These significant buildings by architect Benjamin Braunstein survive mostly intact and offer recessed facades and courtyards that maximize fresh air and light. Architecturally, Marion Court boasts terra-cotta elements that feature animals, leaded glass depictions of castles, and a roof garden where residents would recreate and keep cool come summer. For two to four rooms at Remo Hall and Jupiter Court, rentals cost $46 and up.

Schloh's grandson Bruce Powell explained, "When the Depression hit, my grandfather refused to go bankrupt, so a lot of the money invested in his developments came from family and friends. According to my mother, he didn't buy a new suit for 10 years, since he tried to keep everything afloat." Pictured here with Rego Construction Company colleagues are Charles Hausmann (second from right) and Henry Schloh (far right). (Courtesy of Bruce Powell.)

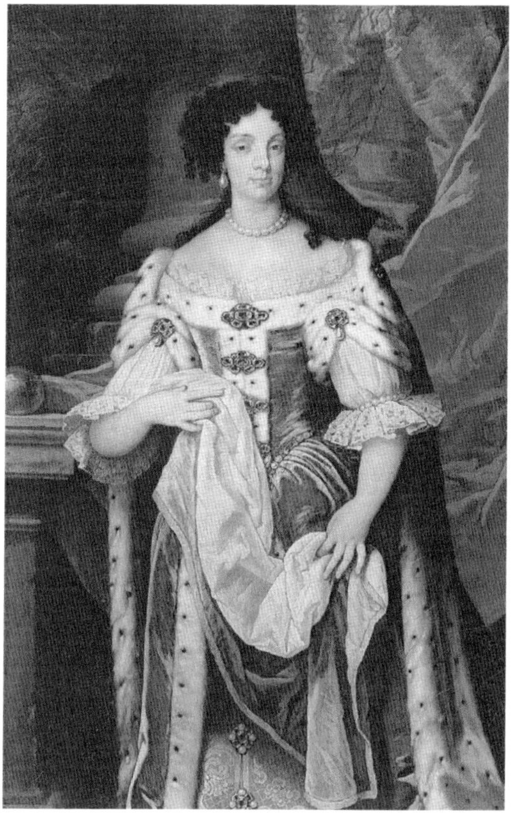

Queen Catherine of Braganza and the Succession of Queens Boulevard

Queens County is believed to have been named on November 1, 1683, after Queen Catherine of Braganza, the queen consort of King Charles II. The borough of Queens became official on January 1, 1898. Queens Boulevard, which spans 7.2 miles and consists of 16 lanes at its widest on Yellowstone Boulevard, originated as a two-lane dirt road in 1873. Its succession of names began with Buttermilk Hollow, followed by Whitepot Pike and Queens Pike. In conjunction with New York City mayor and New York State governor John T. Hoffman, the route was renamed Hoffman Boulevard. During the 1939–1940 World's Fair, it was advertised as "World's Fair Boulevard." (Author's collection.)

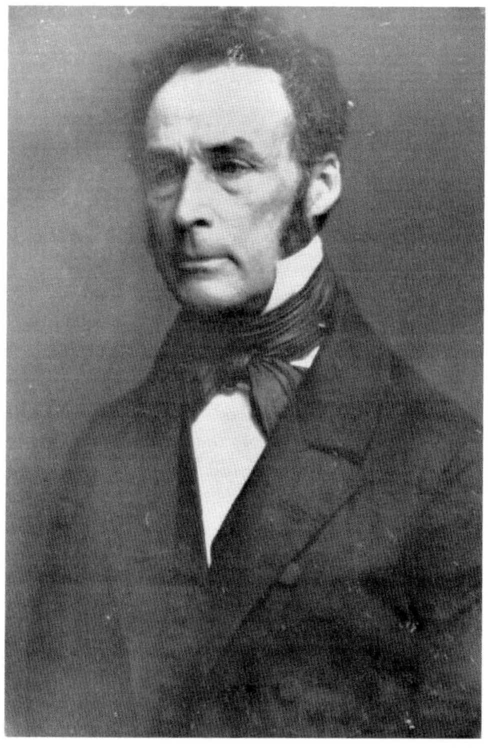

Stephen Alling Halsey

Back in March 1947, 150 children and parents witnessed New York City deputy mayor John J. Bennett shoveling the earth for the new Stephen A. Halsey Junior High School 157 in Rego Park. It was fitting to honor Stephen A. Halsey (1798–1875), a Renaissance man who played an influential role in the early development of Queens. Halsey purchased the Blackwell and Perrot farms, situated between Pot Cove and Hallett's Cove. He configured streets and erected wharves, houses, and factories, which attracted tradesmen and manufacturers. Under his leadership, this settlement became a village known as Astoria in 1839. (Courtesy of Queens Community Board 6.)

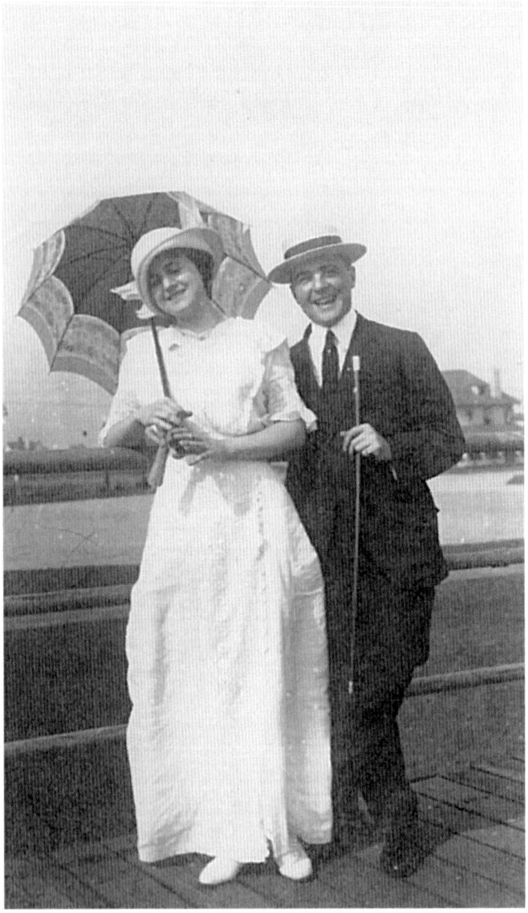

Theobald Henry Engelhardt

Architect Theobald Henry Engelhardt (1886–1964) of 59 Seasongood Road introduced stately Colonial apartment houses that received first-prize awards from the Queens Chamber of Commerce. Most praised are The Lexington House, The Kelvin, The Livingston, and The Portsmouth. Unique appointments are bay windows, porches, wood-burning fireplaces, maid's quarters, and museum-quality lobbies overlooking picturesque communal gardens.

Mayor Michael Bloomberg designated January 16, 2006, as "The Lexington House Day." His proclamation read, "Since 1931, this Forest Hills landmark has been where 'Good neighbors make a house our home.' Residents continue to gather for brunch, tea parties, and rooftop Fourth of July celebrations. Such camaraderie is a credit to The Lexington House and New York City." Louise and Theobald Henry Engelhardt are seen here on August 10, 1913. (Courtesy of Trudy and Bernie Smith.)

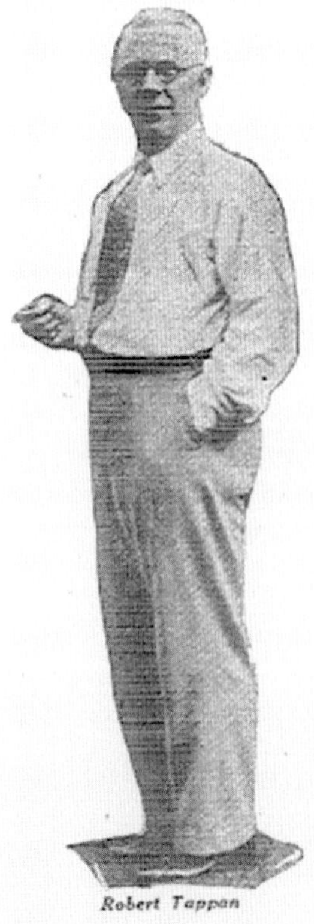

Robert Tappan

Architect Robert Tappan (1884–1961) of 28 Whitson Street designed a foremost achievement of urban planning, known as Arbor Close (1926) and Forest Close (1927), situated between 75th Avenue and 76th Avenue from Austin Street to Queens Boulevard. These brick row houses with leaded glass, pitched slate roofs, and landscaped lawns were awarded by the Queens Chamber of Commerce. Through an arched gateway lies a communal garden, emphasizing the romantic Arts-and-Crafts ambiance.

Along 67th Drive between 108th and 110th Streets are 13 English Country Cottage Revival–style detached houses. A Tappan creation in the Forest Hills Gardens is the English Gothic–style Saint Luke's Church.

To reserve finances and construction time, Tappan was a strong advocate of metal for one-family homes, and invented a system of coordinated unit planning and construction in 1918. His successes were coupled by his Queens Borough vice presidency. (Courtesy of Queens Community Board 6.)

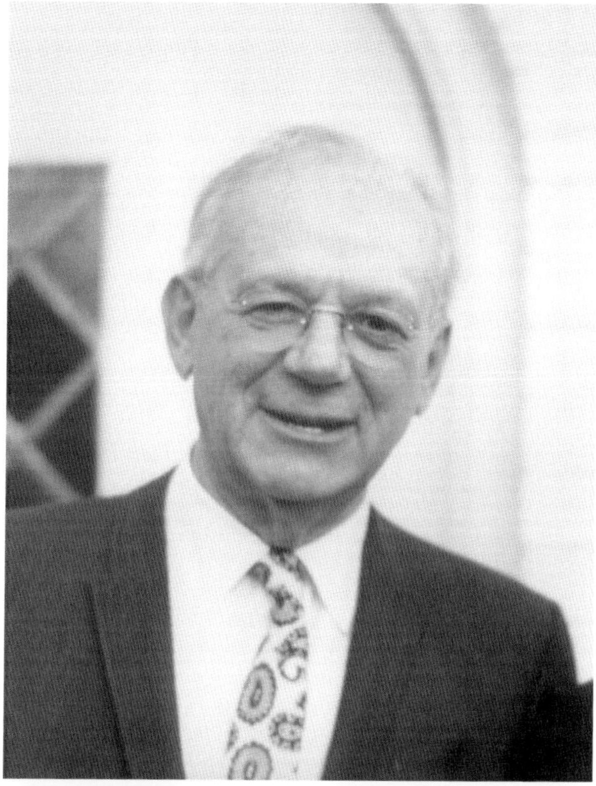

Benjamin Braunstein
Constantinople native Benjamin Braunstein (1892–1972) was an award-winning architect. When the Queens population doubled in the 1920s and further progressed due to the IND subway line and the 1939 World's Fair, Braunstein saw opportunity. He designed a large quantity of significant apartment houses in the Tudor, Colonial Revival, and Art Deco styles. Forest Hills residents witnessed the rise of Sutton Hall, the Holland House, Valeria Arms, The Wakefield, and Tilden Arms. As a client of the Rego Construction Company, he designed Rego Park's earliest apartment houses, which were Remo Hall, Jupiter Court, and Marion Court. Beyond the immediate area, The Mowbray in Kew Gardens and Hawthorne Court in Bayside are standouts. (Courtesy of Edith Magaziner.)

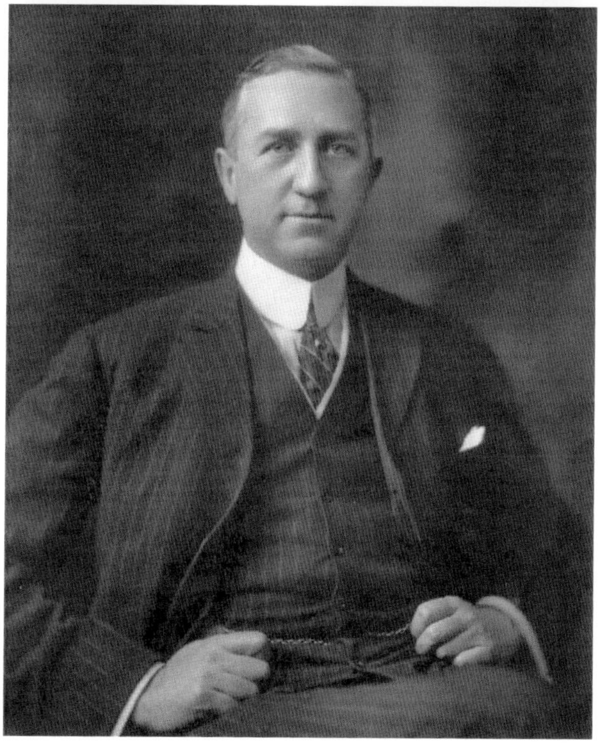

Kenneth MacKenzie Murchison
America's first concrete tennis stadium, the Forest Hills Tennis Stadium, was designed in 1923 by Kenneth MacKenzie Murchison (1872–1938), a West Side Tennis Club member and a foremost public building architect. Murchison's touch gave birth to a 14,000-seat stadium where pivotal moments in tennis and music were witnessed. Other public works include the Long Island Railroad Jamaica Station, Baltimore's Pennsylvania Station, the Hoboken Terminal, and New York City's Beaux-Arts Apartments. As a member of high society, he founded the Beaux-Arts Ball at Hotel Astor, and as a master of 14 instruments, he conducted New York's Mendelssohn Glee Club. (Courtesy of Pati de Wardener.)

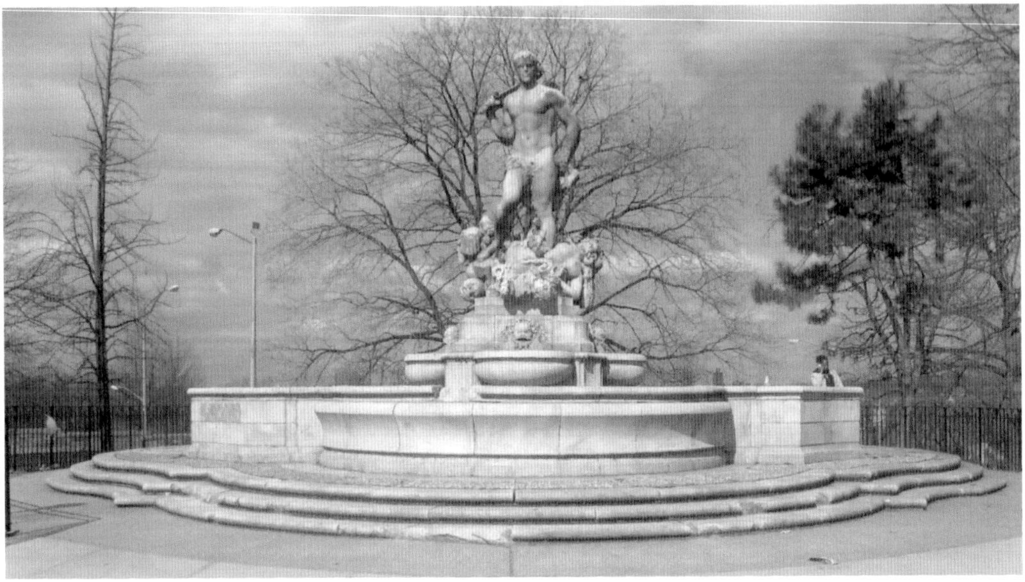

"Where Is Our Civic Virtue?"
This Classical 22-foot stone and marble sculpture was designed in 1920 by the last major American Beaux-Arts sculptor, Frederick William MacMonnies (1863–1937), and sculpted by the Piccirilli Brothers. It stood in Manhattan's City Hall Park until 1941, when it was relocated just west of Queens Borough Hall. Former congressman Anthony Weiner wrongfully called it sexist in 2011, leading to its relocation to Brooklyn's Green-Wood Cemetery. It depicts a muscular nude Hercules who stands over, but not atop, two mermaid-like sirens depicting vice and corruption. *Civic Virtue* is allegorical and denounces societal vice and corruption. (Photograph by Michael H. Perlman.)

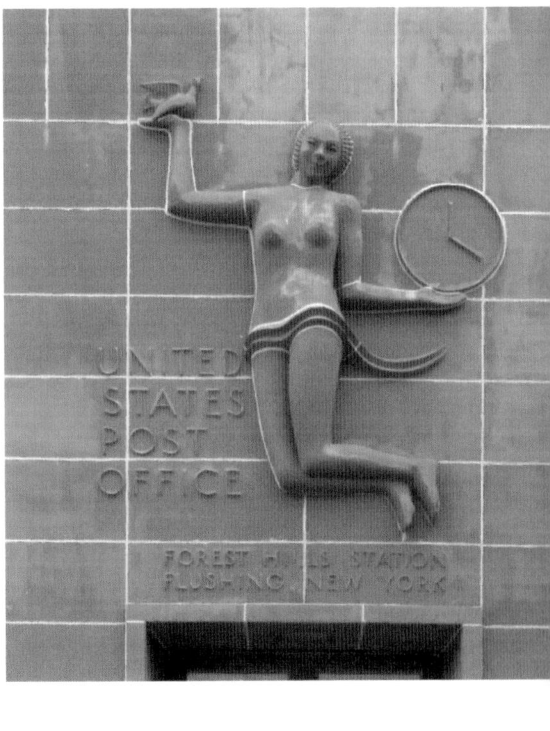

Spirit of Communication
Local residents entering the Forest Hills Post Office are greeted by the *Spirit of Communication*, a terra-cotta relief above the entryway of a site designed by Lorimer Rich (1892–1978). In 1938, famed sculptor Sten Jacobsson (1899–1983) designed the life-sized relief. Its depiction of a nude female with a carrier pigeon and a clock was deemed risqué when first unveiled. Some era post offices featured a mural, whereas Forest Hills received a sculpture commissioned by the Treasury Department Section of Fine Arts. Today, the relief is recognized by the New Deal Art Registry and the Smithsonian American Art Museum. The International-style post office was listed in the National Register of Historic Places in 1988. (Photograph by Michael H. Perlman.)

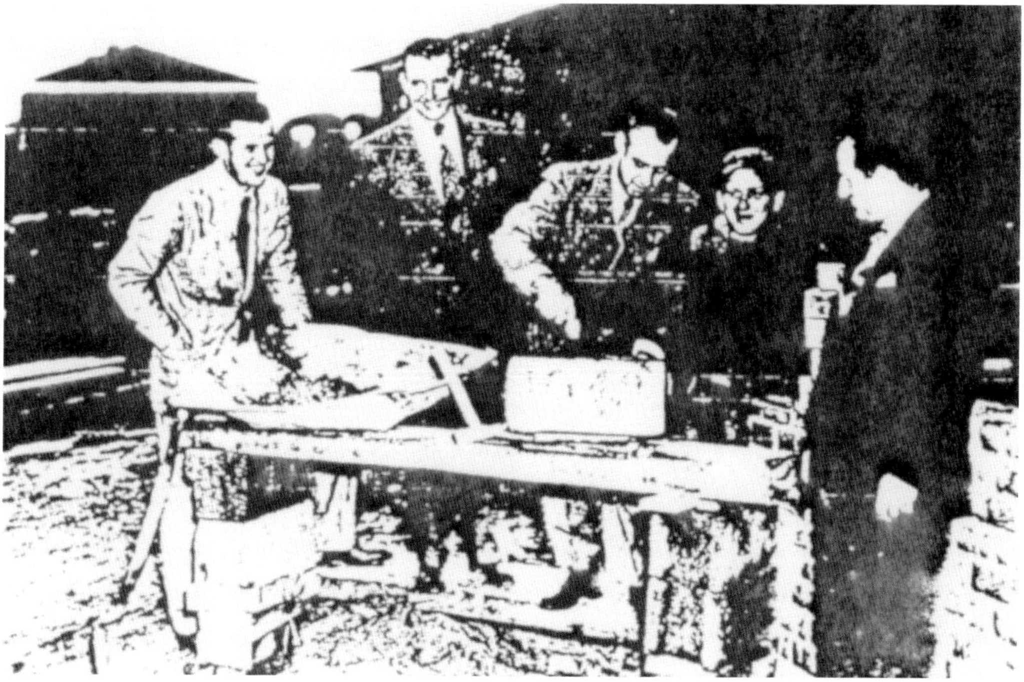

The Wolosoff Brothers of Forest Hills

In the early 1930s, Wolosoff brothers Morty, Alvin B., and Leon, of 69-50 Ingram Street, were the architects and builders of over 200 Neo-Tudor brick row houses and detached homes in Stafford Lawns.

Boundaries comprise Ingram Street to Juno Street between 68th Avenue (Baldwin Avenue) and 69th Avenue (Stafford Avenue), 68th Avenue from Harrow Street to Selfridge Street, Selfridge Street between Loubet Street and Olcott Street, and the Stafford Hall apartment house on 69th Avenue.

A log-burning fireplace, a paneled gallery dining room, and leaded glass studio casement windows exemplified distinction. Stafford Lawns was named after the country town of Stafford in Staffordshire, England. They named the nearby Kew Gardens Hills section in 1937. (Courtesy of Bill Safka.)

The Holland House

A Dutch king granted the land the Holland House sits on at 73-37 Austin Street to Casper Joost Springsteen in the mid-17th century, when Queens was a Dutch colonial province of New Netherlands. After remaining in the Springsteen farming family for seven generations, the four-acre parcel sold for in excess of $1 million. In 1929, the 10-story Old English and Art Deco apartment house, designed by Benjamin Braunstein, was prized for being the tallest in Queens. The Holland House was home to American Thoroughbred horse racing hall of fame jockey Eddie Arcaro (1916–1997) and fashion model Sabina Weber. Singers/actors Bing Crosby and Dixie Lee visited music publisher Rocco Vocco in Penthouse 10A. (Author's collection.)

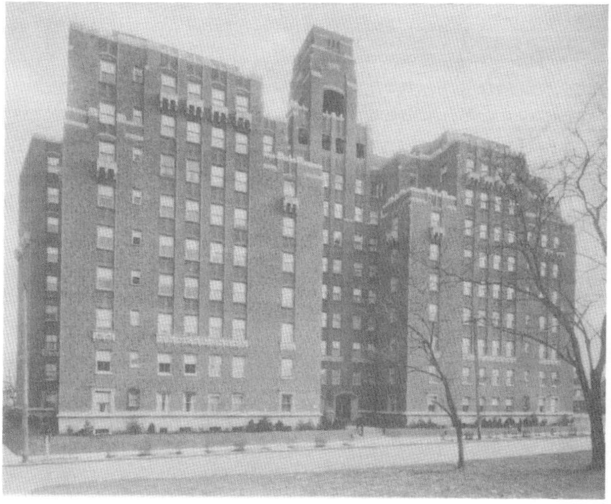

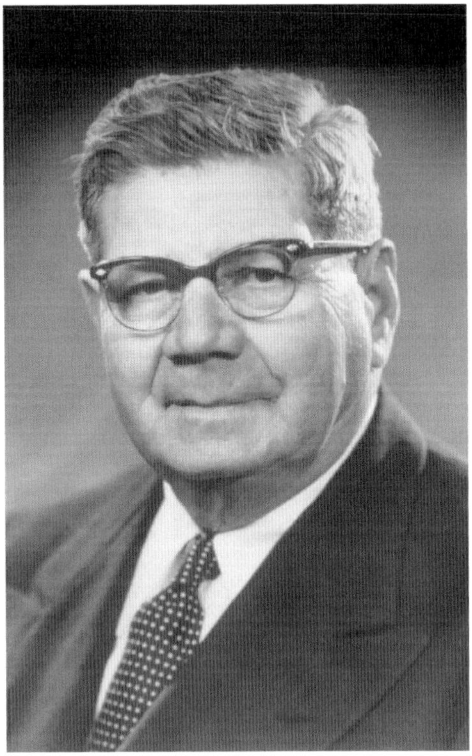

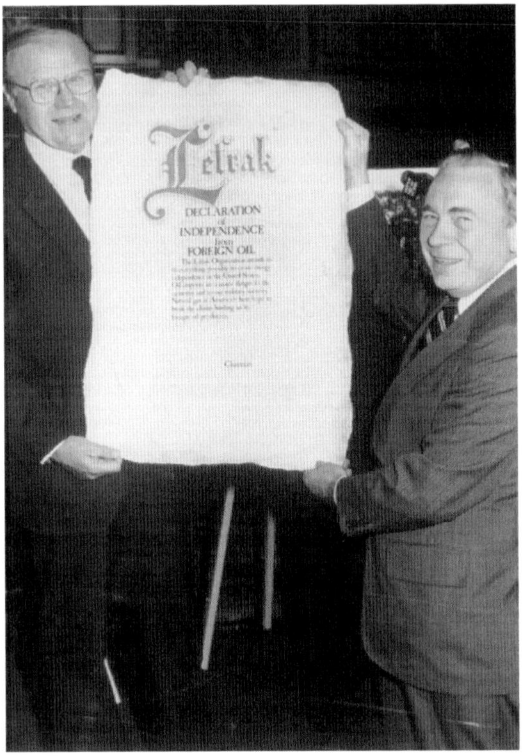

Harry and Samuel Lefrak

A flag proudly waves at Lefrak Memorial Square on Queens Boulevard and 65th Avenue in Rego Park alongside the Lefrak Center office building and a block east of the former Lefrak Tower. A 1965 plaque honors Sarah and Harry Lefrak. Harry Lefrak (1885–1963, pictured above at left) of 103-25 68th Avenue in Forest Hills chaired one of America's largest construction firms, the LeFrak Organization. At the time of his death, he was noted for building more than 400 middle-income apartment houses in the metropolitan area, with several named after states such as The Maryland and The Tennessee in Rego Park. He also established the Lefrak Foundation to benefit charitable and religious organizations, such as the United Jewish Appeal.

Harry's son, Samuel J. LeFrak (1918–2003, on the left in the image at right), also a philanthropist, became president of the Lefrak Organization in 1948. Known as the master of middle-income housing, he built Lefrak City in the 1960s, a contained residential and commercial development on a highly accessible location, consisting of 20 apartment high-rises with geographic names such as Paris and London. (Both courtesy of Jeff Gottlieb.)

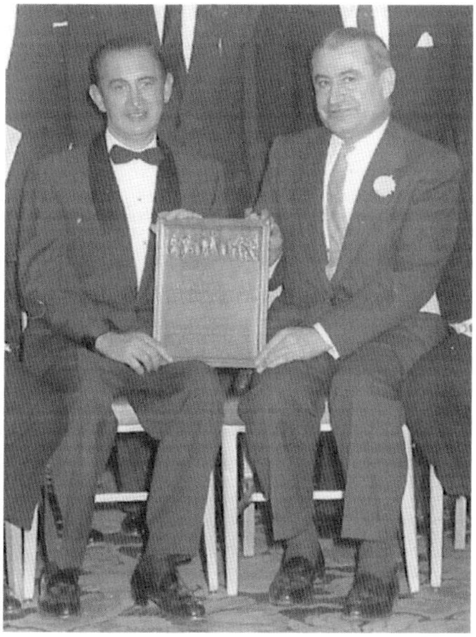

Alfred L. Kaskel and Philip Birnbaum

Among the most noteworthy community visionaries was the award-winning duo, architect Philip Birnbaum (right; 1907–1996) and builder Alfred L. Kaskel (left; 1901–1968).

It is rare for a duo to design and develop a generous section of a neighborhood. Their numerous apartment houses within the confines of Yellowstone Boulevard and 108th Street uniquely merge Colonial and Art Moderne styles, and are attributed as presidential buildings.

From 1939 through 1942, they completed The Thomas Jefferson, James Madison, Andrew Jackson, and The Benjamin Franklin. The George Washington and The Grover Cleveland followed in 1949. As innovators, they designed detailed large lobbies with picture windows overlooking a central courtyard with a sunken fountain and cherubs. They are also noted for curved brick corner terraces, bright and airy exposures, and lobbies with antiques from Europe.

Between 1953 and 1955, they introduced The Woodrow Wilson, The James Monroe, and The Martin Van Buren. In 1952, the 13-story Howard Apartments on 66th Road became the first fireproof buildings of steel and concrete without fire escapes, and were named after Kaskel's son Howard. The Birnbaum family lived in the 99-72 66th Road penthouse. The Anita and Carol apartments in Rego Park were named after Kaskel's daughters. Dara Gardens in Kew Gardens Hills was named after Birnbaum's daughter in 1952.

That year, the award-winning Mid-Century Modern Metropolitan Industrial Bank at 99-01 Queens Boulevard was completed. It was the first regional bank to utilize all industrial materials, distinguished by its colonnade corner with curved glass, stainless steel and Swedish granite fins, triple-height windows, a streamlined teakwood balcony, an Art Deco terrazzo floor, and an interior mural commemorating Colonial scenes of Queens.

For the Pickman family, Birnbaum designed Forest Hills South, a complex of seven Georgian Colonial buildings, which face a park-like campus with fountains north of Queens Boulevard between 76th Drive and 78th Avenue.

In 1965, the towering Mid-Century Modern Kennedy House on Queens Boulevard memorialized President Kennedy. It features a large crystal chandelier in the lobby, bands of terraces, and a roof deck with a swimming pool. "He wanted lobbies of buildings to feel somewhat grandiose, to give a type of prestige to the then rising middle class," said Dara Birnbaum.

As an architect of over 300 buildings throughout New York City, Birnbaum was highly praised for his efficient apartment layouts, where he aimed to eliminate interior hallways, enabling builders to fit additional apartments per floor. (Courtesy of Daniel Kaskel.)

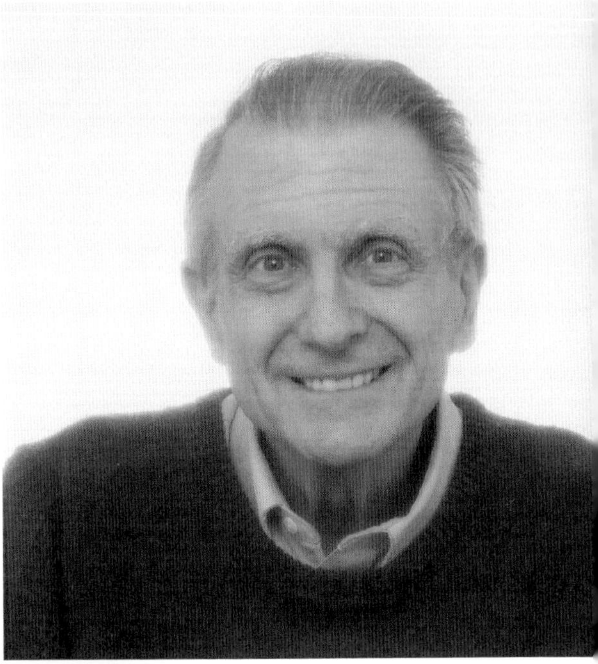

Jeff Gottlieb

Jeff Gottlieb (born 1941), a retired history teacher, builds a legacy as historian and president of the Central Queens Historical Association and the Queens Jewish Historical Society. Regarded as a "walking encyclopedia," he conducts historic tours of downtown Forest Hills, comprised of Austin Street, Continental Avenue, Ascan Avenue, and Queens Boulevard. Other tours cover the Forest Hills Gardens, the Cord Meyer section, Rego Park, Kew Gardens, and Richmond Hill. His bus tours include Jewish Central Queens and Jazz Trail: From Flushing Town Hall to Addisleigh Park. Gottlieb is a resident of Kew Gardens Hills and formerly lived in Forest Hills. (Courtesy of Continental Photo and Video.)

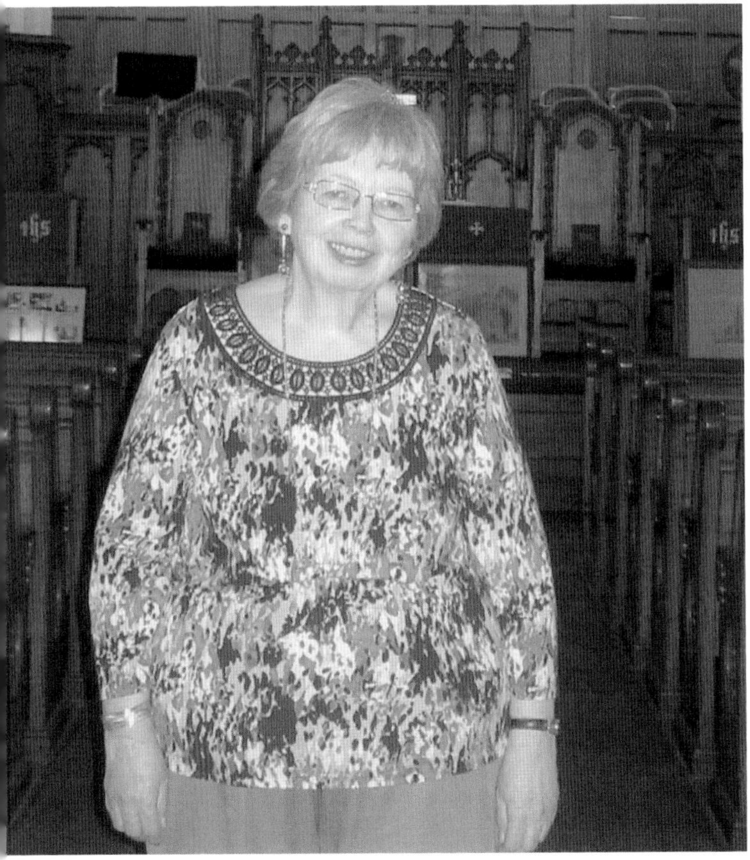

Marjorie Melikian

Rego Park resident Marjorie Melikian serves as historian of the First Presbyterian Church of Newtown, an 1895 edifice that houses a congregation dating to 1652. Newtown was renamed Elmhurst in the immediate area, and once included what became Rego Park and Forest Hills. Melikian conducts walking tours that explore Newtown's colonial roots. She restored their 1788 bell purchased after the Revolution, helped place the church in the State and National Registers of Historic Places in 2013, and launched a concert fundraising series to aid community musicians and the church's restoration. She reintroduced Newtown Pippin apple trees regionally. (Photograph by Michael H. Perlman.)

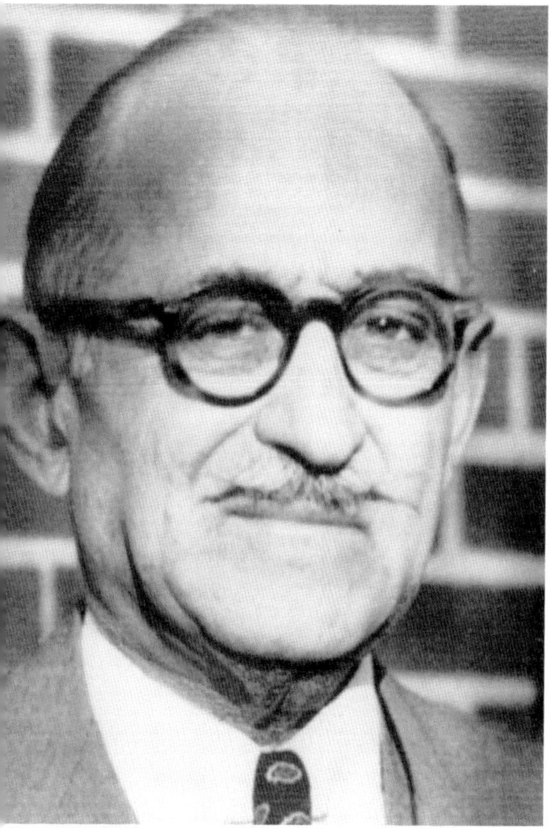

Leo Ehrenreich
A walk along Austin Street leads one to the Ehrenreich-Austin Playground, situated between 76th Avenue and 76th Drive. It honors Leo Ehrenreich (1882–1962). When parks commissioner Robert Moses and Queens Borough president George Harvey were receptive to his petition, the playground plot was acquired on May 2, 1947.

Ehrenreich was the first president of the Santee Regular Democratic Club. As a "one-man civic association," he advocated for Forest Hills and Kew Gardens playgrounds, led a citywide campaign to increase the number of police officers, and launched a successful program to install traffic signals at Queens's 50 most dangerous intersections. (Courtesy of Queens Community Board 6.)

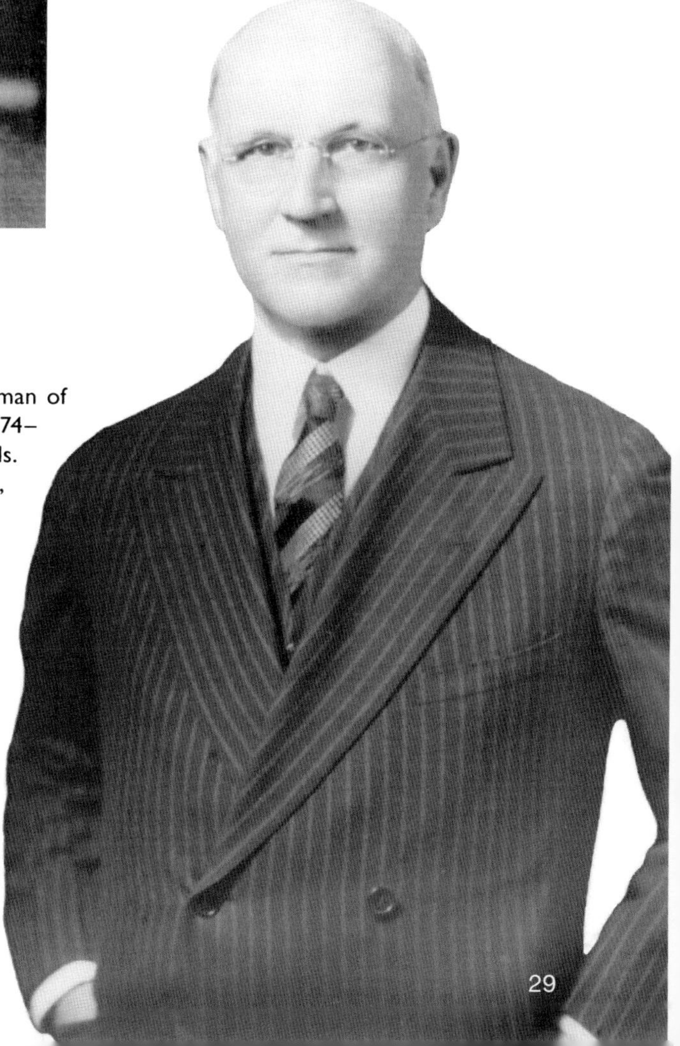

Frank Heustis Sincerbeaux
A well-respected civic leader, attorney, and man of many hats was Frank Heustis Sincerbeaux (1874–1969) of 43 Greenway Terrace in Forest Hills. He founded Public School 99 in Kew Gardens, was vice president of the Forest Hills Gardens Corporation, and was president of the Queens Valley Golf Club. At the Episcopal Church of the Resurrection in Kew Gardens, he earned the title of "Long Island's outstanding layman." He also served as president of the New York School for the Deaf. (Courtesy of Barbara Sincerbeaux.)

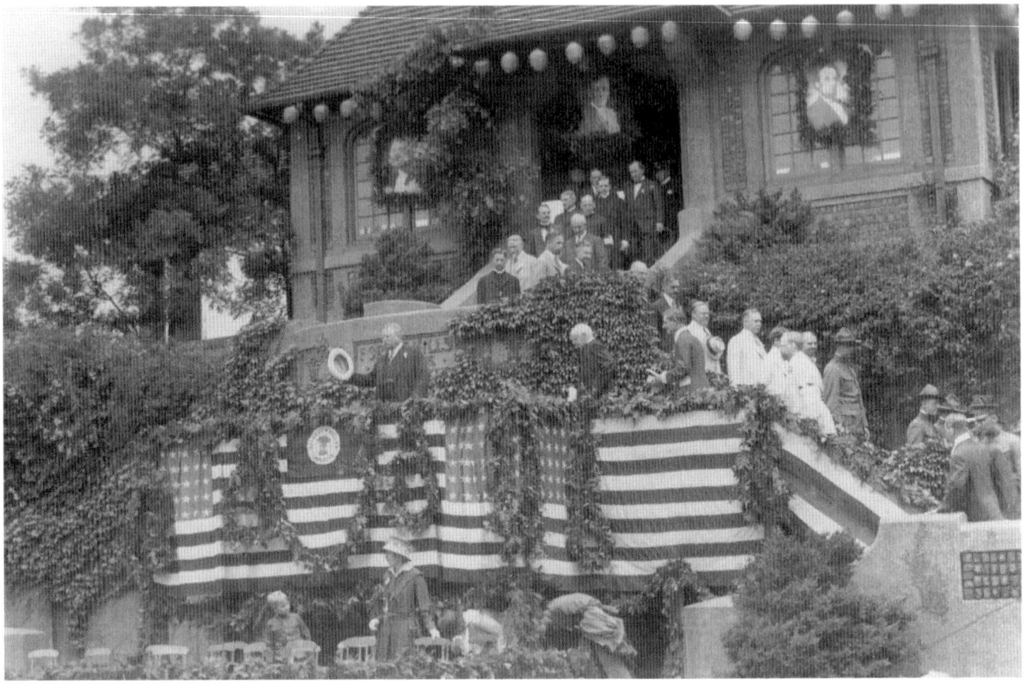

Theodore Roosevelt at Station Square

The 26th US president, Theodore Roosevelt (1858–1919), made a stop in the Forest Hills Gardens. One of Forest Hills's most historic moments transpired on July 4, 1917, when Colonel Roosevelt stood atop the Long Island Railroad Station steps of the exquisitely decorated Station Square and recited his "One Hundred Percent American" speech. To address World War I, he pleaded for a single standard of patriotism and loyalty to the America of Washington and Lincoln. He stated, "There can be no half and half attitude in this war, and no honorable man can afford to take such an attitude . . . Either a man is an American and nothing else, or he is not an American at all." The 3,000 onlookers cheered. Prior to introducing Roosevelt, Dr. Frederick Burgess, bishop of Long Island, read excerpts from Washington's Farewell Address. The Forest Hills Reception Committee included Forest Hills Gardens architect Grosvenor Atterbury, George C. Meyer of Cord Meyer Development Company, John M. Demarest of the Sage Foundation Homes Company, and famed author Lyman Beecher Stowe. (Courtesy of Cord Meyer Development Company.)

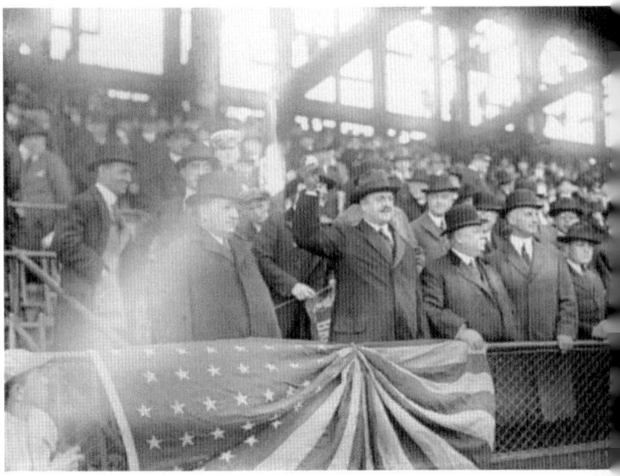

Mayor John Francis Hylan

It is inspirational how an individual who was raised on a farm and arrived in New York with $4.50 would become the 96th mayor of New York City. Mayor John Francis Hylan (1868–1936) lived at 2 Olive Place in the Forest Hills Gardens and served from 1918 to 1925. He played a major role in the creation of a subway owned and operated by the public, which would become the Independent Subway System. (Courtesy of Library of Congress.)

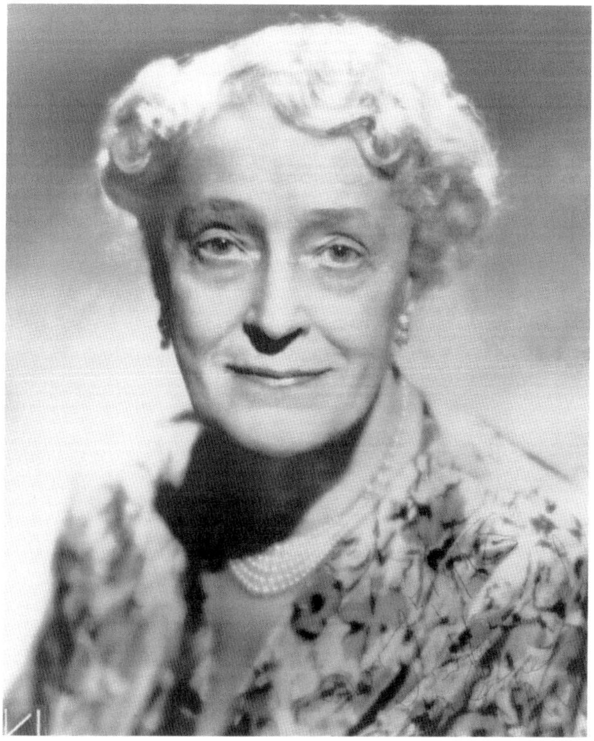

Lucy Allen Smart

A respected local historian who published *History of Forest Hills from Days of the Indians* (1924), Lucy Allen Smart (1877–1960) resided at 45 Deepdene Road and then the Forest Hills Inn. She was the Kew-Forest School's librarian and dean of girls and *The Forest Hills Gardens Bulletin* editor. In 1937, Mayor LaGuardia appointed her as secretary of the board of trustees of the Queensborough Public Library, which was a historic first for females on citywide library boards. On club stages, she gained fame for her portrayals of historic American women including Harriet Beecher Stowe and Dolley Madison. (Courtesy of Queens Community Board 6.)

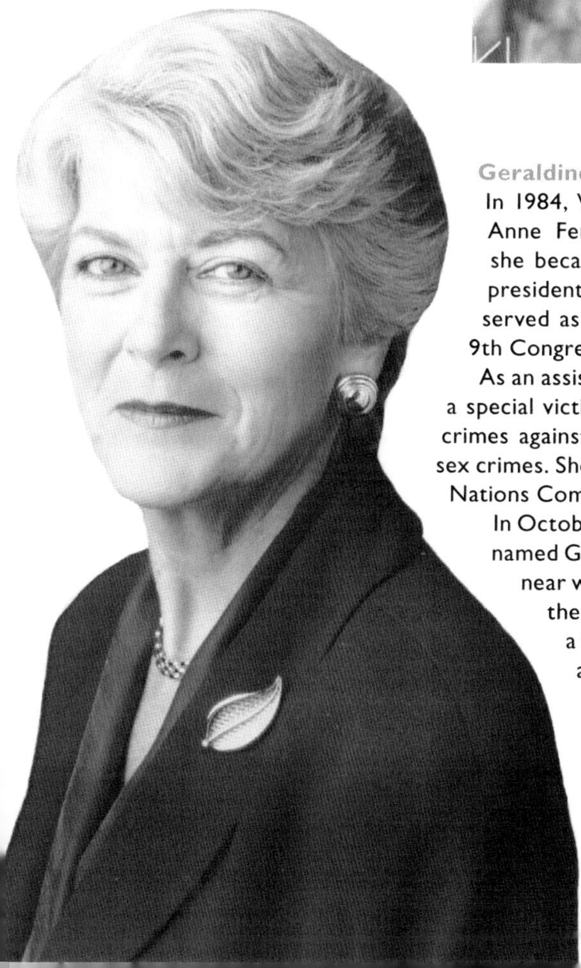

Geraldine Anne Ferraro

In 1984, Vice Pres. Walter Mondale selected Geraldine Anne Ferraro (1935–2011) as his running mate, and she became the first female and Italian American vice president candidate on a major party ticket. She also served as a triple-term Queens congresswoman of the 9th Congressional District from 1979 through 1985.

As an assistant district attorney for Queens, she founded a special victims bureau and supervised the prosecution of crimes against seniors, domestic violence, child abuse, and sex crimes. She also served as a US ambassador to the United Nations Commission on Human Rights.

In October 2012, Austin Street at Ascan Avenue was co-named Geraldine Ferraro Way at a dedication ceremony near where she once resided at 22 Deepdene Road in the Forest Hills Gardens. "Geraldine Ferraro was a tireless advocate, dedicated public servant, and a pioneer who broke through gender gaps and energized a generation of women through her historic nomination as vice president," said Councilmember Karen Koslowitz. (Courtesy of Queens Community Board 6.)

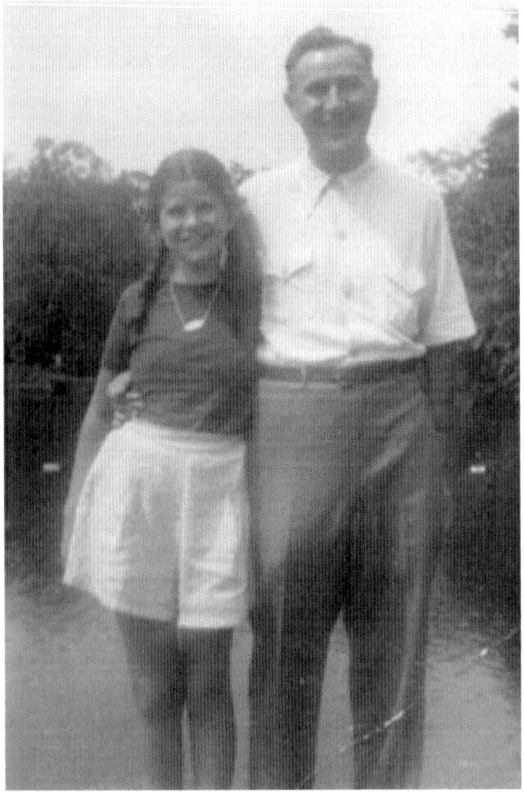

Arthur J. Katzman

"The conscience of city government" was the nickname earned by Arthur J. Katzman (1904–1993), who served New York City Council for 29 years after being elected in 1961. His residence was The Park Briar at 110-45 Queens Boulevard in Forest Hills.

Katzman advocated for the creation of Yellowstone Park between Yellowstone Boulevard, 68th Avenue, and 68th Road. What was slated for residential development opened as a park on May 27, 1968. The park's Arthur J. Katzman Playground marks his legacy.

Katzman was the recipient of the LaGuardia Medal by Mayor Edward Koch and the Daughters of the American Revolution Good Citizens Award in response to outstanding community service as a naturalized citizen. He is pictured here with Marcia Katzman. (Courtesy of Marcia Katzman Allen.)

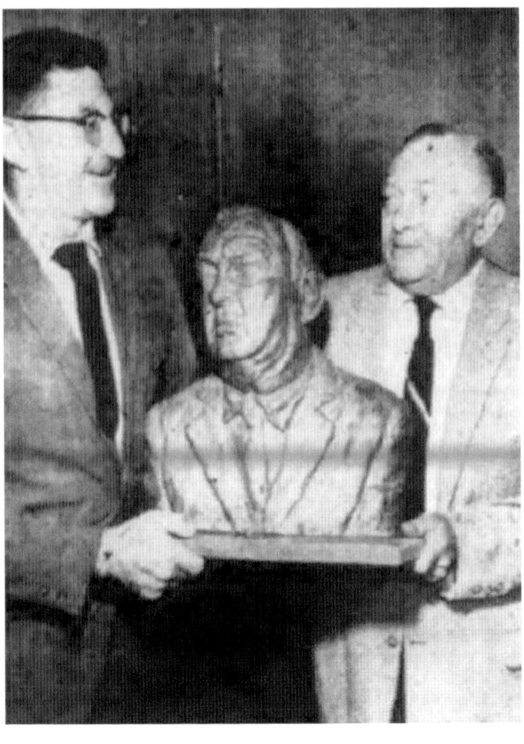

Meet the Federoffs at Federoff Triangle

On the bustling Queens Boulevard in Forest Hills lies a triangular park bounded by 67th Road and 102nd Street. It is a retreat for families, friends, and lovers who congregate under Sycamore trees.

A plot of asphalt in the 1950s became an unnamed greener park in the 1960s. Then it underwent an incarnation in September 1970 when city council introduced a bill to name the park in honor of Gussie Federoff (1889–1967) and Barnett Federoff (c. 1895–1970), who lived nearby.

Gussie was born in Kiev and married Barnett. As a member of Hadassah, which advocates for women's issues and provides medical training, she raised funds for the United Jewish Appeal. Barnett was the first president of the Senior Citizens Society of Lost Battalion Hall in Rego Park. Here, Lost Battalion Hall director David Siegel (left) presents a bust to Barnett Federoff in 1963. (Courtesy of Queens Community Board 6.)

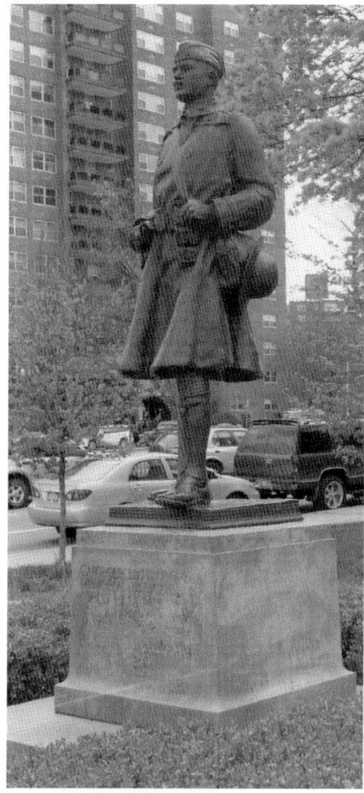

Capt. Gerald MacDonald

Forest Hills's serene green spot amidst the hustle and bustle of Queens Boulevard between Yellowstone Boulevard and 70th Road was named MacDonald Park on April 25, 1933, after Capt. Gerald MacDonald (1882–1929), a World War I veteran. He was an officer of engineers at the Battle of Meuse-Argonne and erected bridges and dug trenches. On May 26, 1934, a bronze Gerald MacDonald statue was dedicated to those who served in the war. American Legion Post 630 allocated $1,500 at the request of his brother, World War I veteran Henry MacDonald.

The historic site was the scene of memorable community events. In 1969, Mayor John V. Lindsay addressed an audience of 300, and in September 1964, US Attorney General Robert F. Kennedy addressed 700. In 2011, "Queen of Freestyle" Judy Torres, also a 103.5 WKTU on-air personality, performed at the "One Thing That's Green" event, which attracted over 800 volunteers who planted trees. (Photograph by Michael H. Perlman.)

Forest Hills Tree Giveaways

Since 2011, a tradition of biannual Forest Hills Tree Giveaway events has blossomed in MacDonald Park, where volunteers donated 1,200 trees to the public, planting the seeds for next generation's mature trees. This signifies how community partnerships enhance the city's environment and aesthetics. Rego-Forest Preservation Council and Four Borough Neighborhood Preservation Alliance are in partnership with New York Restoration Project and MillionTreesNYC. Tree certificates name trees after local notables, historic sites, and streets. (Author's collection.)

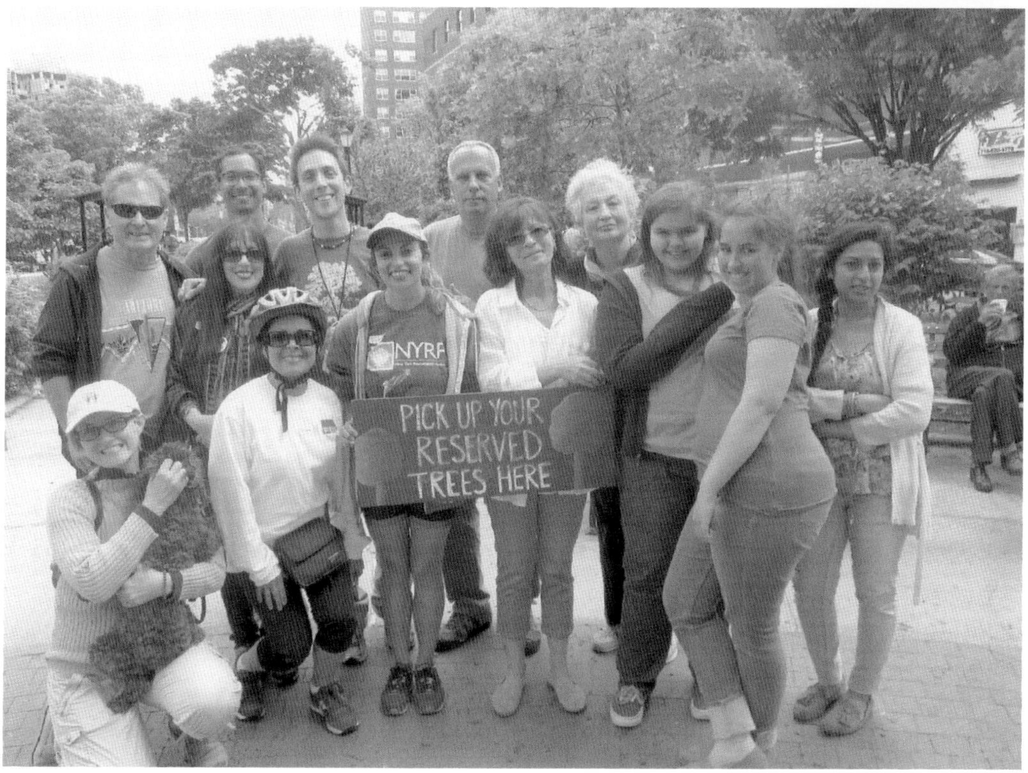

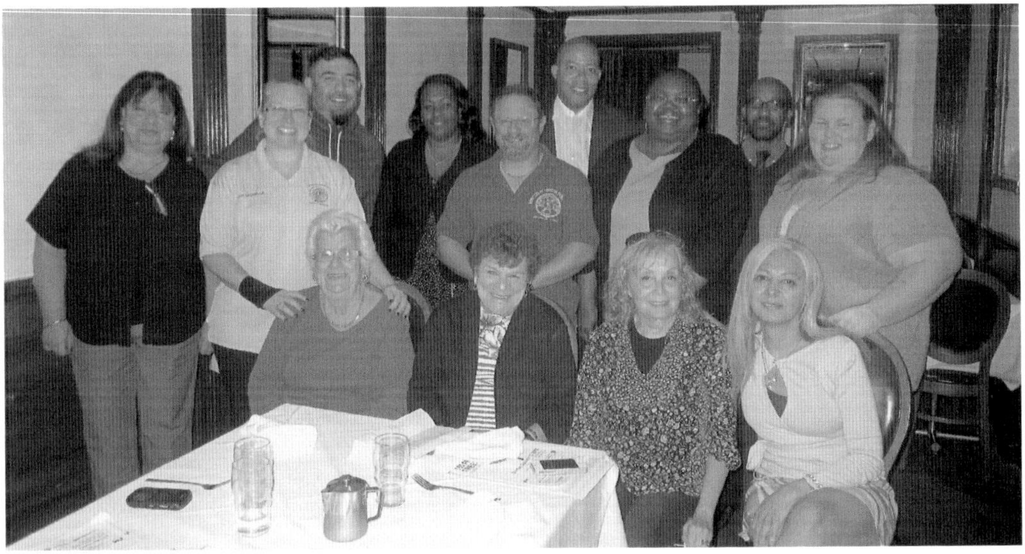

Rego Park–Forest Hills Lions Club

Founded in 1949, the Lions Club coordinates annual summer festivals for foster care children at Forestdale in Forest Hills, feeds the needy, cares for the elderly, recycles eyeglasses, and contributes to the Lions Eye Banks for corneal transplants. "Volunteers don't get paid because they are worthless, but because they are priceless," said Lion Robert Libin, whose grandfather was a charter member. "Alone we can do so little, together we can do so much," stated Helen Keller at the Lions' 1925 International Convention. (Photograph by Michael H. Perlman.)

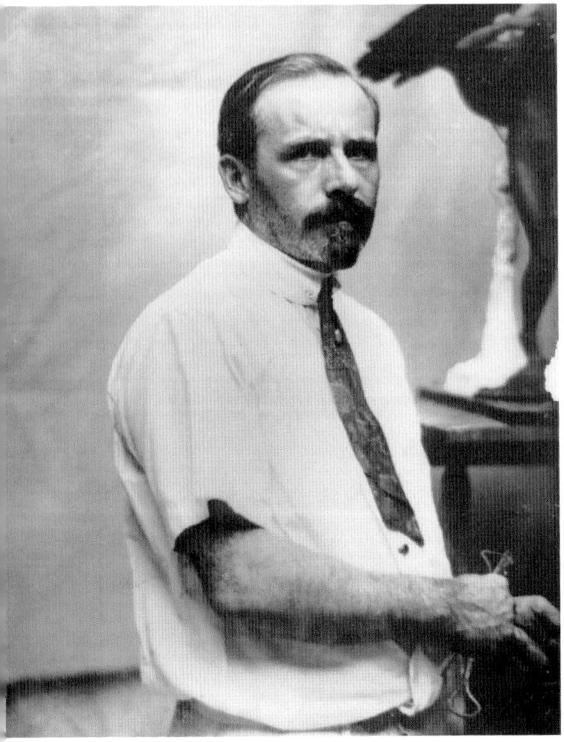

Adolph Alexander Weinman

On Flagpole Green, the World War I Soldiers & Sailors Memorial commemorates 102 community residents. It was designed by Adolph Weinman (1870–1952), a profound American sculptor who lived at 236 Greenway South and maintained a studio at 234 Greenway South. It reads, "Erected by the citizens of Forest Hills in recognition of the patriotic spirit and loyal devotion of the men of this community who served in the Military Forces of The United States in The Great War."

Another commission was Weinman's *Pietà* on Our Lady Queen of Martyrs Church. Atop Manhattan's Municipal Building stands his *Civic Fame* sculpture. He also designed the silver Mercury dime and Walking Liberty half dollar, the 1904 Louisiana Purchase World's Fair Exposition medals, and *The Rising Sun* and *Descending Night* allegorical scenes. (Courtesy of Queens Community Board 6.)

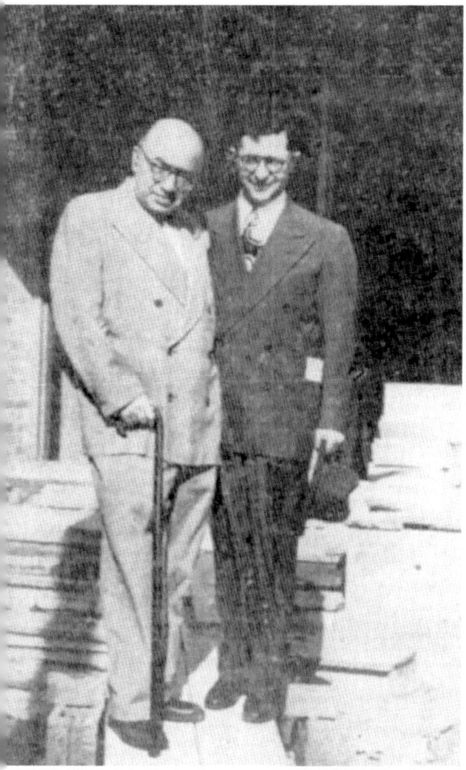

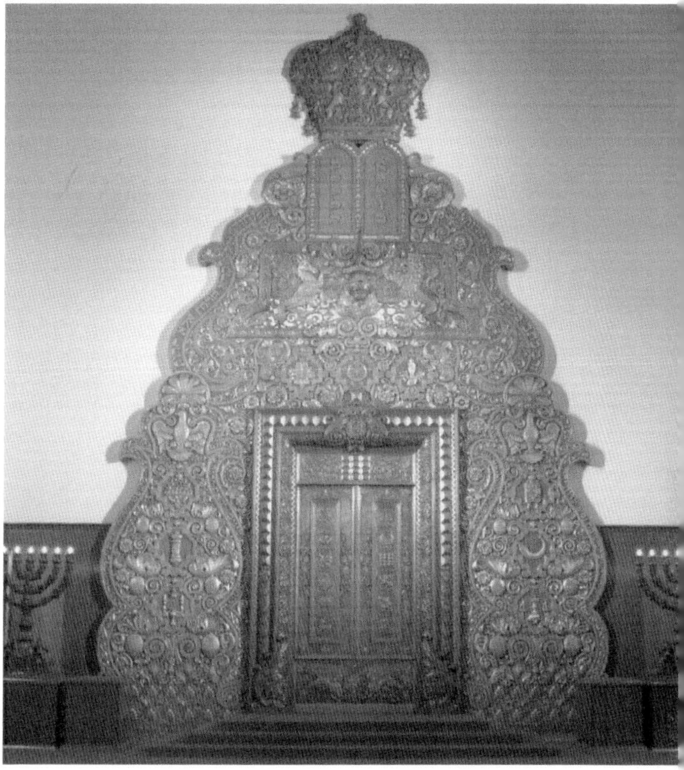

Arthur Szyk and Rabbi Ben Zion Bokser

Between 1933 and 1984, Rabbi Ben Zion Bokser (1907–1984, pictured above left, on the right) served Forest Hills Jewish Center (FHJC). Descending from Poland, he would later make his home at 96-01 68th Avenue. He was an influential rabbi of Conservative Judaism and chairman of the Committee on Jewish Law and Standards of the Rabbinical Assembly.

At Queens College, he was a religious studies and political science professor. Some of his books were *Judaism: Profile of a Faith* and *Jews, Judaism and the State of Israel.*

The corner of FHJC is co-named Rabbi Ben Zion Bokser Square, which New York City mayor Ed Koch signed into a bill in 1984.

Stepping inside the 1,400-seat sanctuary, the over 20-foot ornate golden *Aron Kodesh* (*Holy Ark*, pictured above right) was designed by famed artist Arthur Szyk (1894–1951, above left, on the left), a native of Poland. The *Holy Ark* was his first 3-D creation for a synagogue and resembles a Torah breastplate depicting Judaic traditions and holidays. It is regarded as one of the greatest works of 20th-century Judaic art.

The Arthur Szyk Society referred to his art as a means to promote ethnic and religious tolerance, human dignity, and social justice. Syzk worked in the tradition of 16th-century miniaturist painters utilizing text and illustrations. The famed *Szyk Haggadah*, given to the synagogue, became a work of hope and courage during World War II. (Left, courtesy of the Arthur Szyk Society; right, photograph by Michael H. Perlman.)

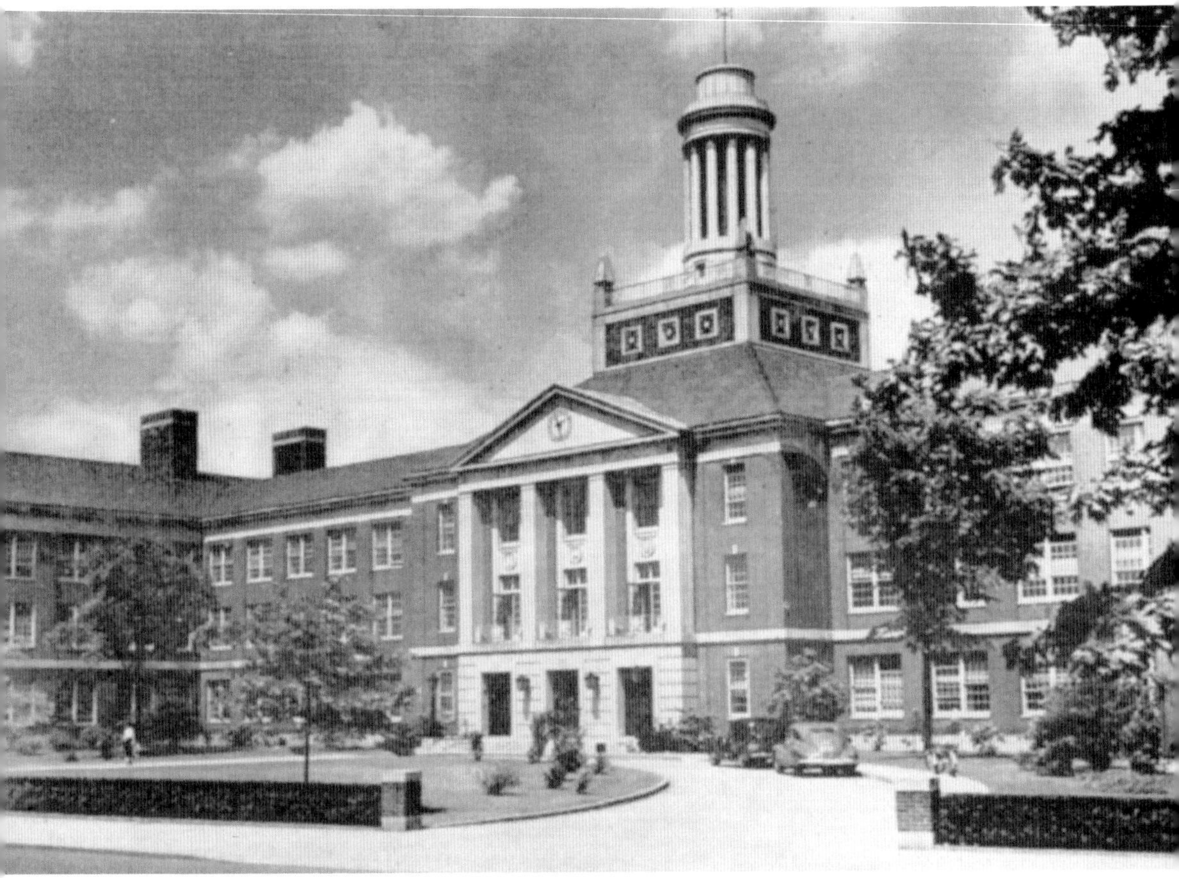

Forest Hills High School
The three-story Georgian Colonial–style Forest Hills High School (FHHS) at 67-01 110th Street, designed by the notable New York City Board of Education architect Eric Kebbon at a sum of $3,225,000, more closely evokes a forested college campus with columns, pediments, and an illuminated cupola. Opened on February 3, 1941, FHHS would generate an extensive resume of alumni ranging from Burt Bacharach and the Ramones to Simon & Garfunkel; Bob Keeshan, who portrayed Captain Kangaroo; and Marty Ingels.

The cornerstone ceremony was on May 12, 1940, during the period of the 1939–1940 World's Fair. On scene were New York City mayor Fiorello H. LaGuardia, who addressed a diverse crowd and laid the cornerstone; Newtown High School Band and Choir and Richmond Hill High School Chorus, which performed patriotic numbers; and religious figures such as Rabbi Solomon Landman of Temple Isaiah of Kew Gardens, Rev. John Wells Rahill of the Church-in-the-Gardens, and Rev. Joseph McLaughlin of the Church of Our Lady Queen of Martyrs.

In 1998, Pres. Bill Clinton praised the school's academic and extracurricular excellence, and it received recognition as one of 124 Blue Ribbon schools nationally. In 2000, First Lady Hillary Clinton delivered the commencement address. Today, it has an enrollment of 3,708 students.

For over 60 years, the 1,176-seat auditorium has accommodated *SING!*, a musical production featuring students who compete on a grade basis. Folk-rock legend Paul Simon took the stage in the late 1950s, and Hollywood producer Leslie Urdang coordinated *Senior SING!* in 1972. FHHS competes in the Public Schools Athletic League, and students participate in sports ranging from basketball and track to tennis and baseball in the generously sized field. (Author's collection.)

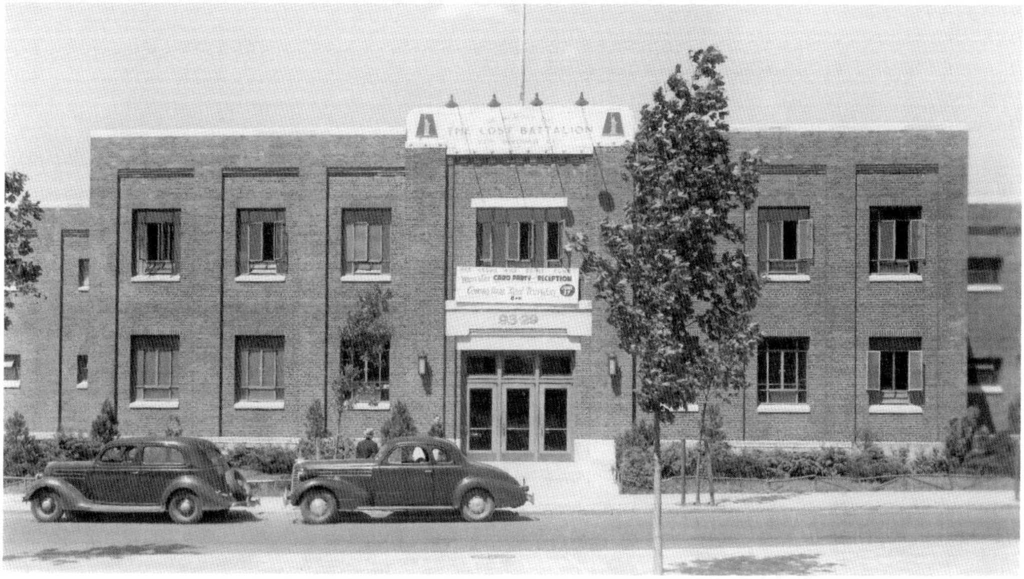

The Lost Battalion Hall Recreation Center

In 1939, the Works Progress Administration funded Lost Battalion Hall at 93-29 Queens Boulevard in Rego Park, which honors the 77th Division of the US Army for its heroism in World War I. This division fought in the Battle of the Argonne in France. More than half its 550 American soldiers perished and are members of "The Lost Battalion." A tributary limestone installation with two bronze tablets of the Statue of Liberty adorns the facade, and the interior features a WPA mural of the Lost Battalion in action.

Historically, Lost Battalion Hall featured a firing range and drill hall for the Queens Veterans of Foreign Wars and the American Legion. The Civilian Defense Volunteer Office welcomed enrollees for World War II here. In 1941, 2,000 people celebrated Pres. Franklin D. Roosevelt's birthday with a dance to aid an infantile paralysis drive. Other events included square dance festivals in the 1940s, an appearance by professional basketball player Bobby McDermott in 1950, boxing matches, a Perquackey contest in 1966, and testimonials for Presidents Truman and Eisenhower. (Courtesy of Jeff Gottlieb.)

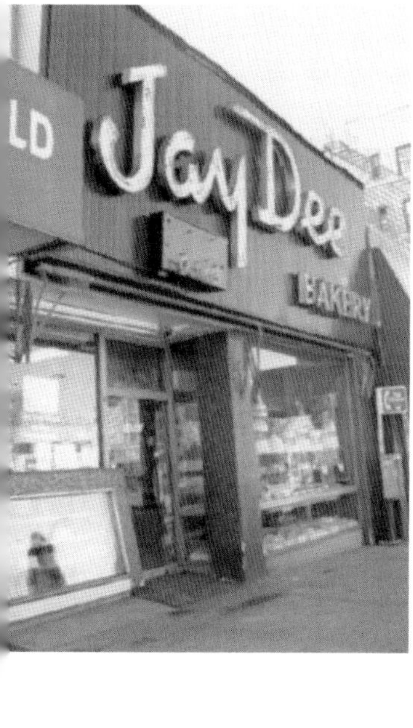

Jay Dee Bakery

In pink neon, massive Art Deco letters spell out "Jay Dee Bakery," a cornerstone at 98-92 Queens Boulevard from the early 1950s through 2009. Philip Kampin and Maurice Goldstein were the owners in 1952. It recalls an era when rye bread, Napoleons, and assorted cookies were freshly prepared, and the staff and patrons exchanged stories. Jay Dee catered numerous social functions. The window was a neighborhood showcase filled with multilayer cake models. The facade's whimsical Ravenna glass mosaics in green, orange, and gold were works of art, and Moderne curves characterized the interior ceiling and walls, where indented clouds displayed cake models. (Courtesy of Forgotten New York.)

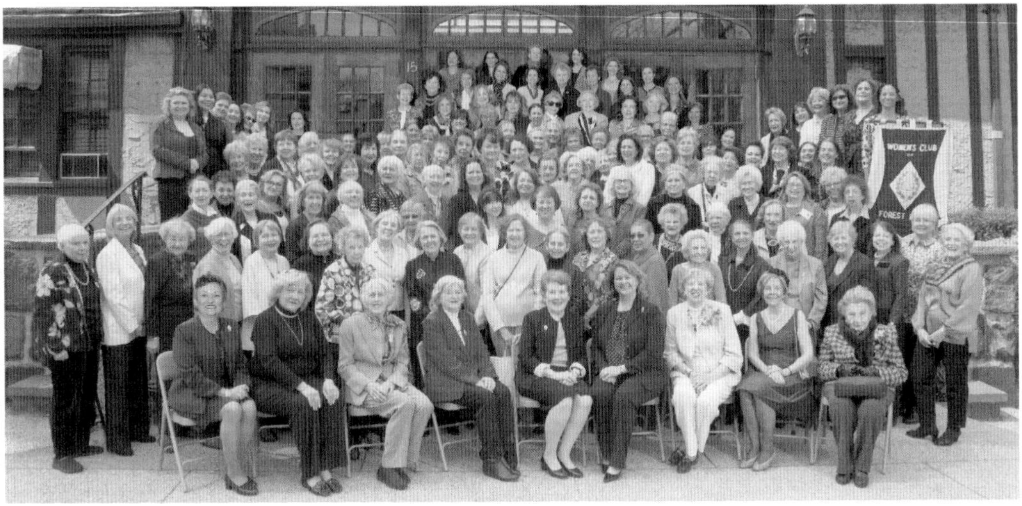

The Women's Club and the Men's Club at the Community House

This nonsectarian Tudor clubhouse at 15 Borage Place in the Forest Hills Gardens has served as a second home for notables and locals since August 12, 1926. Designed by Forest Hills Gardens architect Grosvenor Atterbury, it features special events at Hof Hall and Smith Hall, a heated indoor pool, educational spaces, and a gym. The Women's Club of Forest Hills and the Men's Club of Forest Hills, which celebrated their 100th anniversary in 2013, foster bonds between an extensive membership and the community through philanthropic, social, intellectual, and artistic initiatives.

Men's Club historians recall encounters with Broadway performers including Lee Sullivan, Hal LeRoy, Bert Wheeler, and Arthur Treacher, and a notable member, humorist Don Marquis. In 2014, the Community House accommodated the centennial celebration of Public School 101 (2 Russell Place), featuring the music of Forest Hills notable Betina Hershey Russo. (Both courtesy of Church-in-the Gardens Community House.)

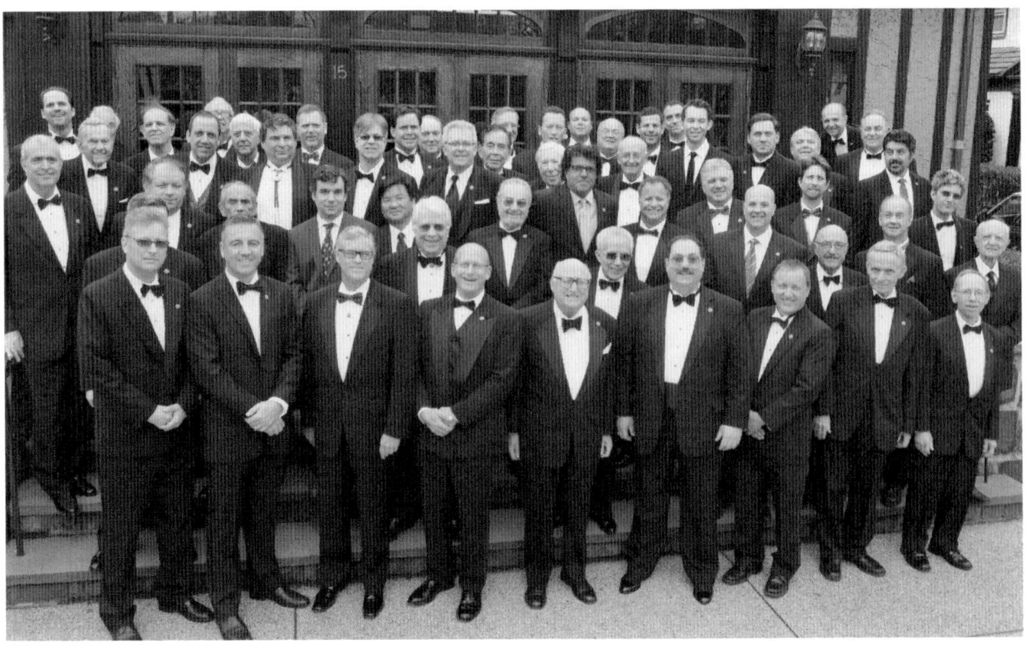

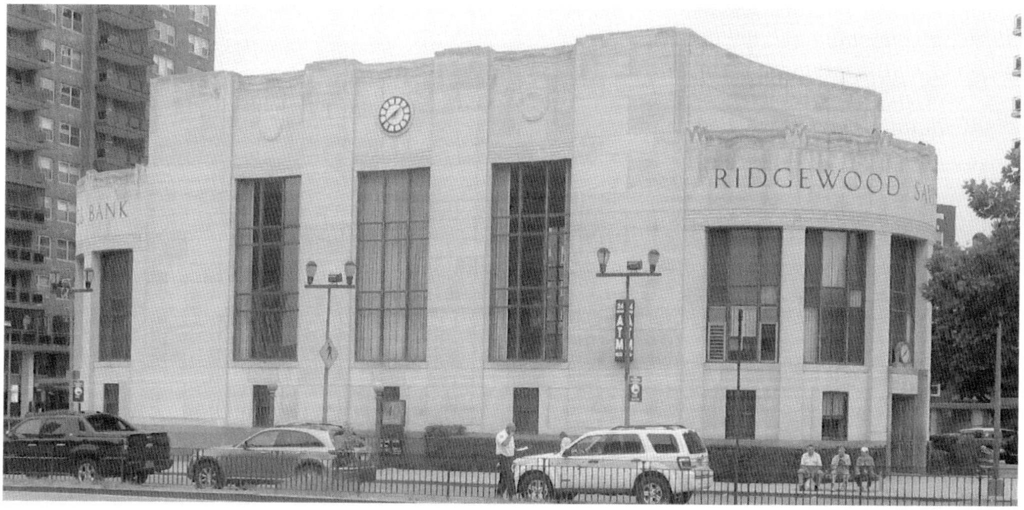

Ridgewood Savings Bank

Halsey, McCormack & Helmer, a noteworthy New York firm that specialized in bank architecture, presented Forest Hills with the three-story Modern Classical–style Ridgewood Savings Bank at 107-55 Queens Boulevard in 1940. This New York City Landmark bank, which originated in 1921 in Ridgewood, valued Forest Hills growth reflected by the IND subway line in 1936 and the 1939 World's Fair.

Some distinctive features are flat eagles and modernistic clocks on the convex and concave facade, and a streamlined ceiling designed by the famed muralist Angelo Magnanti (1879–1969).

Staff members volunteer in soup kitchens, compile food collections, and coordinate family festivals. Representatives visit schools to teach students from kindergarten through college about how "saving is the secret of wealth" (the bank's slogan), and to help establish their accounts. (Photograph by Michael H. Perlman.)

Tower Diner and the Gatanas Family

Opened in 1993, Tower Diner at 98-95 Queens Boulevard in Forest Hills is a representation of Americana. Owners Spiro and John Gatanas and their parents have creatively adapted the Colonial-style Emigrant Savings Bank while preserving authentic features such as the imposing clock tower, easily spotted along Queens Boulevard. This is a must-stop for extensive American and cultural foods, including chicken souvlaki, turkey burgers, and pasta primavera. Earlier incarnations were Manna-Hatin Restaurant, a nightly dancing spot that featured Billy Rose's Aquabelles from the 1939 World's Fair's Aquacade, and Croft Chemists, which housed a soda fountain. (Photograph by Michael H. Perlman.)

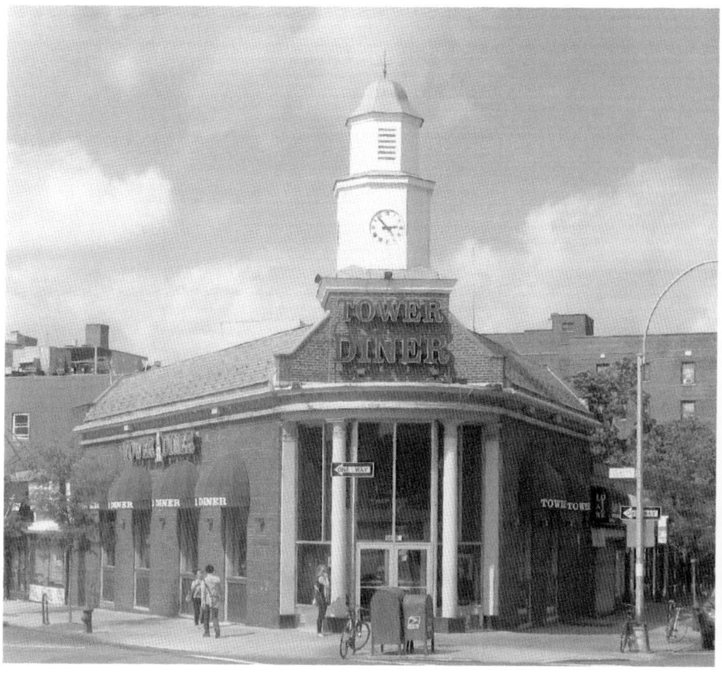

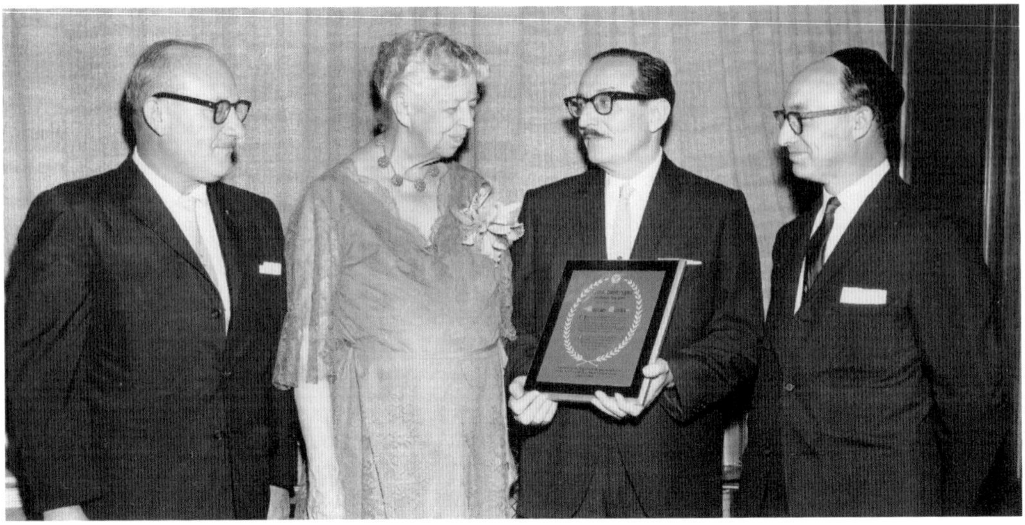

Rabbi Josiah Derby and Alexander Raymond Katz

Rego Park Jewish Center at 97-30 Queens Boulevard (pictured below) was founded when the 1939 World's Fair contributed to a population boom.

Rabbi Josiah Derby (1913–2002), a native of Ukraine, immigrated to the United States in 1921. As a rabbinical student, he became the synagogue's first spiritual leader from 1941 to 1983. He gave women a greater presence in the synagogue and played an influential role in the Conservative movement. His establishment of the Solomon Schecter School of Queens became the first Conservative day school countrywide.

Listed in the National Register of Historic Places in 2009, the synagogue is a showcase of Judaic art and Art Deco and Bauhaus-inspired architecture. Adorning the facade are stained glass windows and a colorful mosaic mural depicting Old Testament scenes and symbols. Both were designed by the prolific 20th-century artist Alexander Raymond Katz (1895–1974), noteworthy for his ornamental treatment of the Hebrew alphabet in conjunction with Judaic symbols.

Chairman of the board Ruth Loewenstein's cherished memories include Rabbi Josiah Derby, Cantor Morris Lowy, a visit by Eleanor Roosevelt, a renowned choir, a thriving Hebrew school, and clubs including the Sisterhood and the Men's Club. Pictured above from left to right are Harris Herman, Eleanor Roosevelt, Marcus Marks, and Rabbi Derby at the United Jewish Appeal dinner. (Above, courtesy of Rego Park Jewish Center; below, photograph by Michael H. Perlman.)

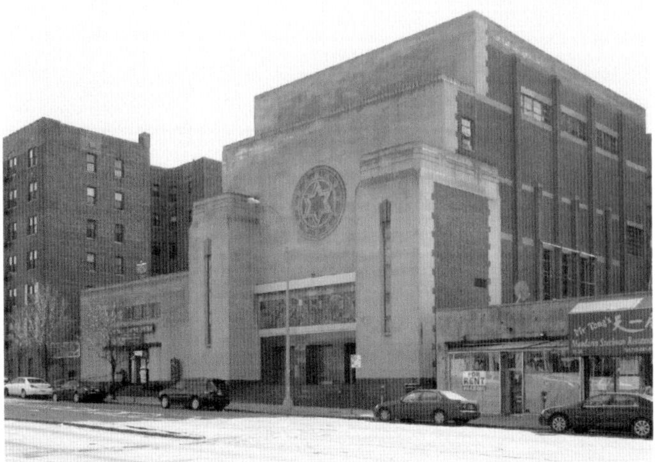

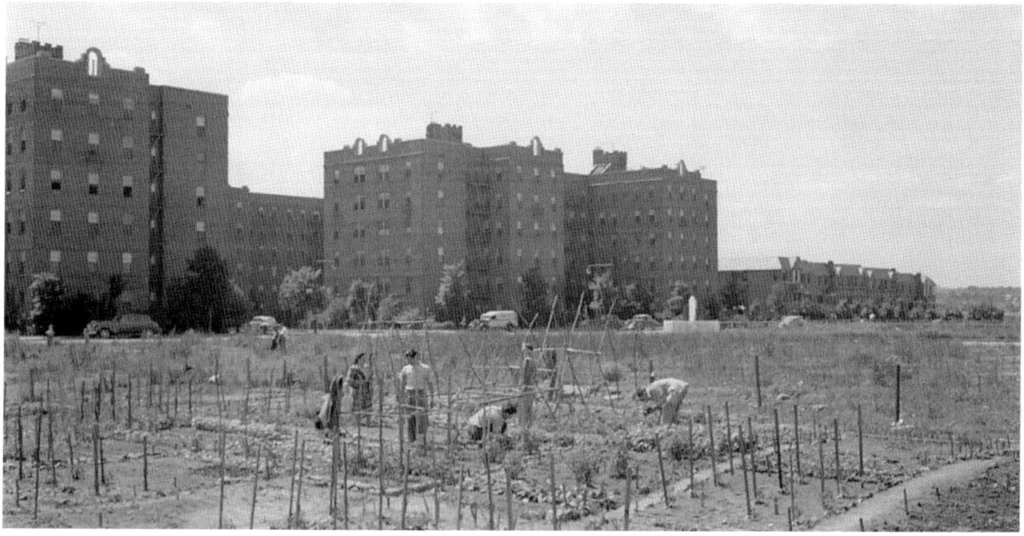

Victory Gardening with Ruth M. Noble

Forest Hills and Rego Park were among numerous communities nationwide where families and neighbors bonded by turning the soil of backyards and communal gardens to grow produce, conserve food, and help provide relief for World War II servicemen. Forest Hills had 33 communal plots and hundreds of individual gardens. Some were established near the Queens Gardens Apartments and Thorneycroft Apartments complexes. Lots were transformed from dumping grounds to diverse gardens offering corn, beets, lettuce, cabbage, tomatoes, herbs, and coffee. In July 1943, Ruth M. Noble, honorable chairman of the Forest Hills Victory Gardens Committee, coordinated the multi-generational RKO-Civilian Defense Volunteer Office Victory Garden Contest. "War Gardens for Victory—Grow Vitamins at Your Kitchen Door," read a US Office of War Information poster. The US Department of Agriculture's short film *Victory Garden* emphasized its benefits. With the aid of Hollywood, *Food and Magic* was among 47 documentaries produced between 1942 and 1945, in addition to cartoons such as *Jack Wabbit and the Beanstalk*. (Courtesy of Library of Congress.)

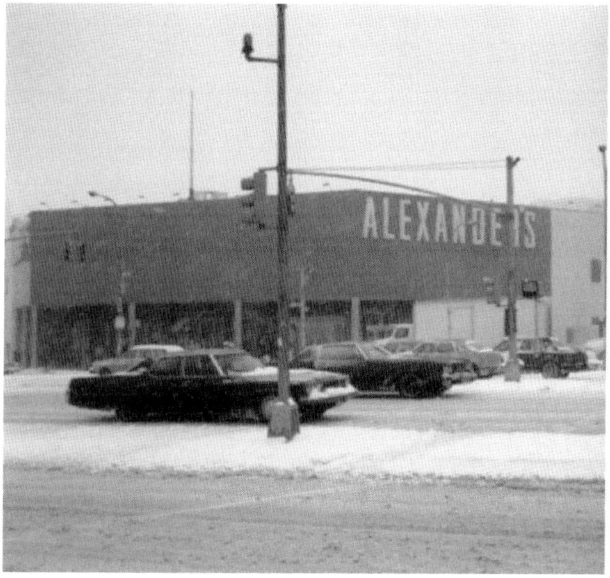

Alexander's

Rego Park was known for its mix of unique mom and pop shops, but in 1959, Alexander's opened on Queens Boulevard and 63rd Road. Behind its red and white glazed brick facade, the "World's Largest Apparel Store" did not sacrifice quality fashions with personalization. Alexander's paid homage to store president George Farkas's father, Alexander.

Alexander's turned its shops into a Hollywood stage and screened a 17-minute, 16 millimeter narrated color film featuring models of Parisian and Italianate imports. By 1962, fashion shows were in full swing. George Farkas displayed his Rembrandt and van Gogh collection and called it "an atmosphere of elegance." At long counters, The Apple Tree restaurant satisfied patrons' taste palates. Alexander's closed in 1992. (Courtesy of Rego-Forest Preservation Council.)

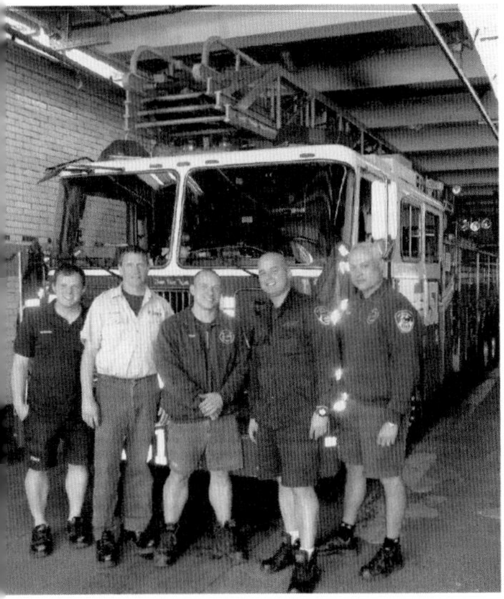

Engine Company 305, Hook and Ladder Company 151

The landmarked Neo-Medieval-style Forest Hills firehouse at 111-02 Queens Boulevard symbolizes heroism. Designed by John R. Sliney, it was dedicated in 1923 under Mayor John F. Hylan and fire commissioner Thomas J. Drennan.

Fire Department of New York firefighter John DePierro was the longest serving firefighter from 1969 until his 2012 retirement. Firefighter John Cabrera stated, "What makes work enjoyable is the great camaraderie, which helps when we respond to a fire."

On September 11, 2001, Engine Co. 305 witnessed the casualties of senior firefighter Peter Nelson and firefighter Joe Hunter. After Hurricane Sandy in 2012, no challenge proved too difficult when facing the hardest hit communities of The Rockaways and Belle Harbor. From left to right, Dan Trabucchi, Lt. John Gleave, Henry Hank Rider, Anthony Quinones, and John Cabrera are pictured in 2012. (Photograph by Michael H. Perlman.)

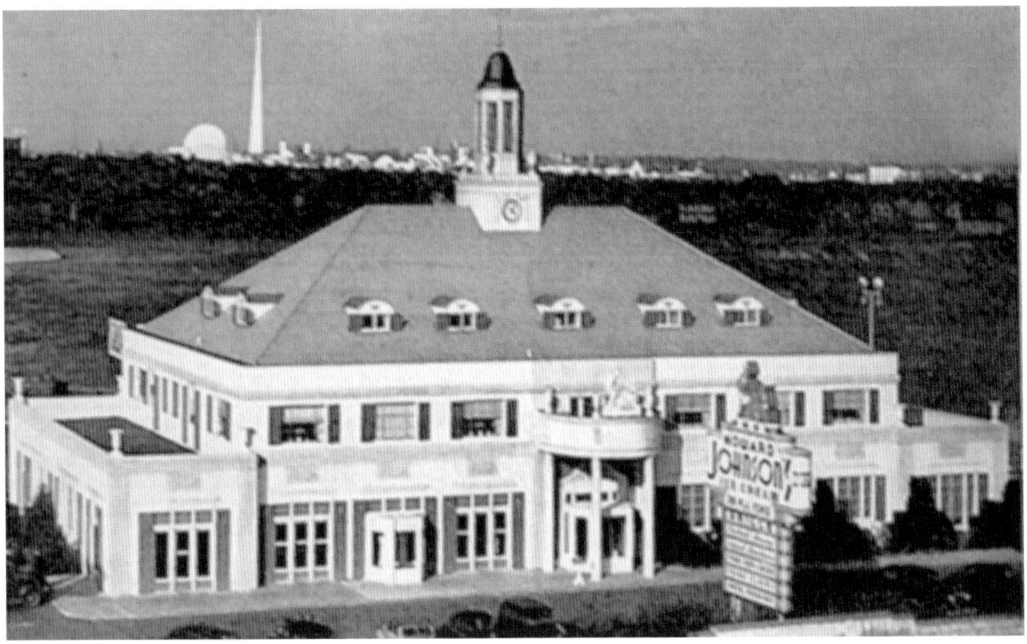

Howard Johnson's

Rego Park residents were fortunate to have "the largest roadside restaurant in the U.S." at 95-25 Queens Boulevard, which opened in 1940. The Trylon & Perisphere monuments of the 1939 World's Fair are visible in the background. The three-story, $300,000 restaurant occupied a 1,000-seat Georgian Colonial mansion designed by the chain's chief architect, Joseph G. Morgan. It was owned by Howard D. Johnson, who commissioned the Fair's esteemed seafood chef, Pierre Franey.

An Art Deco roadside neon sign boasted 28 flavors (such as chocolate chip, butter pecan, and burgundy cherry ice cream), a grille, and a cocktail lounge. The Colonial Room and Empire Room hosted weddings. Crystal chandeliers, murals designed by the famed colorist Andre Durenceau, and a winding grand stairway were regal appointments. By 1974, standardization and a change in tastes called for fast food, leading to this icon's demolition. (Courtesy of Queens Chamber of Commerce.)

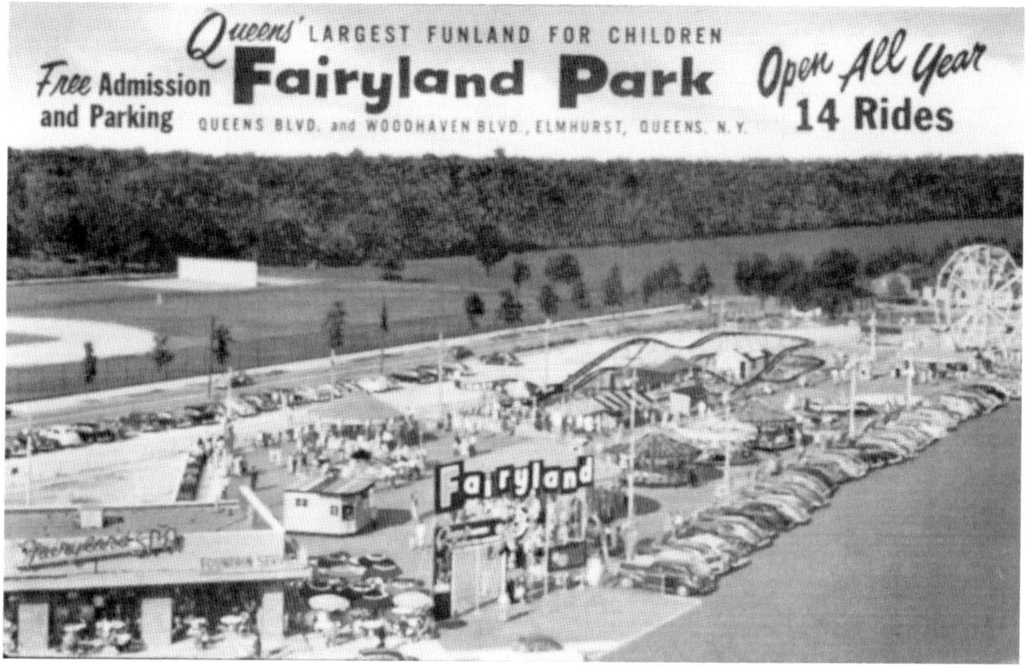

Amusements at Fairyland

After World War II, what a relief it was for Queens families to venture to the Fairyland amusement park. It was 1950, and partners Bernard Berkley and Al McKee capitalized on the highly visible intersection of Woodhaven Boulevard at Queens Boulevard and 57th Avenue. Popular rides were the Roller Coaster, Merry-go-Round, Ferris Wheel, the Jeep and Water Boats, the Auto Fire Engine, and the Train. Open seven days a week, amusement-goers could enjoy 14 rides at 14¢ a ride. On a good Sunday, 15,000 patrons would attend. By the 1960s, it expanded to 24 rides, but in 1968, Fairyland was shuttered to make way for the Queens Center Mall. Yielding $250,000 annually, Fairyland was deemed the most successful amusement park nationwide in 1953. (Courtesy of Bob Holden.)

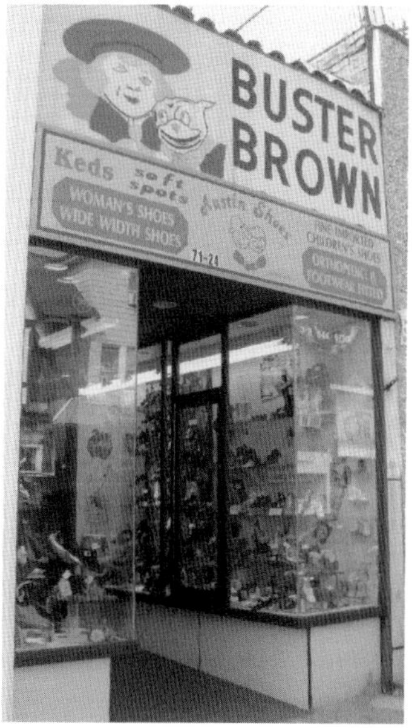

Buster Brown

Buster Brown Shoes, a mom and pop shop at 71-24 Austin Street in Forest Hills, closed its doors in 2010. In 1878, the youthful George Warren Brown dedicated his savings towards launching a shoe company. At the 1904 St. Louis World's Fair, a Brown Shoe Company executive encountered cartoonist and modern comic strip inventor Richard Outcault, who created "Buster Brown," and acquired the name. Actors who dressed as Buster along with his dog, Tige, performed countrywide and marketed Buster Brown shoes in shoe shops and theaters. Several generations felt like a notable wearing the brand. (Courtesy of Greg Godfrey.)

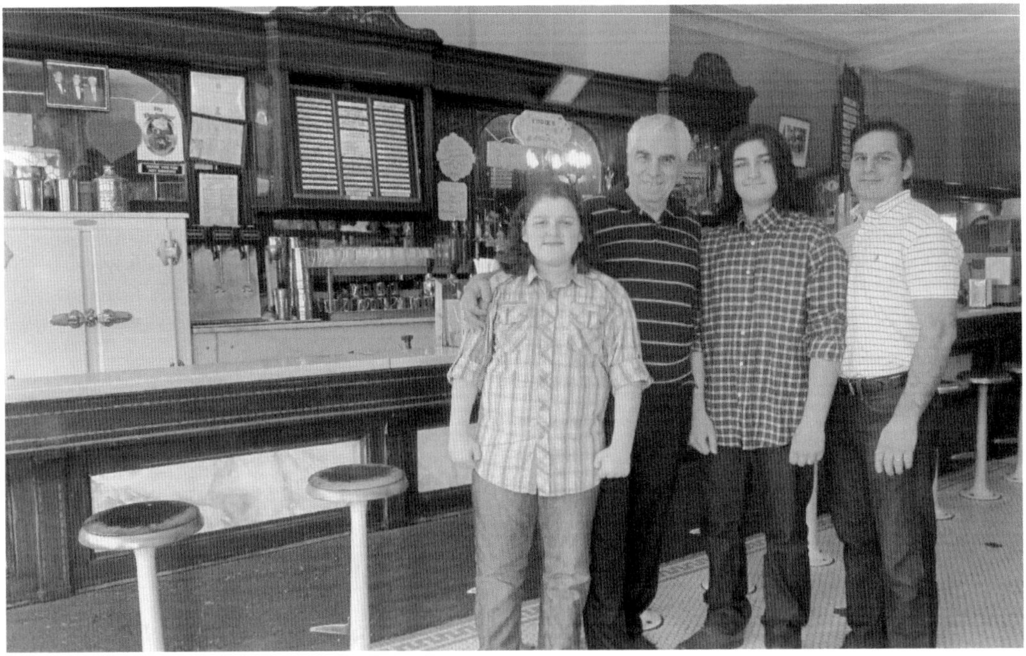

Eddie's Sweet Shop and the Citrano Family

At 105-29 Metropolitan Avenue, this Forest Hills ice cream parlor is the earliest and most intact parlor citywide. Potentially since 1925, generations of children to elders have satisfied their sweet tooth on the cast-iron swivel stools in front of a mahogany and marble counter. Other period features are a honeycomb mosaic floor, ornate mirrored wooden built-ins, leaded glass, a tin ceiling, an electric Frigidaire freezer, and a wall clock by the pioneer Seth Thomas Clock Company.

In 1949, the shop was named Witt's Confectionery after a favorite local, William Witt. It was sold to the Citrano family in 1968 and renamed Eddie's Sweet Shop. Today, it is owned by father and son Giuseppe and Vito Citrano. Three generations worked alongside one another until Vito's paternal grandfather, Vito Citrano Sr., passed away in 1995.

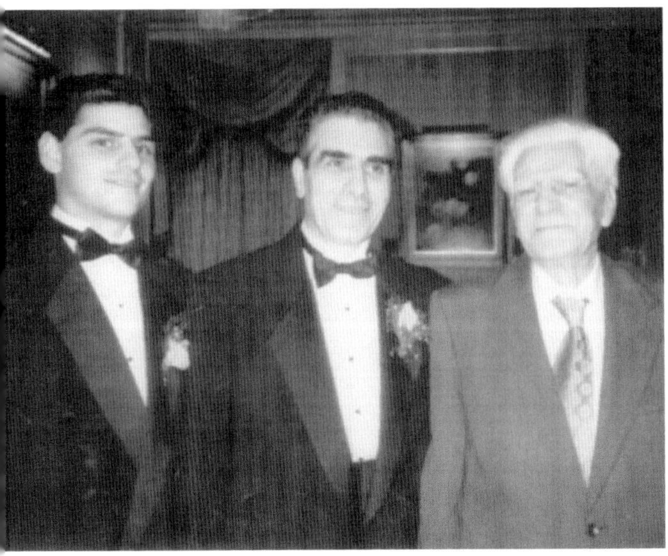

Referring to nearly 20 homemade flavors, Vito explained, "My father showed me not to be afraid to work hard. When it's time to make hot fudge, I will keep stirring until it's right."

Patrons' memories range from enjoying sundaes after movies at the Cinemart to watching Neil Armstrong walking on the moon on a vintage television. Eddie's Sweet Shop has been featured in *Brighton Beach Memoirs*, *Remember Me*, and Hostess, Coca-Cola, and Louis Sherry Ice Cream commercials.

Shown above in 2014 are Joseph Citrano, Giuseppe Citrano, Brandon Citrano, and Vito Citrano. At left in 1992 are Vito Citrano, Giuseppe Citrano, and Vito Citrano Sr. (Above, photograph by Michael H. Perlman; left, courtesy of the Citrano family.)

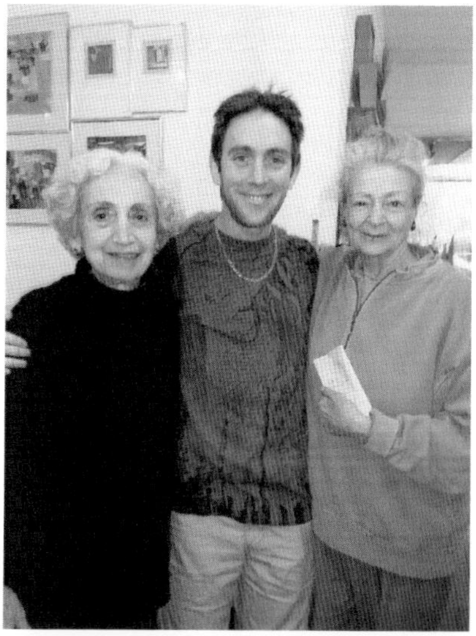

Stoa Jewelry

Upon entering Stoa Jewelry at 71-60 Austin Street in Forest Hills, a patron would be greeted by partners Marie Sinanian and Rena Monogenis, whose amiable personalities transcended their custom-made jewelry. "We would design every type of jewelry that can be worn, from looks that are classic to way out there. Customers became the mamas, the papas, and an acquired family," said Monogenis. Stoa's clientele included Geraldine Ferraro and Renée Richards. In 2013, after a 45-year run, a thank-you note on their artistic window display also marked the finale of Austin Street's mom and pop shops from the time it was The Village. Michael H. Perlman is pictured here with Marie Sinanian (left) and Rena Monogenis. (Photograph by Sol Perlman.)

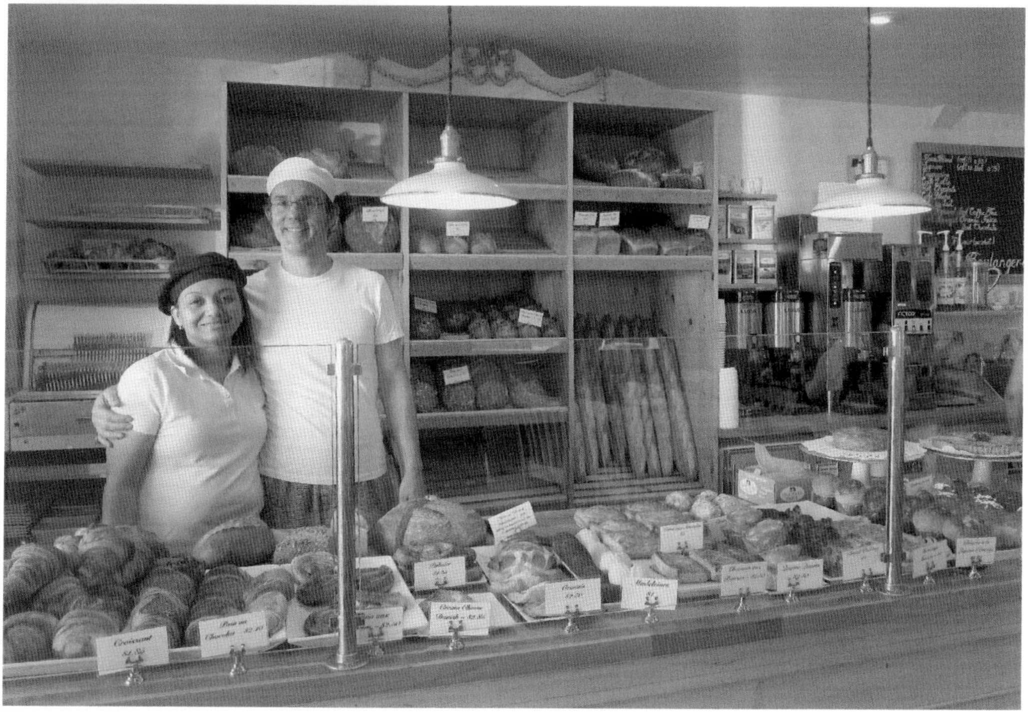

La Boulangerie

A touch of the French countryside can be found in the Tudor-inspired Forest Hills. With a mission of introducing a family-oriented, novelty bakery café in the age of large corporations, Francois Danielo and Nadia DeJesus, pictured here, opened La Boulangerie at 109-01 72nd Road in 2011. Patrons gather around a wooden communal table and observe the art of baking while French music classics play. A diverse menu offers croissantes, tarte aux abricots, salad niçoise, crème patissiere, and imported hot chocolate. This charming shop is home to artistic community events. The Gavroche Duo, which features Forest Hills notables Valentine Biollay on vocals and Sunny Knable on the accordion, specializes in performances of French standards with modern American jazz influences. (Photograph by Michael H. Perlman.)

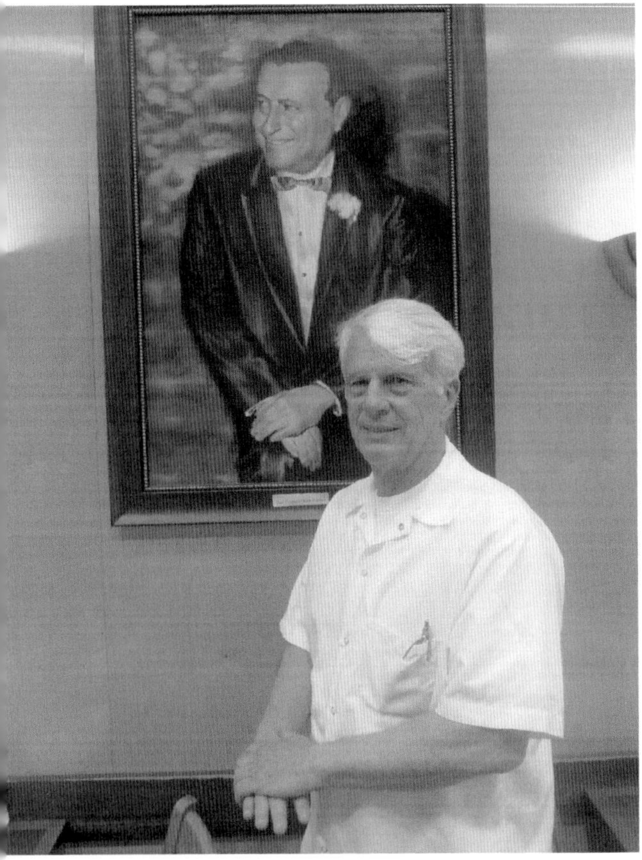

Jay Parker of Ben's Best Delicatessen
Jewish delicatessens may be dwindling, but at 96-40 Queens Boulevard, Ben's Best, which opened in 1945 and incorporated in 1947, has become a Rego Park institution. Jay Parker (pictured), son of the late Benjamin Parker (in portrait), acquired the business in 1984 and keeps his father's vision alive. He stated, "Customers have been here for 40 years and pick up the conversation from where they left off. Seventy years ago, you walked through the door and got the same product you will get today. Consistency is the word." His personal favorites are goulash and his grandfather's stuffed cabbage recipe. Pastrami, corned beef, chicken soup with matzo ball, and the Knishwich are among many patron favorites. Ben's Best processes orders nationally, and its catering services included Air Force One under the Clinton administration. Jerry Lewis, Gov. Nelson Rockefeller, Governor Pataki, and Mayor Ed Koch are some notables who have been spotted here. (Photograph by Michael H. Perlman.)

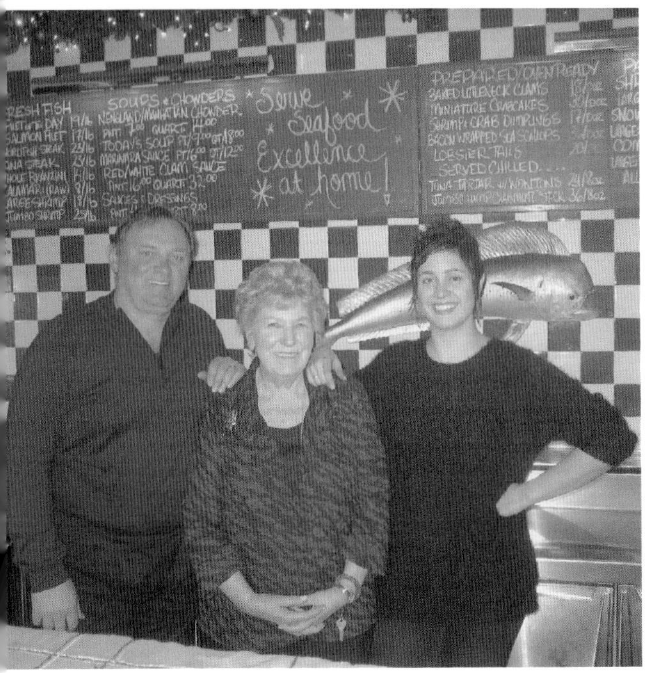

The Barnes Family of London Lennie's
In December 1959, Joan Marilyn Barnes and her husband, Leonard Barnes, acquired a small wooden-floor fish market on Woodhaven Boulevard and renamed it Rego Park Seafood. Fish and chips were 99¢. After undergoing expansions, it was renamed London Lennie's in 1968. At 63-88 Woodhaven Boulevard, it is now considered the premier seafood restaurant of Queens. "When I was five, I would go to the Fulton Fish Market with my dad. Today, there are not many people who grew up in the business and became a restaurateur," said owner Leslie Barnes. Between 130,000 and 140,000 meals are served annually. Popular events are the Crawfest, Crabfest, and Oysterfest. Jimmy Heath, Connie Francis, Mayor Giuliani, Gerry Cooney, Miracle Met Ed Charles, and LL Cool J have been spotted here. From left to right are Leslie Barnes, Joan Marilyn Barnes, and Teagan Barnes. (Photograph by Michael H. Perlman.)

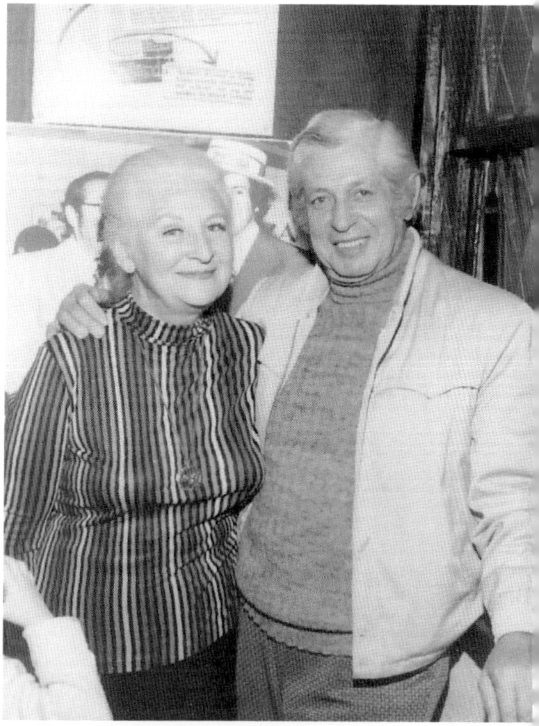

All Aboard the Hamburger Train with Jack and Frances Lewis

The Hamburger Train, which opened at 96-58 Queens Boulevard in December 1954, was Rego Park's culinary delight stationed outside the subway entrance. It had a hooting model train complete with blinking locomotive lights, which delivered food along a counter from the kitchen directly to the patrons. The crew wore regulation railroad uniforms.

Since Jack Lewis operated a complex model railroad system through their Saunders Street apartment, his wife Frances Lewis came up with the concept of the Hamburger Train. This became a highlight for children and families, and was a destination for many birthdays. For 75¢, a patron could enjoy The Train Beefburger, or for $1.25, The Pullman (deluxe burger with bacon, tomato, and fries). From the Ice Cream Parlor Car, a 55¢ Soda-Licious Double Scoop featured French ice cream sodas. Omelets and sandwiches were also served.

Grandson Mark Lewis recalled, "I remember standing at the corner of the counter and nervously accelerating the train by the controls, and carefully stopping the car in front of the customer, which carried the plate." (Both courtesy of Mark Lewis.)

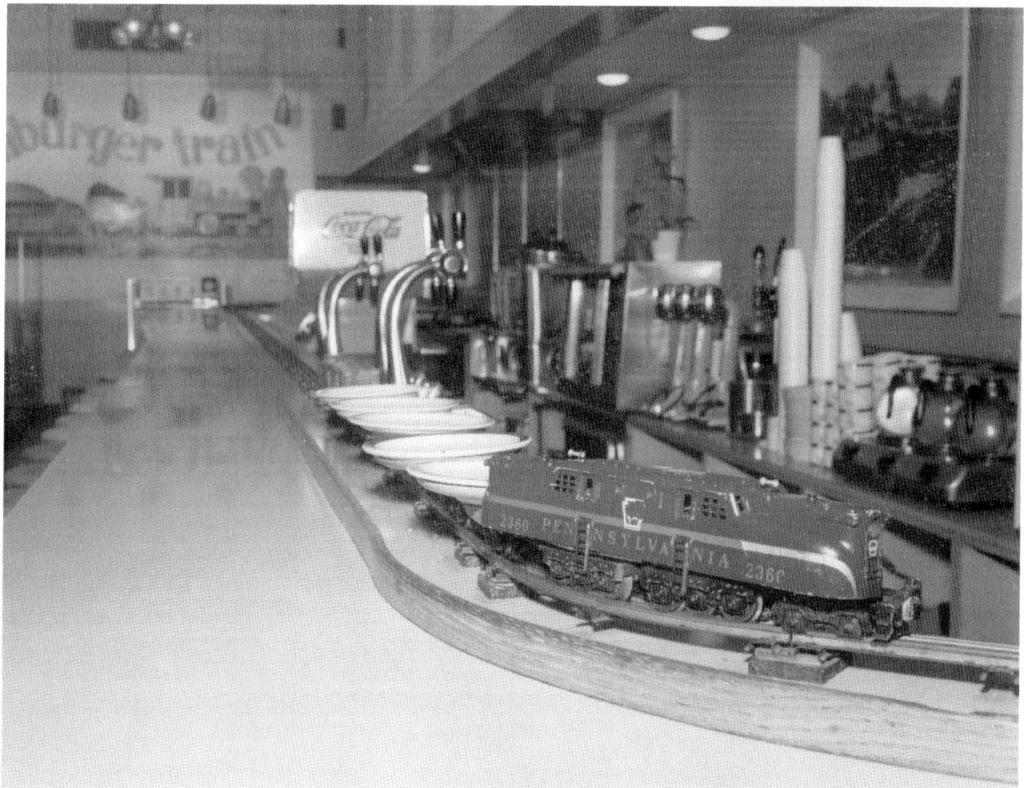

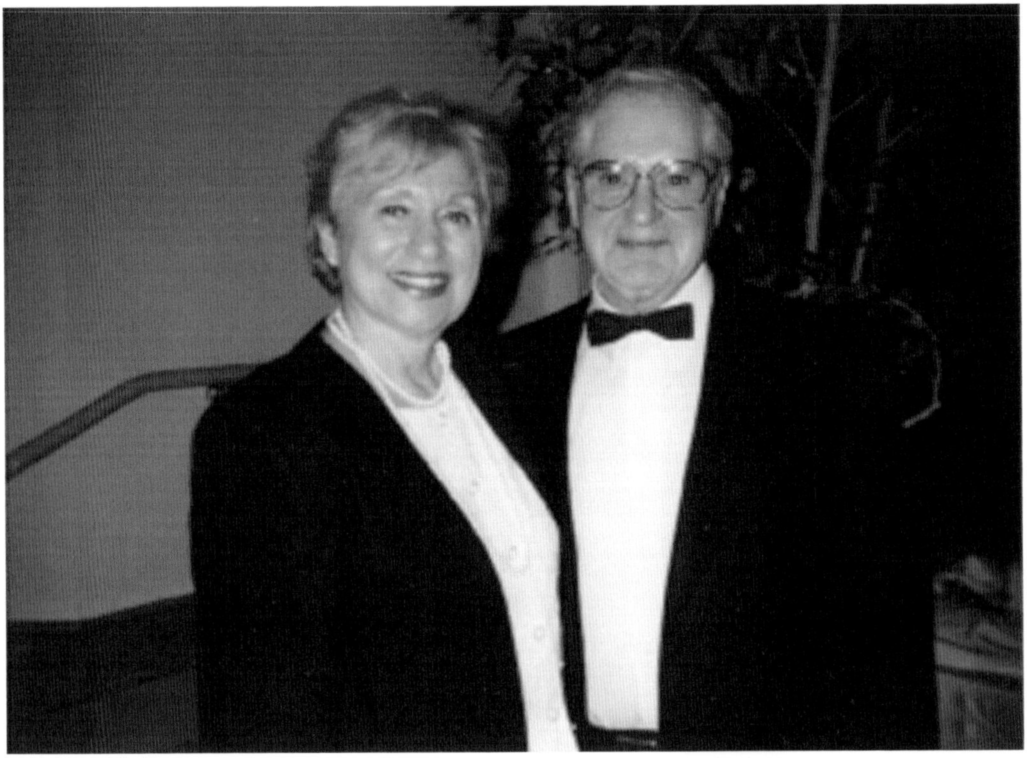

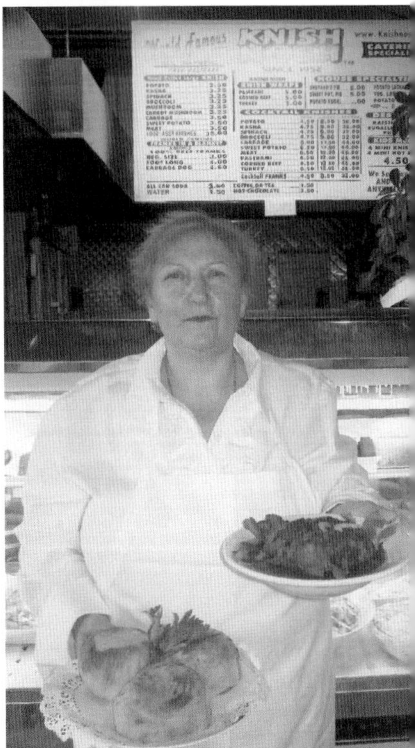

Knish Nosh

Knish Nosh at 100-30 Queens Boulevard (originally at 101-02 Queens Boulevard) in Forest Hills has brought the knish into a food group of its own, and is recognized countrywide. According to Al Heller, son of the late owner Sam Heller, Hy and Stanley Tabb are believed to be the original owners from 1945. In 1951, Sam Heller and his childhood friend Harvey Wallis purchased Knish Nosh after Sam's wife, Nettie Heller, agreed that the product was good. By 1990, Sam became the sole owner.

In 1952, a knish was 20¢, and the first varieties were potato, kasha, and liver. Today there are a dozen varieties, along with a frank-in-a-blanket and raisin rugelach. Al stated, "Through dad's approximate half-century making knishes, he was loyal to his customers and workers including manager Ernest French. Dad's nickname was 'The Godfather of Queens Boulevard.' " Sam's wife, Nettie, still resides in Rego Park.

Today, Romania native Ana Vasilescu is the chef. A full line of kosher food includes soups, salads, and entrees such as Chef Ana's Garlic Chicken and Stuffed Cabbage. She explained, "My grandma encouraged me to cook as a young girl. Julia Child and Jacques Pépin are some of my largest influences." Above are Nettie and Sam Heller around 1990; at right is Ana Vasilescu. (Above, courtesy of Al Heller; right, photograph by Michael H. Perlman.)

CHAPTER TWO

Arts and the Social Scene

Enter the social scene, where couples, friends, and families could plan a day bowling at Hollywood Lanes or Cameo Bowling; see a movie at the Trylon, Forest Hills, Midway, or Cinemart; or venture over to Fairyland Amusement Park under Bernard Berkley and Al McKee's leadership. Locals could also enjoy dinner and a show at Boulevard Tavern, where "The Singin' Rage, Miss Patti Page" would perform. If a person were lucky, they could enjoy the sounds of The Drifters or Tito Puente at the Stratton Bar, owned by Joe Vogel.

Forest Hills High School was attended by legendary punk rock band the Ramones. Their debut was at CBGB, the legendary Manhattan club, but they did not forget their hometown's Jahn's ice cream parlor.

Legendary drummer Buddy Rich once lived at 105-07 66th Road. Despite not learning to read music, he let his heart take the lead when playing with prominent big bands such as Tommy Dorsey and Artie Shaw. While bopping to Stevie Wonder's "I Just Called To Say I Love You," realize that he may have lived close by at Birchwood Towers. In 1966 and 1968, he energized 14,000 concertgoers at the Forest Hills Tennis Stadium. Among the Grand Slam winners were Don Budge and Steffi Graf. The sound of tennis balls can still be heard at the West Side Tennis Club.

A former Forest Hills resident and Smithsonian Institution inductee is singer and actress Carol Channing, who played the role of Dolly Gallagher Levin in the Broadway show *Hello, Dolly.* That is also a memorable tune for theatergoers.

At the Church-in-the-Gardens in Forest Hills, visitors may have encountered Tony Award–winner Thelma Ritter, who was noted for her New York accent and her comedic roles, and starred in the Alfred Hitchcock film *Rear Window.* The church accommodates Musica Reginae Productions, which introduced Queens to prestigious concerts featuring young artists since 2000, and showcases traditional to contemporary music with inspirations from classical, chamber, opera, and jazz. Influential figures include president Daniel Olson; Dr. Barbara Podgurski, executive and artistic director; and maestro David Close, who is also Our Lady Queen of Martyrs Church's organist and music director. Next door, at the Community House, patrons may feel enriched by the talents of musician Betina Hershey Russo, who is also director of The Garden Players musical theater program, which shapes our youth.

Actor Albert Sidney Howson was in 21 plays for major names, which included Shubert, Frohman, Belasco, and Proctor. He appeared in *Hamlet*, *Twelfth Night*, and *As You Like It.* Wearing another hat, he was president of the Forest Hills Gardens Celebrations Association. On Flagpole Green, he applied his drama skills to annual Memorial Day speeches, where he would quote Shakespeare and wear a cape.

Richard Haas, the famed architectural muralist, designed the mosaic mural on the facade of a bank at 108-36 Queens Boulevard. In 2014, his mural turned 25. It is also a window into historic Forest Hills Gardens scenes, and pays tribute to the Twin Towers, depicted in the backdrop.

Before calling it a day, tune in to Carroll O'Connor, and if old enough, Archie Bunker from the classic sitcom *All in The Family*, who may have been a classmate at Public School 3 in Forest Hills.

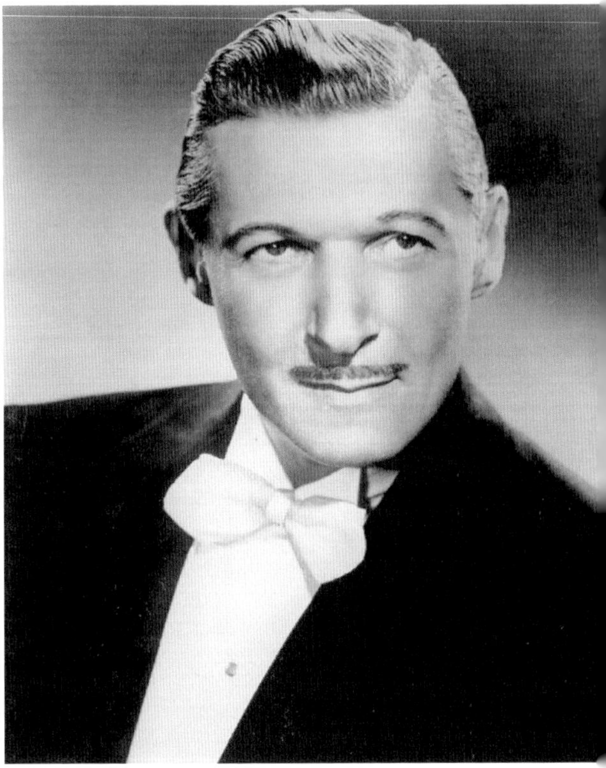

Jan August

Jan August (1904–1976), a self-taught pianist who resided in Lane Towers at 107-40 Queens Boulevard in Forest Hills, had a touch for merging Classical with Latin rhythms. He founded Jan August and his Rhythm Section, played in New York City's Capitol and Roxy Theatres, and guest-starred with the Queens Symphony Orchestra at Forest Hills High School in 1957. August recorded "Malaguena" and "Babalu." He performed "Misirlou" for President Truman, and between 1947 and 1951, sold eight million records. (Courtesy of Mercury Records.)

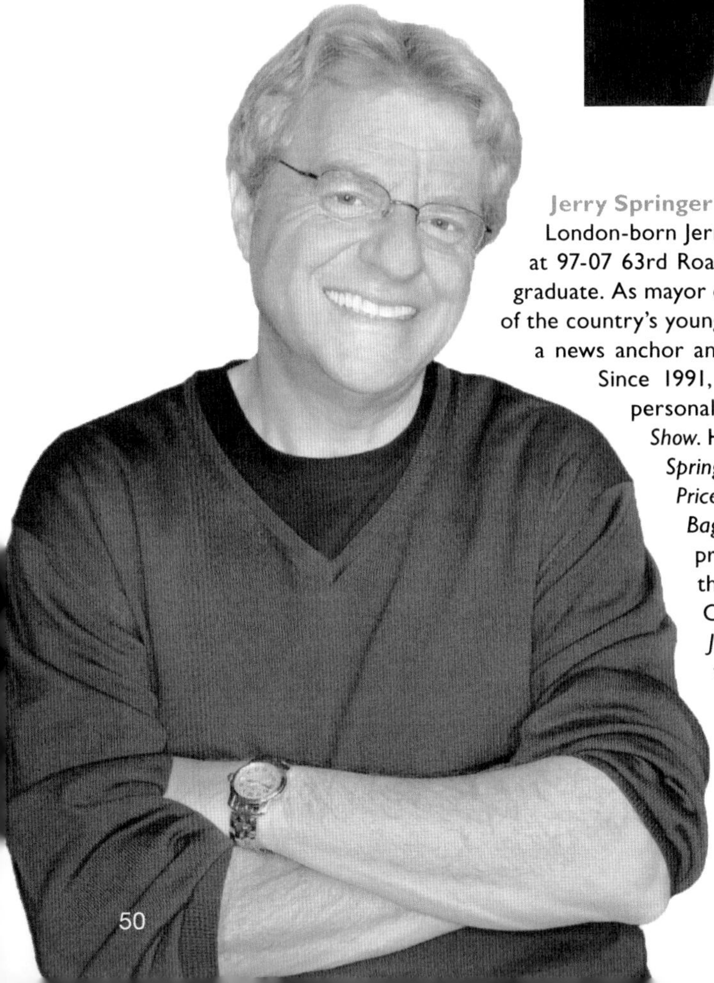

Jerry Springer

London-born Jerry Springer (1944) once lived in Park City at 97-07 63rd Road, and is a 1961 Forest Hills High School graduate. As mayor of Cincinnati at age 33 in 1977, he was one of the country's youngest. Changing his career path, he became a news anchor and managing editor of NBC in Cincinnati. Since 1991, he achieved prominence as a television personality on his daily talk show, *The Jerry Springer Show*. He starred in the film *Citizen Verdict*, hosted *Springer on the Radio*, *America's Got Talent*, *The Price Is Right Live*, and most recently hosts *Baggage* and *Tabloid*. His comedic skills were prevalent when he starred as Billy Flynn in the musical *Chicago*. He won the Laurence Olivier Award for the British musical *Jerry Springer: The Opera*. Emmy Award–winning newscaster, country artist, game show host, and lawyer are among his many credentials. (Courtesy of Jerry Springer.)

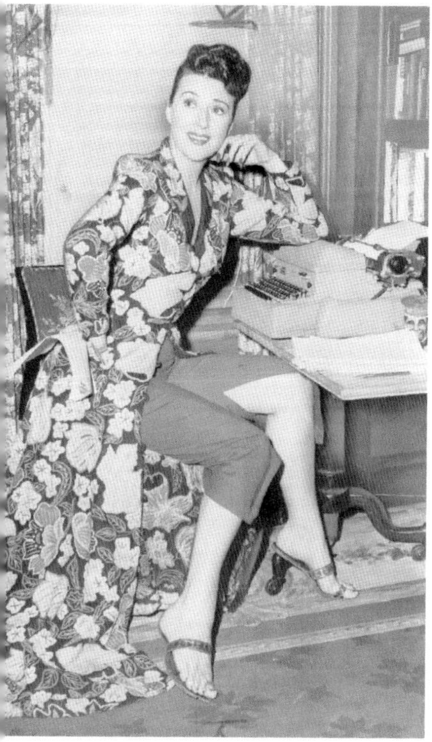

Gypsy Rose Lee and June Havoc

Sisters Gypsy Rose Lee (1911–1970, pictured at left) and June Havoc (1912–2010, below) lived on Dry Harbor Road and 84th Street in Rego Park. Havoc, born Ellen Evangeline Hovick, was a child vaudeville performer, actress, dancer, and theater director. American audiences were entertained with her Broadway and Hollywood appearances. She starred in films including *Brewster's Millions* (1945), *Gentleman's Agreement* (1947), and *When My Baby Smiles at Me* (1948). Broadway appearances include *Pal Joey* (1940). Havoc was inducted into the Theater Hall of Fame in 2001. Her childhood as Baby June was chronicled in the musical *Gypsy* (1959), which was named after and also predominantly starred her older sister, Gypsy Rose Lee, born Rose Louise Hovick, who became a burlesque queen, but only after facing their stage mother, Rose Hovick's, influences. *Gypsy*, also a film, was based on Lee's 1957 memoir. As an actress, her motion picture appearances include *Ali Baba Goes to Town* (1937), *Stage Door Canteen* (1943), and *Screaming Mimi* (1958). At the 1939 World's Fair's Hall of Music, Lee starred in a Michael Todd musical, *Streets of Paris*. (Left, courtesy of Library of Congress; below, photograph by Paramount, courtesy of Mark Sonntag Collection.)

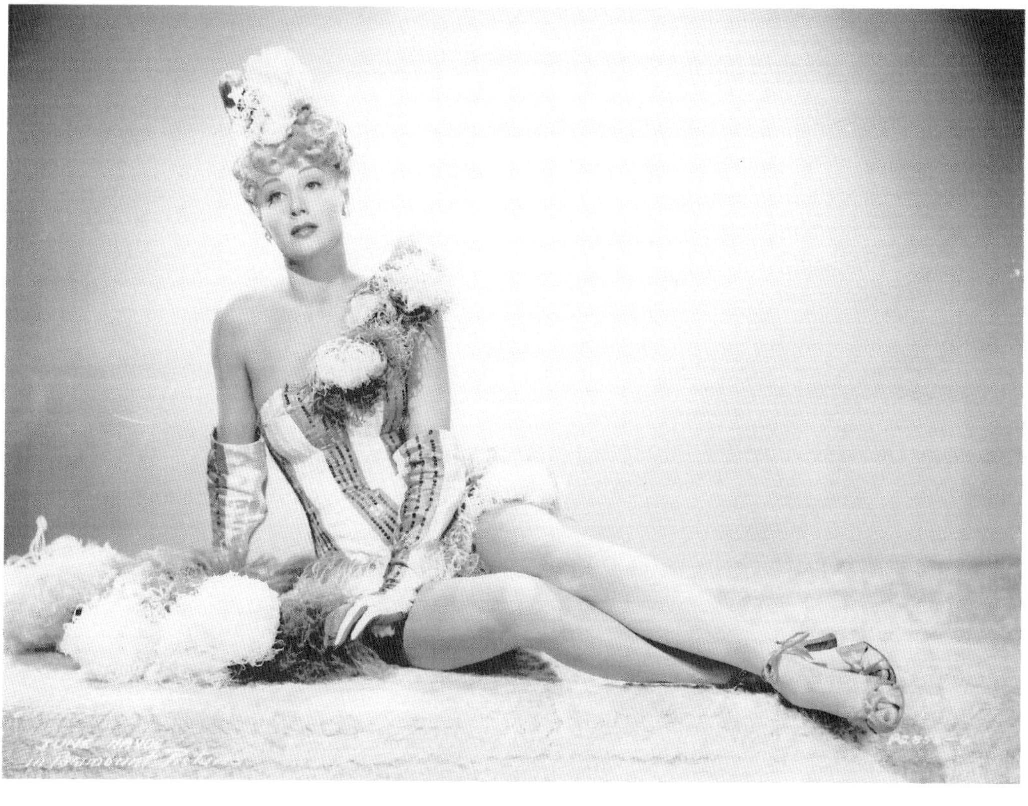

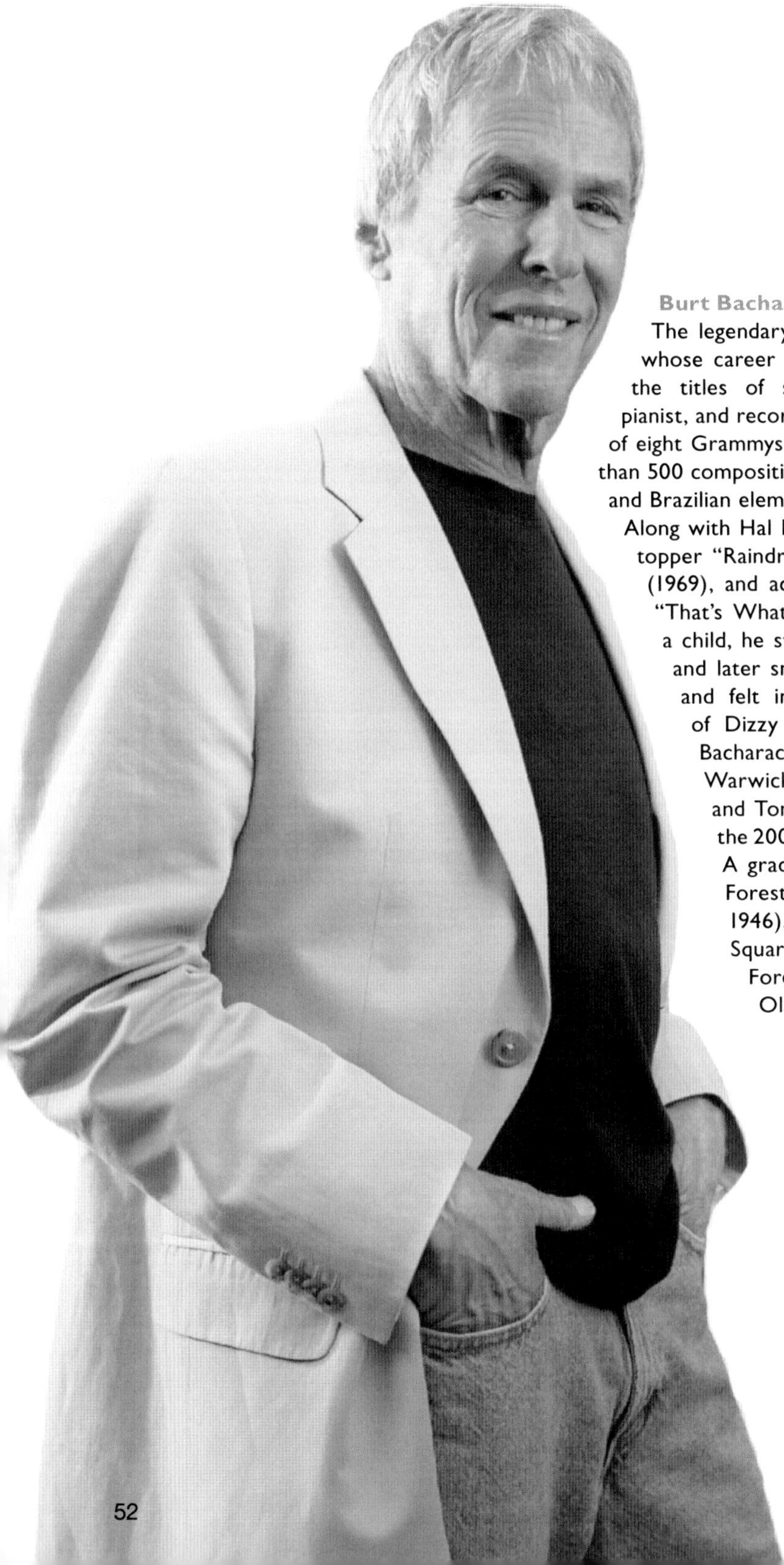

Burt Bacharach

The legendary Burt Bacharach (born 1928), whose career spans six decades, has earned the titles of songwriter, composer, singer, pianist, and record producer. He is the recipient of eight Grammys and three Oscars. With more than 500 compositions that merge jazz, pop, rock, and Brazilian elements, he scored 52 Top 40 hits. Along with Hal David, he composed the chart-topper "Raindrops Keep Fallin' on My Head" (1969), and achieved Song of the Year with "That's What Friends are For" in 1986. As a child, he studied piano, cello, and drums, and later snuck into Manhattan jazz clubs and felt inspired by the bebop sounds of Dizzy Gillespie and Charlie Parker. Bacharach has worked with Dionne Warwick, Vic Damone, Steve Lawrence, and Tom Jones. He was honored with the 2008 Lifetime Achievement Award. A graduate of Public School 101 and Forest Hills High School (class of 1946), he lived at The Grosvenor Square at 150 Burns Street in the Forest Hills Gardens. (Courtesy of Olaf Heine.)

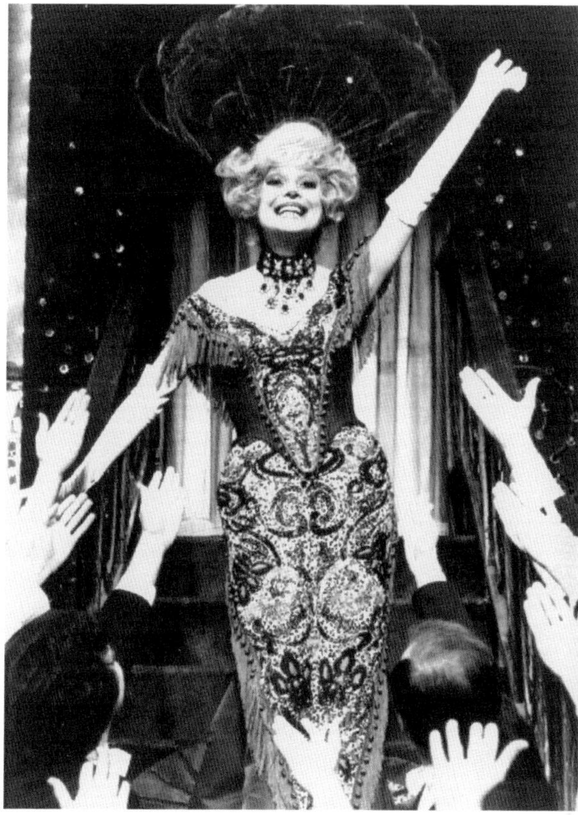

Carol Channing

Legendary singer and actress Carol Channing (born January 31, 1921), a Forest Hills resident as of 1955, starred in the Broadway show *Gentlemen Prefer Blondes* as Lorelei Lee, and most notably as Dolly Gallagher Levi in *Hello, Dolly!*, which consisted of over 5,000 consecutive runs. The musical earned 10 Tonys, including Channing's for Best Actress in a Comedy in 1964. She also played Muzzy in the film *Thoroughly Modern Millie*, resulting in a Golden Globe Award. In 1995, she received a Lifetime Achievement Tony Award, and in 2009 was inducted into the Smithsonian Institution. In 2012, the documentary *Carol Channing: Larger Than Life* was released. (Courtesy of Carol Channing Productions.)

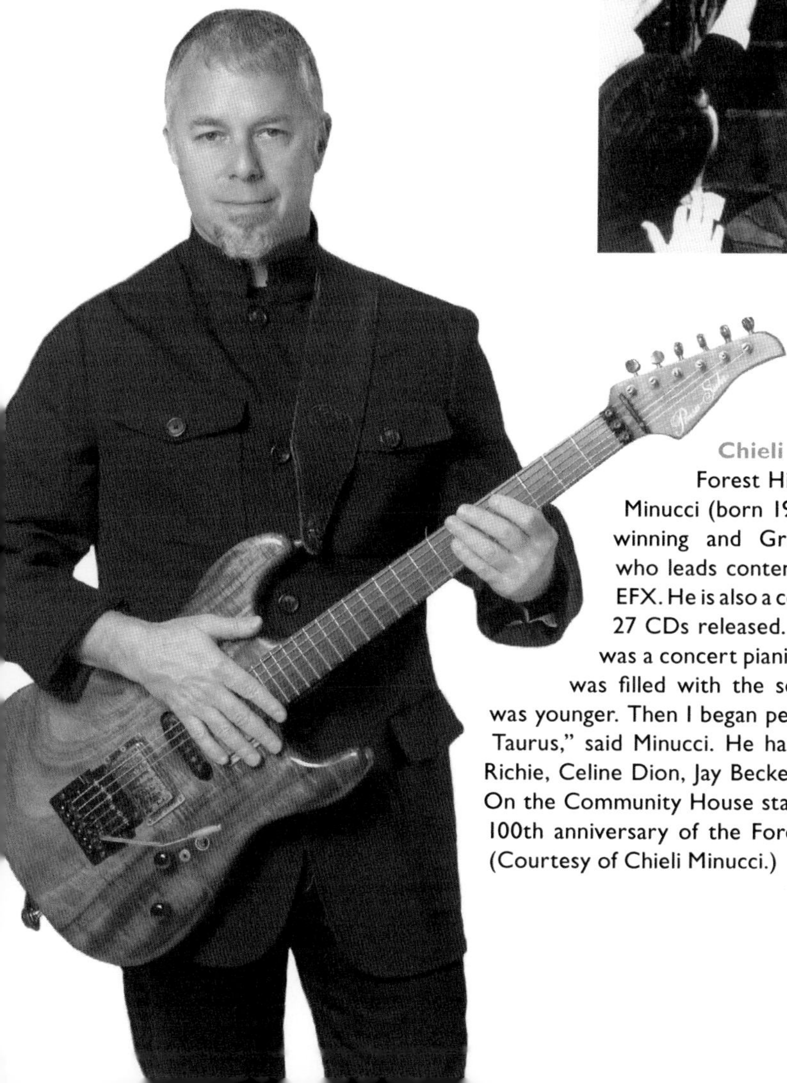

Chieli Minucci

Forest Hills Gardens resident Chieli Minucci (born 1958) is a three-time Emmy-winning and Grammy-nominated guitarist who leads contemporary jazz group Special EFX. He is also a composer and producer with 27 CDs released. "My father, Ulpio Minucci, was a concert pianist/composer, and my home was filled with the sound of the piano when I was younger. Then I began performing in the local band, Taurus," said Minucci. He has collaborated with Lionel Richie, Celine Dion, Jay Beckenstein, and Jennifer Lopez. On the Community House stage, he commemorated the 100th anniversary of the Forest Hills Gardens in 2009. (Courtesy of Chieli Minucci.)

A Century of Tennis Icons in Forest Hills

With a backdrop of crisp blue skies and trees in bloom, a tennis ball–themed flag reading, "100 Years in Forest Hills," was raised and waved in pride alongside the American flag. At 1 Tennis Place in the Forest Hills Gardens, generations of the West Side Tennis Club (WSTC) shared in the honor of the flag raising ceremony on April 21, 2013.

The West Side Tennis Club was founded in 1892 on Manhattan's West Side. After outgrowing its third home, land was secured in the Forest Hills Gardens in 1913 for a stately $25,000 Tudor clubhouse designed by Grosvenor Atterbury, which overlooked tennis courts and temporary grandstands. The club and the United States Lawn Tennis Association partnered to finance the 14,000-seat Forest Hills Tennis Stadium for $150,000. It was completed on August 11, 1923, in time for the Wightman Cup, where an American victory took center court.

Kenneth Murchison, a foremost public building architect and WSTC member, was appointed to design the first concrete tennis stadium in the United States. The builder was the Foundation Company, which specialized in superstructures and substructures. The Massachusetts Institute of Technology designated it "America's Tennis Stadium."

The horseshoe-shaped stadium features a distinctive colonnade of archways, which appear golden at sunset. Glazed terra-cotta shields display the WSTC logo, and eagles brace the flagpoles.

The clubhouse walls are graced with photographs and have become a tennis player hall of fame, which bears homage to the generations of players on its field. Names include Bill Tilden, Helen Jacobs, Ted Schroeder, Rod Laver, John Newcombe, Chris Evert, Martina Navratilova, Jimmy Connors, Art Larsen, Ken Rosewall, John McEnroe, Andre Agassi, Bobby Riggs, and Tony Trabert. Helen Wills Moody was the first female American athlete to be recognized as an international celebrity. In 1938, Don Budge coined the term "Grand Slam" after his victories in the nationals in England, France, Australia, and the United States. In 1953, Maureen Connolly Brinker was the first woman to win a Grand Slam. The stadium was the birthplace of the US Open, where Billie Jean King played the first "open" match in 1968.

Tennis was once a segregated sport, but racial barriers were broken when Althea Gibson became the first African American to win a US national tennis title in 1957, and Arthur Ashe became the first African American man to achieve the US Open title in 1968. The stadium was home to the Singles Championships, National Championships, and the Davis and Wightman Cups. (Photograph by Michael H. Perlman.)

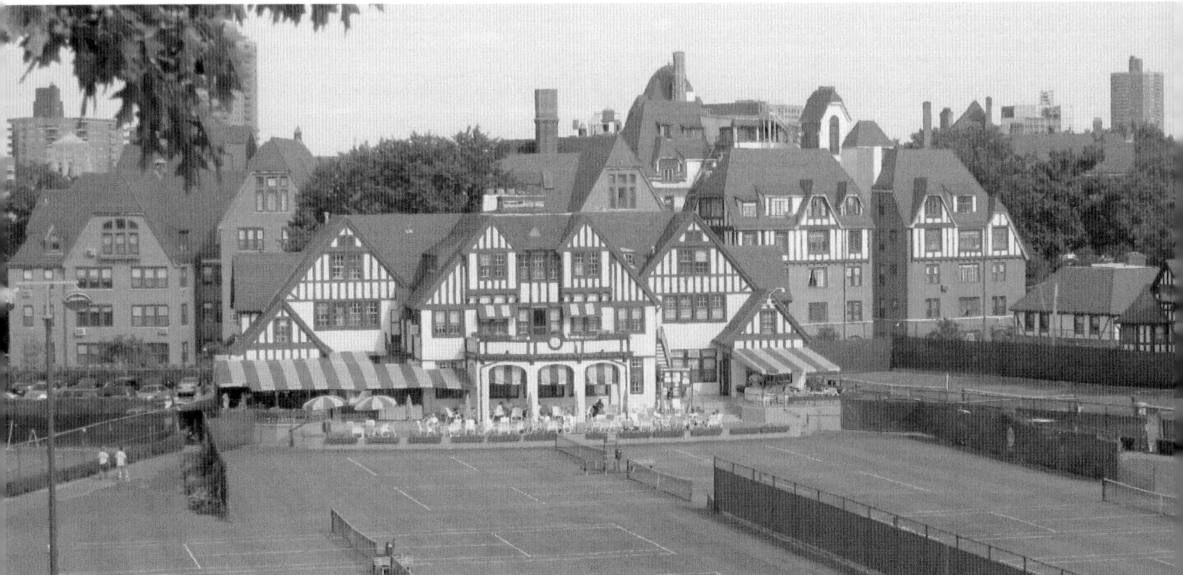

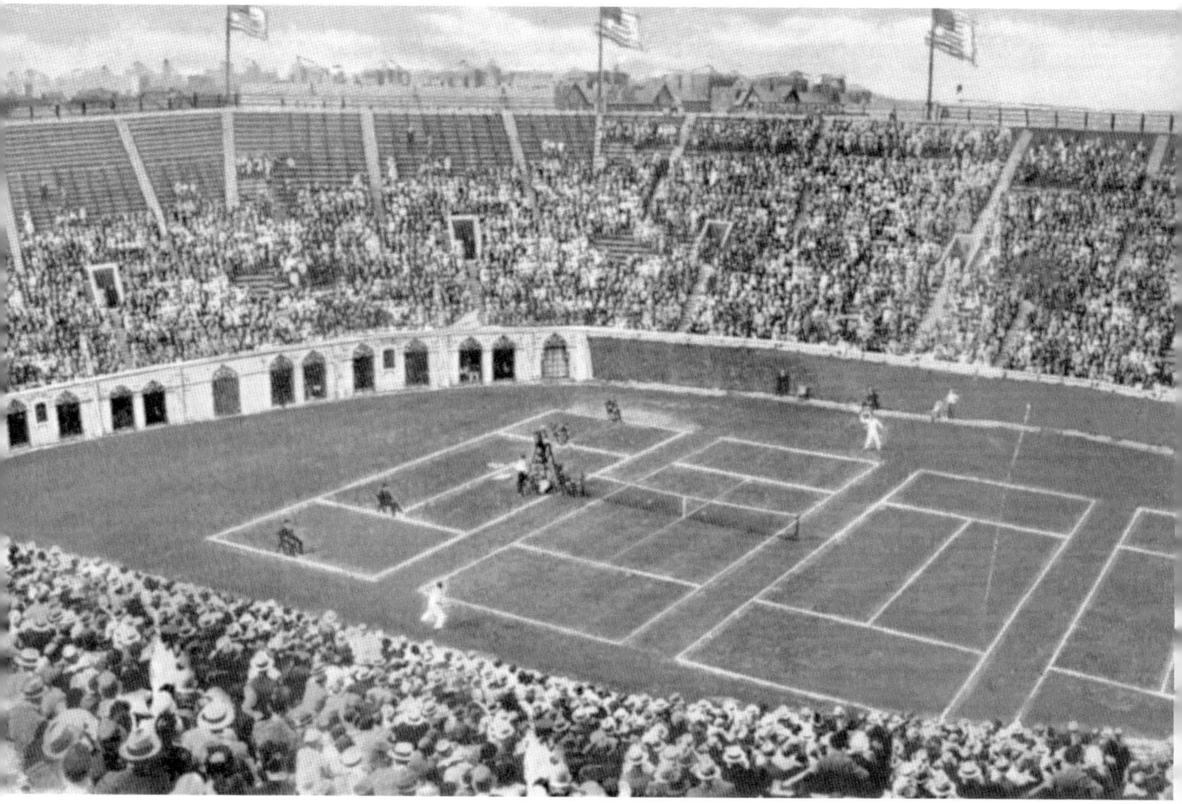

A Mic and a Spotlight at the Tennis Stadium

Cinematography also made its mark with Alfred Hitchcock's film *Strangers on a Train* (1951) and *The Royal Tenenbaums* (2001) at the West Side Tennis Club's historic courts.

The Forest Hills Music Festival originated in 1960 and became a summer tradition, where thousands of fans would cheer to the likes of Frank Sinatra, The Beatles, Barbra Streisand, Simon & Garfunkel, Diana Ross, Judy Garland, Ella Fitzgerald, Joan Baez, Trini Lopez, The Who, The Rolling Stones, The Doors, Johnny Mathis, Bob Dylan, Jimi Hendrix, The Monkees, Bette Midler, Perry Como, Donna Summer, and Peter, Paul, & Mary, among other icons.

As the spectators at the US Open grew, it was transferred to Flushing Meadows Park in 1978. The Tournament of Champions was held through 1990, but fewer concerts were held as of the late 1990s. After undergoing restoration work, Forest Hills regained some of its glorified musical past with the arrival of Mumford & Sons in August 2013, and a summer concert series in 2014, which the Zac Brown Band opened. In the fall of 2014, groundskeeper Jim Sheridan was commemorated for his 50 years of diligent work in maintaining and improving the grounds. He reminisced, "When The Beatles landed in a helicopter on the grass courts, it blew down some fencing. I once stood underneath the stadium's archways near the stage, and saw Roger Daltrey of The Who warming up." Referencing the property's historic appeal for commercial shoots, he continued, "John McEnroe was barraged by machines throwing tennis balls at him. It was a losing battle." (Author's collection.)

Simon & Garfunkel

Singer and guitarist Paul Simon (born 1941, pictured at right) and singer Art Garfunkel (born 1941, left), who graduated from Forest Hills High School, offered the definitive folk-rock sound of the 1960s and 1970s. The duo took the stage at the Forest Hills Tennis Stadium in August 1967 and 1968 and in July 1970, as part of the annual Forest Hills Music Festival. During their teen years, they began writing music and scored a Top 50 hit. Under Columbia Records in 1964, their first album was *Wednesday Morning, 3 AM*. Their signature folk-rock song, "The Sound of Silence," became the No. 1 song in America and led to their stardom. It was followed by the release of their 1966 album *Sounds of Silence*. Also in 1966, *Parsley, Sage, Rosemary and Thyme* was released, featuring "Scarborough Fair," and in 1968, their album *Bookends* featured "Mrs. Robinson" and "A Hazy Shade of Winter." Their 1970 album *Bridge over Troubled Water* featured the title track, as well as "Cecilia" and "El Condor Pasa."

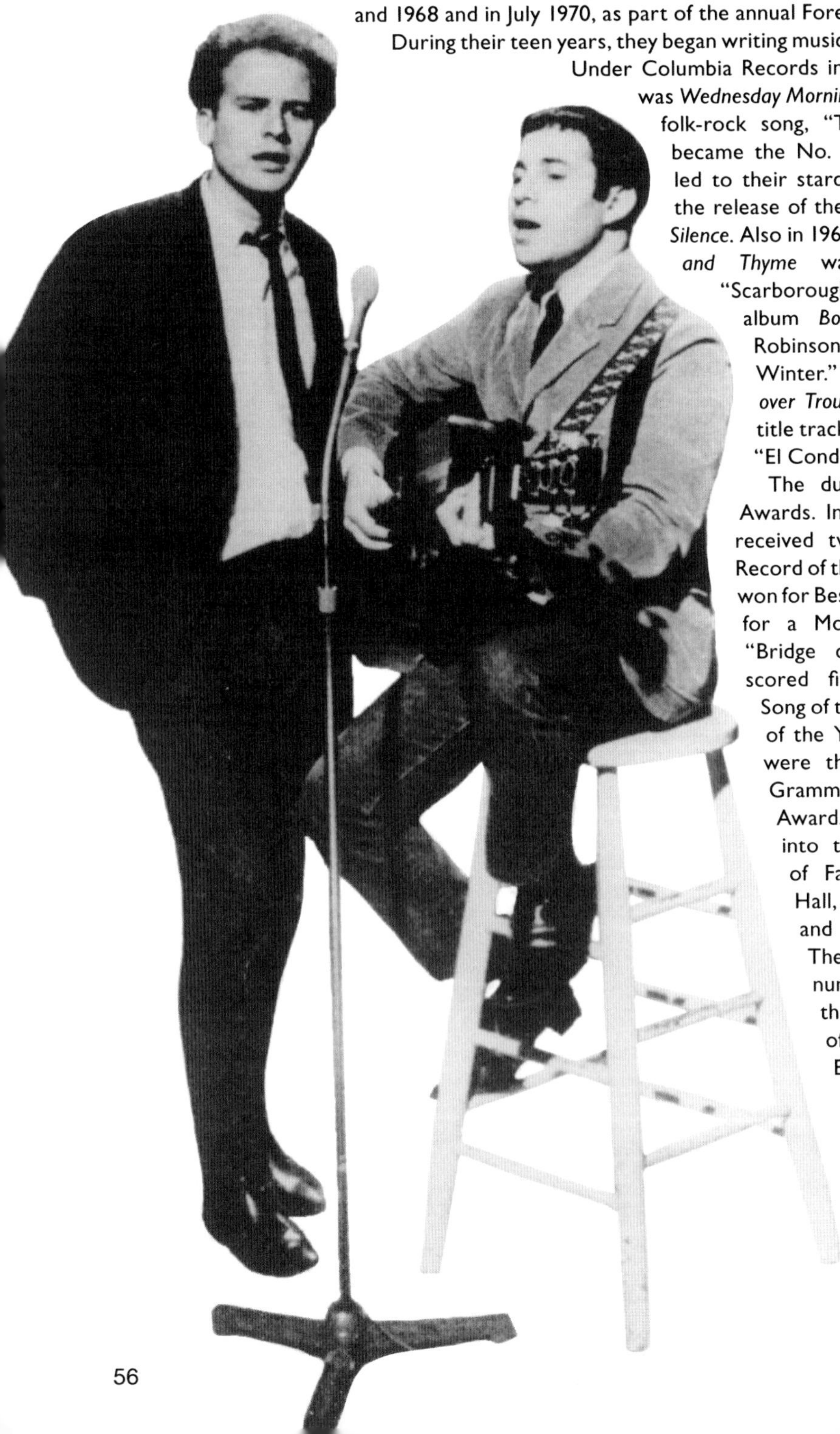

The duo earned 10 Grammy Awards. In 1968, "Mrs. Robinson" received two Grammys, including Record of the Year, and *The Graduate* won for Best Original Score Written for a Motion Picture. In 1970, "Bridge over Troubled Water" scored five Grammys including Song of the Year, as well as Album of the Year. Simon & Garfunkel were the 2003 recipient of a Grammy Lifetime Achievement Award. The duo was inducted into the Rock and Roll Hall of Fame in 1990. Carnegie Hall, Boston Symphony Hall, and Manchester's Odeon Theatre are among the numerous venues where they performed. (Courtesy of Queens Community Board 6.)

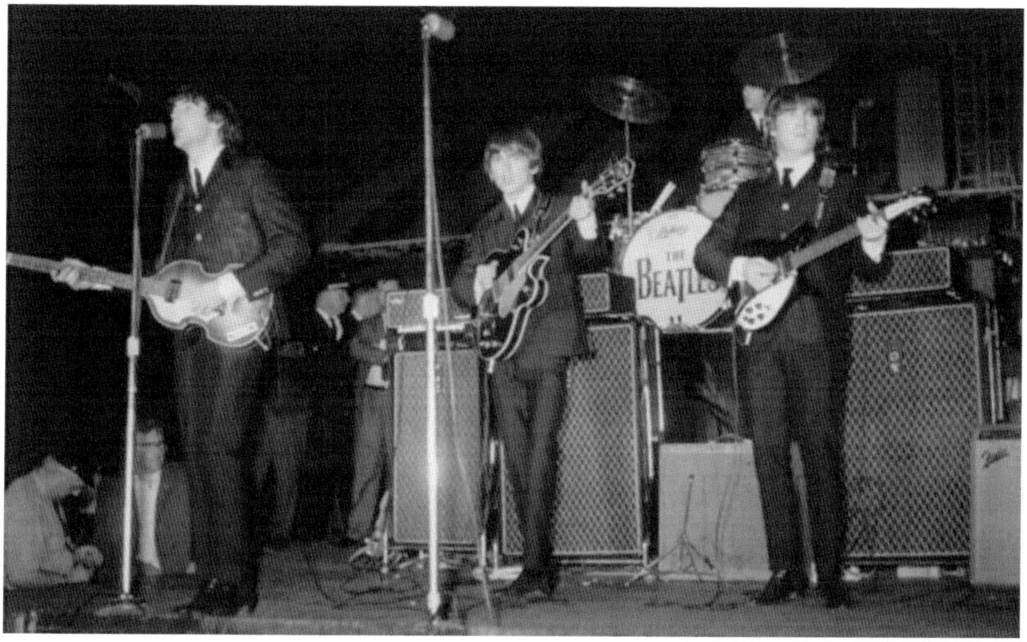

The Beatles
The Beatles landed on the grass courts by helicopter at the Forest Hills Tennis Stadium on August 28, 1964. Twelve numbers, which included "She Loves You," "I Want to Hold Your Hand," "All My Loving," and "Twist and Shout," were practically drowned out by thousands of screaming girls. More fans had their chance to see them take the stage on August 29. Fashionable fans holding up Beatles portraits anxiously waited outside the Forest Hills Music Festival office at 118-30 Queens Boulevard on May 1, 1964, for tickets to go on sale. (Courtesy of West Side Tennis Club.)

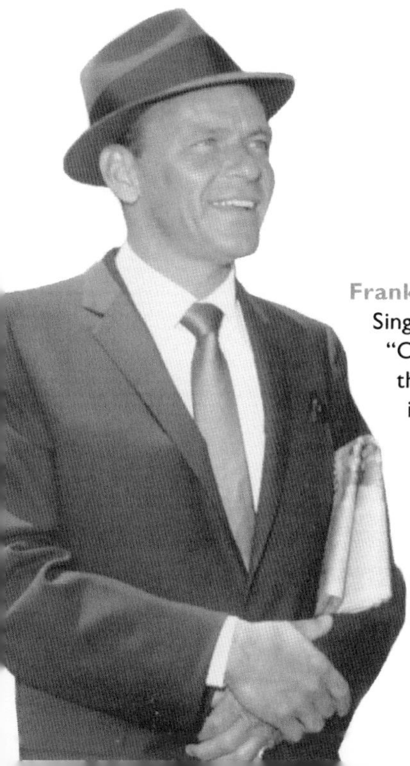

Frank Sinatra
Singer, actor, and filmmaker Frank Sinatra (1915–1998), also known as "Ol' Blue Eyes," charmed 15,000 fans in three July 1965 concerts at the iconic Forest Hills Tennis Stadium. He sang 18 numbers, which included "Luck Be a Lady," "Fly Me to the Moon," and "I've Got You under My Skin." He also appeared twice in July 1977, singing hits such as "My Way" and "Night and Day." He has been called the No. 1 pop singer of the 20th century. (Author's collection.)

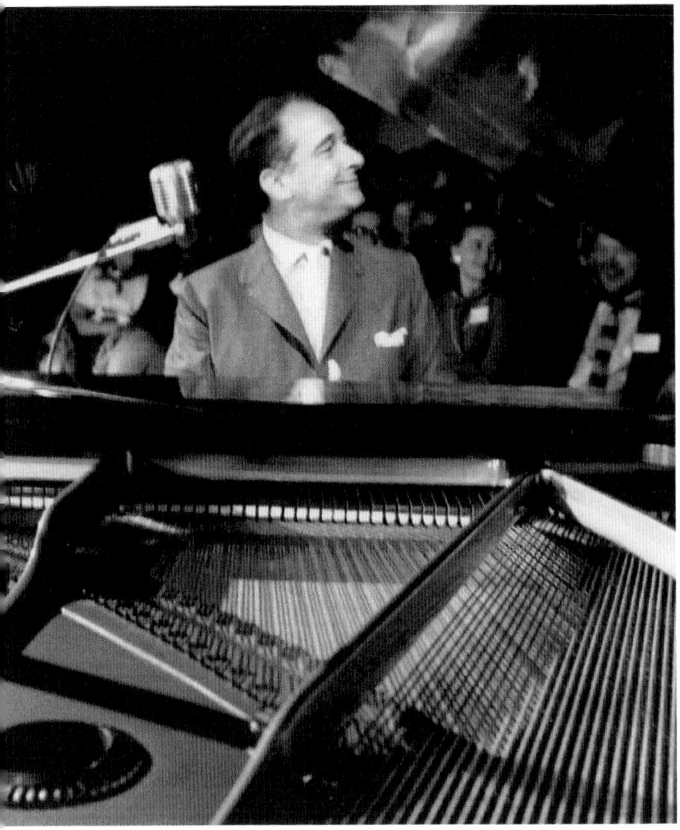

Victor Borge

"Laughter is the shortest distance between people," once stated the Danish-born world-class pianist, composer, humorist, and actor Victor Borge, born Borge Rosenbaum (1909–2000). At the August 1961 Forest Hills Music Festival, Forest Hills Tennis Stadium patrons acquired a taste of his innovative talent consolidating piano playing with humor. Borge's first performance was on Bing Crosby's radio show in 1941, and then he then starred in his one-man Broadway show *Comedy in Music*, which delivered a record-breaking 849 solo performances. He was the recipient of the 22nd annual Kennedy Center Honors for his lifetime contribution to the arts and culture, which President Clinton presented in 1999. His star on the Hollywood Walk of Fame bears tribute. (Courtesy of Joe Clark.)

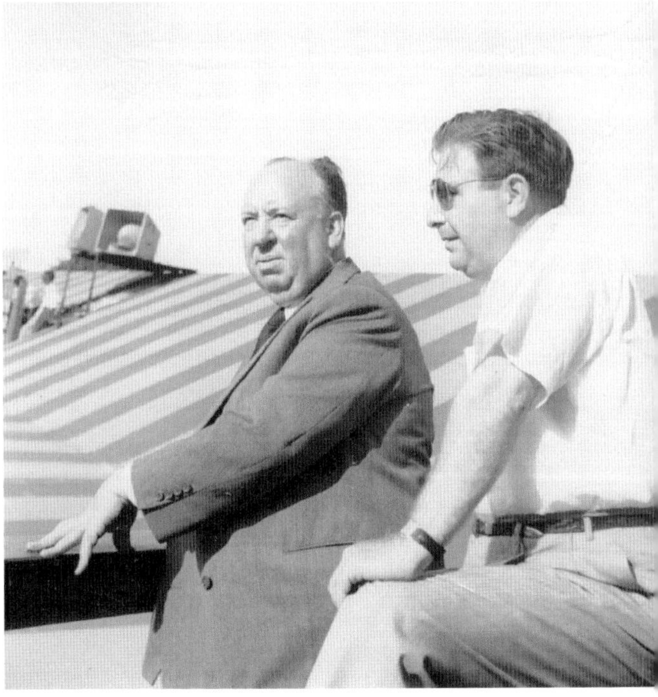

Alfred Hitchcock

Producer and director Alfred Hitchcock (1899–1980, pictured at left) made a stop at the Forest Hills Tennis Stadium to feature the 1950 Davis Cup in his psychological crime thriller *Strangers on a Train*, which was released by Warner Bros. in 1951. (Courtesy of West Side Tennis Club.)

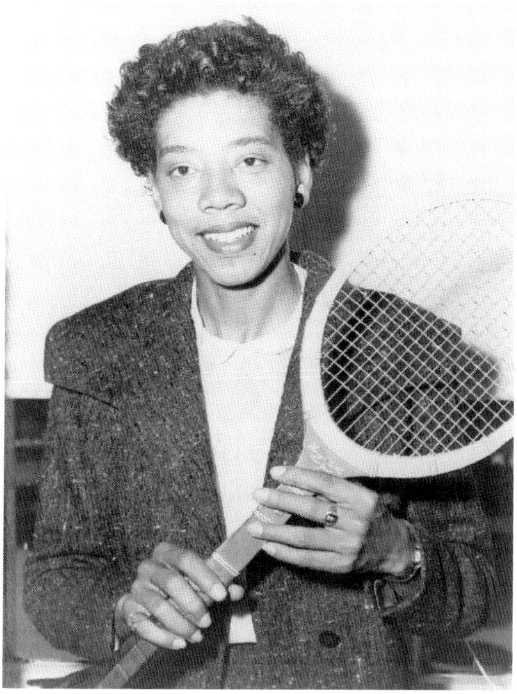

Althea Gibson (ABOVE)
Tennis was once a segregated sport, but that all changed when racial barriers were broken at the Forest Hills Tennis Stadium. Althea Gibson (1927–2003) became the first African American to win the US national tennis title in 1957. At the time, Vice Pres. Richard Nixon presented her with an award. She was inducted into the International Tennis Hall of Fame. (Courtesy of Library of Congress.)

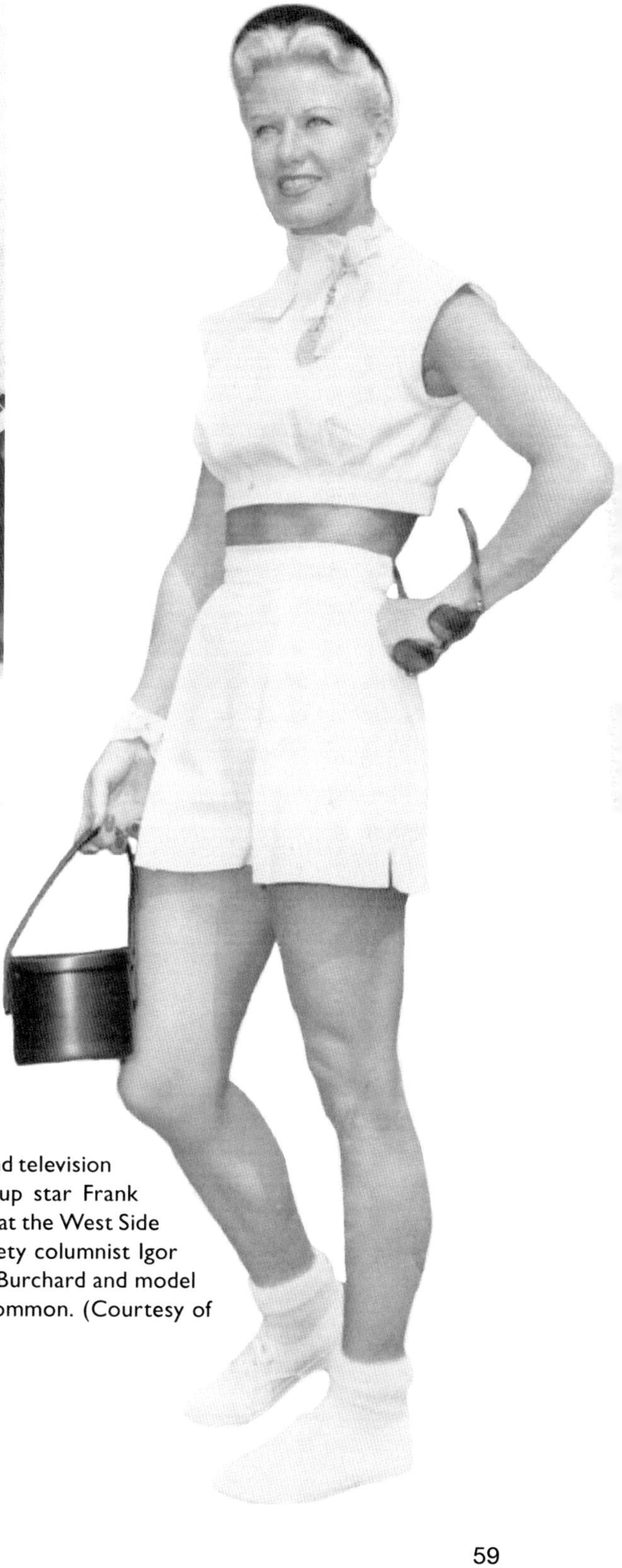

Ginger Rogers (RIGHT)
In 1950, Ginger Rogers (1911–1995), an iconic film and television actress, singer, and dancer, teamed with Davis Cup star Frank Shields in the national mixed doubles championship at the West Side Tennis Club. She also teamed with New York society columnist Igor Cassini to achieve a victory over sports writer Jim Burchard and model Jean French. Celebrity tournaments were not uncommon. (Courtesy of West Side Tennis Club.)

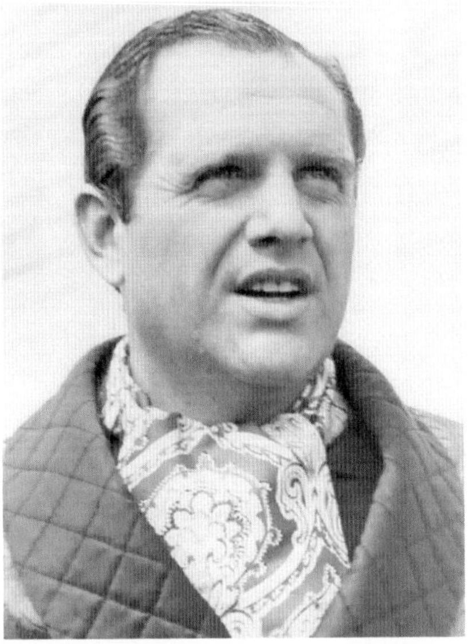

Alan King

Actor, comedian, author, and philanthropist Alan King (1927–2004) was known for his wit and "angry humor" rants. In his youth, he delivered impersonations on street corners for pennies. He visited his parents in Forest Hills and was frequently spotted wearing a straw hat in his Rolls Royce, en route to the Forest Hills Tennis Stadium. (Courtesy of *ABC Stage 67*.)

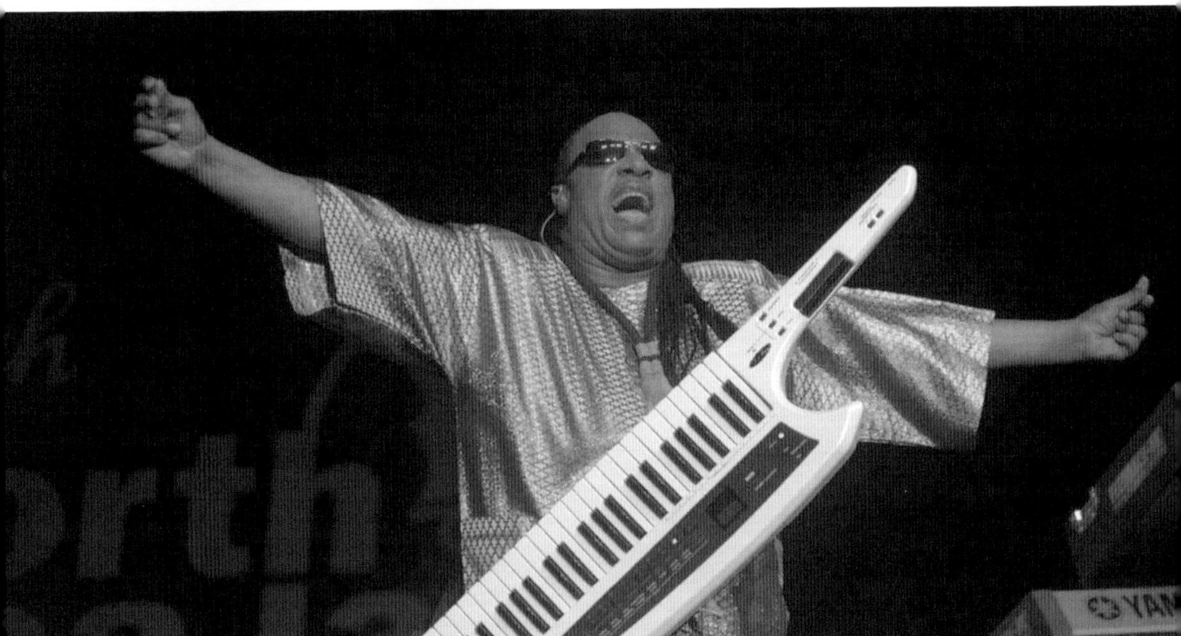

Stevie Wonder

Stevie Wonder, born Stevland Hardaway Morris in 1950, lived in Birchwood Towers at 102-10 66th Road in Forest Hills around 1970. At the 1966 and 1968 Forest Hills Music Festivals, 14,000 concertgoers were energized by his performances at the Forest Hills Tennis Stadium. Blind since birth, he is a soulful singer/songwriter, multi-instrumentalist, and producer. At age 49, he was the youngest recipient at the Kennedy Center Honors for a lifetime contribution to arts and culture. He was inducted into the Songwriters Hall of Fame in 1983 and has a star on the Hollywood Walk of Fame. He received a record-breaking 22 Grammys and sold over 100 million albums and singles such as "My Cherie Amour" (1969), "You Are The Sunshine of My Life" (1973), "I Just Called to Say I Love You" (1984), "Part-Time Lover" (1985), "We Are the World" (1985), and "That's What Friends Are For" (1985). (Photograph by Tom Beetz.)

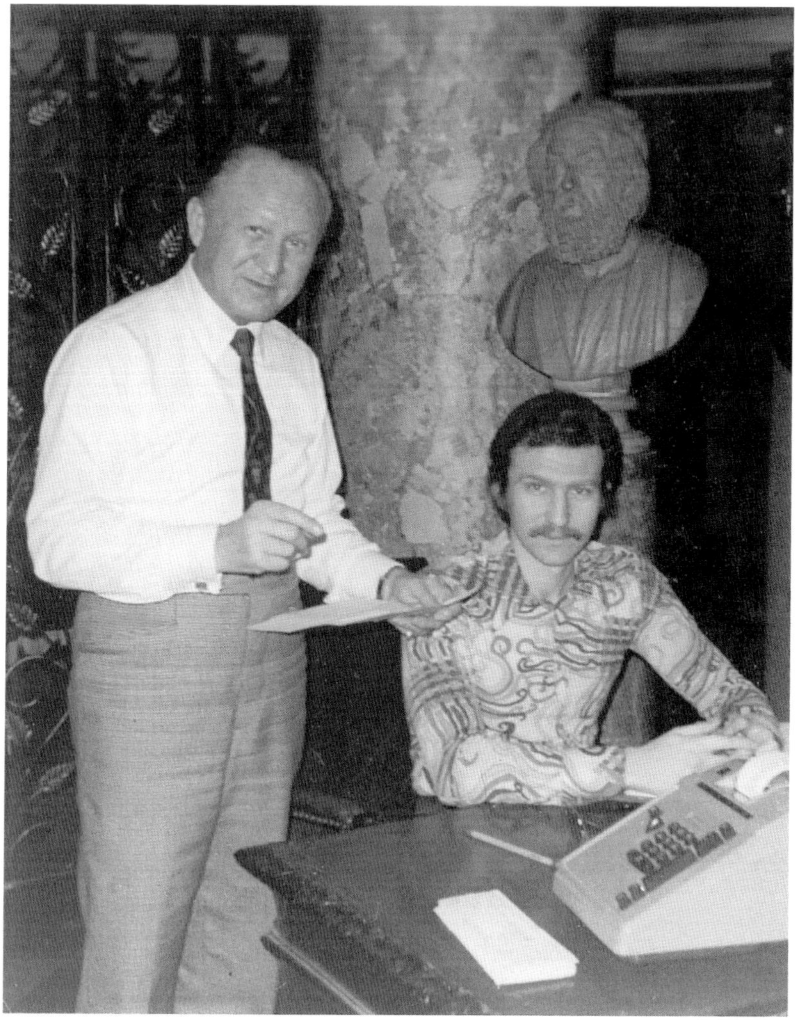

The Legacy of James Kriegsmann Sr. and Jr.

The Kriegsmann family exemplifies a family business that played a prominent role in photographing celebrities. James Kriegsmann Jr. (born 1942, pictured at right), who was raised at 25 Greenway South in the Forest Hills Gardens, continues the legacy of his father, James Kriegsmann Sr. (1909–1994, left). He explained, "I can still picture the reception area with the large photographs on the wall, and the studio with my father behind his 8-by-10 studio camera directing one of his celebrity clients. Nothing could compare to what my father did, which was to get paid to do something you loved." James Kriegsmann Jr. photographed over 35,000 notables, including Halle Berry, Spike Lee, Renée Fleming, Mike Myers, Vic Damone, Ben Vereen, Colleen Dewhurst, Dick Cavett, and Robert Reed.

His father photographed almost every television star in the 1940s and 1950s, such as Milton Berle, Sid Caesar, Dean Martin, and Jerry Lewis. He also photographed big bands, such as the Tommy Dorsey Orchestra, and the singers who performed with them, including Frank Sinatra. Hollywood stars included Doris Day and Judy Garland, as well as nearly all rock-and-roll singers. As the official photographer of the original Cotton Club, Billie Holiday, Louis Armstrong, and Cab Calloway were some of his subjects. Motown performers of the 1960s and 1970s included The Supremes, The Temptations, The Shirelles, and The Platters. Other greats were Ray Charles, Gov. Nelson Rockefeller, and Simon & Garfunkel. He also left his mark on the US postage stamp of Ella Fitzgerald. (Courtesy of James Kriegsmann Jr.)

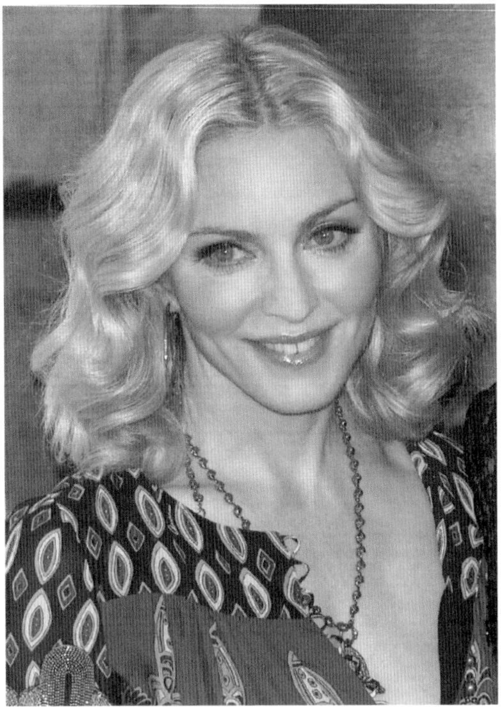

Madonna
"Queen of Pop" Madonna's career began at neighborhood entertainment venues such as Heskel's Restaurant, a hotspot at 70-28 Austin Street in Forest Hills. Disc jockey Billy Ouellette of Let Us Entertain You Inc. was the original DJ, who worked at Heskel's from 1979 to 1989. Besides spinning records, he coordinated the music and mics for live shows. He explained, "I had the pleasure of working with Madonna back in 1983. Madonna performed 'Holiday,' 'Burning Up,' and 'Physical Attraction' with her two male dancers at a Saturday evening show. She was full of energy and charisma, and took the crowd by storm." Besides Madonna, DJ Billy collaborated with The Village People, The Weather Girls, The Trammps, Vicki Sue Robinson, The Cover Girls, and TKA at Heskel's. (Courtesy of David Shankbone.)

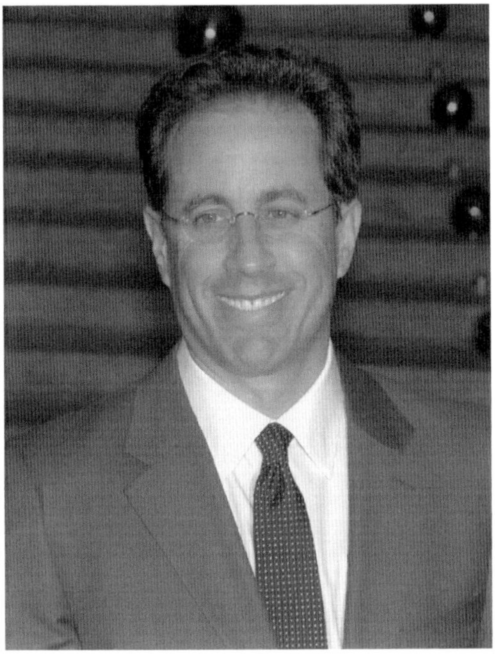

Jerry Seinfeld
At age 10, comedian, actor, producer, and author Jerry Seinfeld (born 1954) began surrounding himself with televised stand-ups, and was particularly amused by the classic duo Bud Abbott and Lou Costello. He entertained American audiences with his classic sitcom *Seinfeld* (1989–1998), where he portrayed a somewhat fictional rendition of himself. His observational humor aims a spotlight on awkward social obligations and personal relationships. When Seinfeld aired, he received an Emmy, a Golden Globe, and SAG Awards. His stand-up work landed him a Lifetime Achievement Award. Seinfeld once called Forest Hills home. (Courtesy of David Shankbone.)

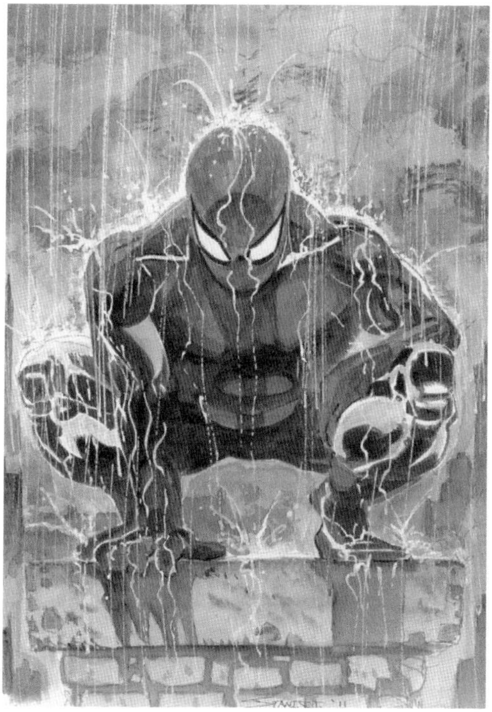

Peter Parker
Notables can also take the form of those rendered in Hollywood. The fictitious humble photojournalist Peter Parker is the alter ego of Spider-Man in the self-titled 2002 film. Parker resided at 20 Ingram Street in the Forest Hills Gardens, which was also featured in the June and July 1989 issues of Marvel Enterprises' *The Amazing Spider-Man*. He attended Forest Hills High School from 1962 to 1965. How coincidental that the home's true residents were Andrew and Suzanne Parker, along with their two daughters. (Courtesy of Artist John Stanisci.)

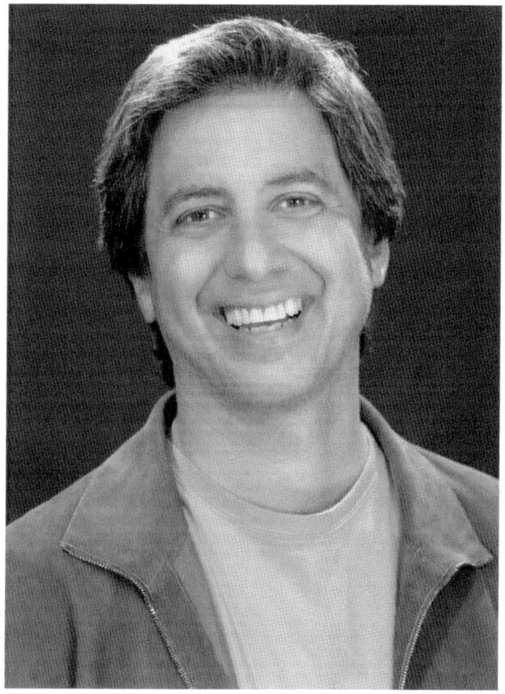

Ray Romano
Forest Hills was the home of Ray Romano (born 1957). "My comedy is always about people, family, and the relationships you have with everyone in your life. Forest Hills was a great place to witness, experience, and share all of those special things," said Romano.

Most noted for his role on *Everybody Loves Raymond* (1996–2005), he is also a screenwriter and a stand-up comedian. He won an Emmy for Outstanding Lead Actor in 2002, as well as People's Choice Awards from 2002 through 2006. In a June 2004 issue of *TV Guide*, his character Ray Barone came in at the No. 10 spot in the list of 50 Greatest TV Dads of All Time. As of 2012, Romano appeared in the television series *Parenthood*, and was the voice of Manny in the animated film *Ice Age: Continental Drift*. (Photograph by Tom Caltabiano.)

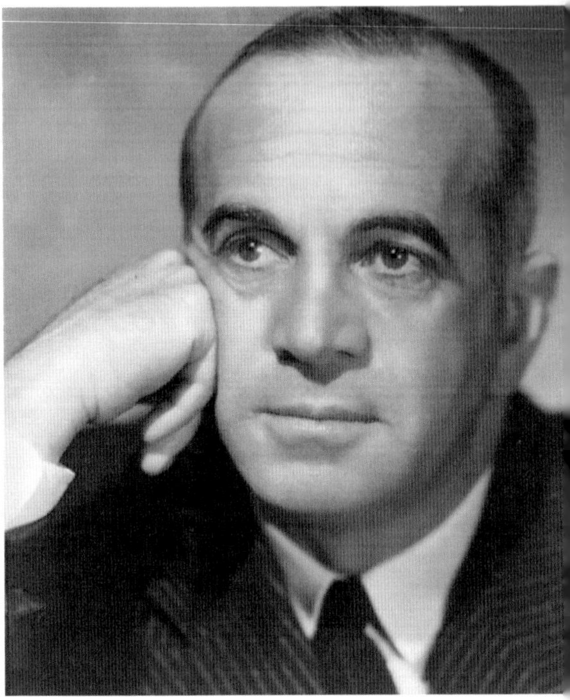

Al Jolson

In 1927, the first feature-length motion picture with synchronized dialogue was "The Jazz Singer," which starred Lithuania native Al Jolson (1886–1950). He owned a Tudor Gothic mansion at 68-12 110th Street (demolished 2006). "The World's Greatest Entertainer" achieved success in Broadway shows, films, commercial recordings, and radio programs. He was the first entertainer to sing for US troops during World War II and to the GIs in Korea.

George Gershwin's song "Swanee" became synonymous with Jolson's musical legacy when he incorporated it into his Broadway show *Sinbad.* He recorded it for Columbia Records in 1920 and sang it in the films *The Jolson Story* and *Rhapsody in Blue*. (Courtesy of International Al Jolson Society.)

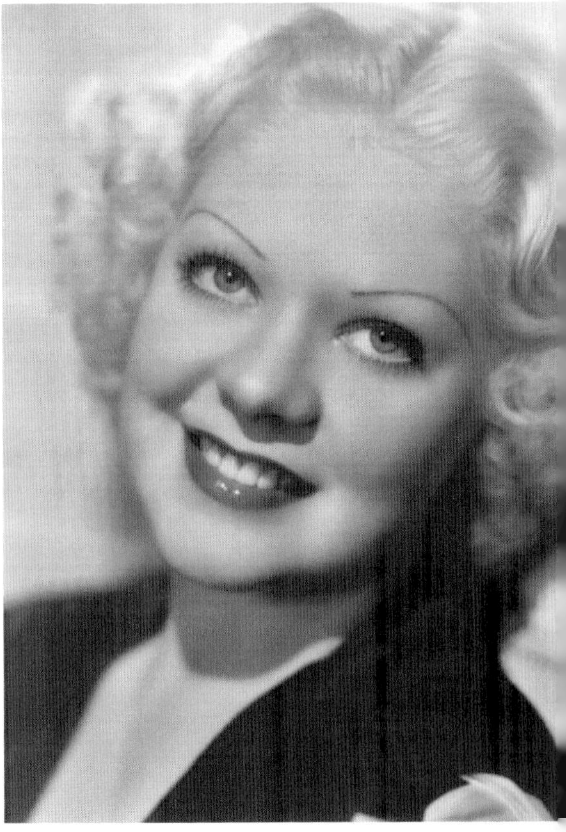

Alice Faye

America's No. 1 female song plugger was Alice Faye (1915–1998), according to composers George Gershwin and Irving Berlin. This vaudeville star, actress, and singer called 63rd Avenue in Rego Park home.

Faye starred with Al Jolson in *Rose of Washington Square* (1939) and was named a top 10 Hollywood draw. She also starred in Technicolor musicals such as *Week-End in Havana*.

At the peak of World War II, she sang "You'll Never Know" in *Hello, Frisco, Hello,* earning an Academy Award. With song titles such as "Blue Love Bird," she introduced 23 hit parade favorites in movies. She and her husband, singer and bandleader Phil Harris, starred on NBC's comedy radio program *The Phil Harris–Alice Faye Show.* (Photograph by Gene Norman.)

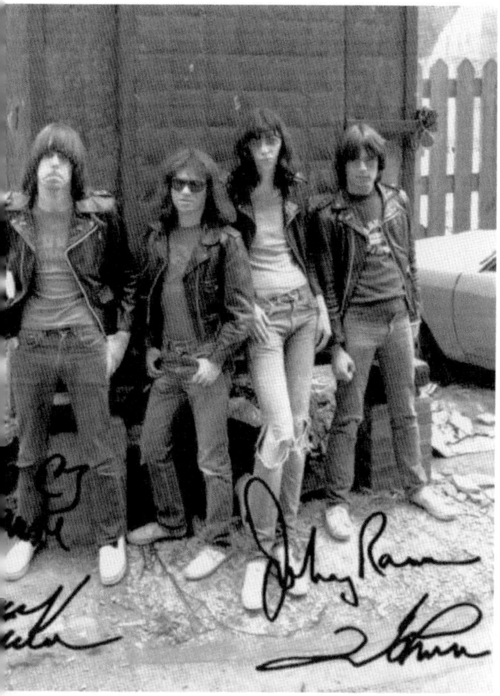

The Ramones

The legendary punk rock band the Ramones emerged from Forest Hills High School. They were often spotted at Jahn's ice cream parlor in Rego Park or consuming burgers nearby at Wetson's. The Ramones were unrelated, despite their shared last name. Formed in 1974, original members were founder, producer, and drummer Tommy Ramone (1952–2014), guitarist Johnny Ramone (1948–2004), lead singer and songwriter Joey Ramone (1951–2001), and bassist and songwriter Dee Dee Ramone (1951–2002). Their debut gig was at famed underground Manhattan club CBGB on August 16, 1974. Memorable singles included "Blitzkrieg Bop" (1976), "I Wanna Be Your Boyfriend" (1976), "Rockaway Beach" (1977), and "Rock 'n' Roll High School" (1979). In 2002, the Ramones were inducted into the Rock and Roll Hall of Fame. Johnny Ramone's first wife, Rosana Cummings, quoted Johnny, "When you make great music, you live forever." (Photograph by Ian Dickson.)

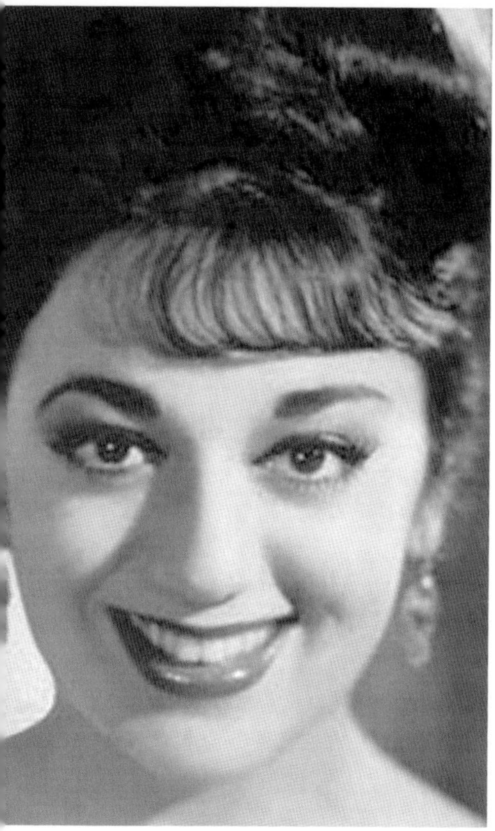

Tatiana Troyanos

American mezzo-soprano Tatiana Troyanos (1938–1993) captivated audiences from 1963 to 1993, and became a mainstay at the Metropolitan Opera House by 1976. Some of her roles were Sesto in Mozart's *La Clemenza di Tito* and Adalgisa in *Norma*. Her recordings range from *Carmen* to *Le Nozze di Figaro* to *Cosi Fan Tutte*. Abroad, she performed in Aix-en-Provence, France, and at the Hamburg State Opera in Germany. Troyanos was nicknamed "Totsie" at Forest Hills High School, where she graduated in 1956. Early on, she lived at the Brooklyn Home for Children, which is now known as Forestdale in Forest Hills. (Courtesy of Library of Congress.)

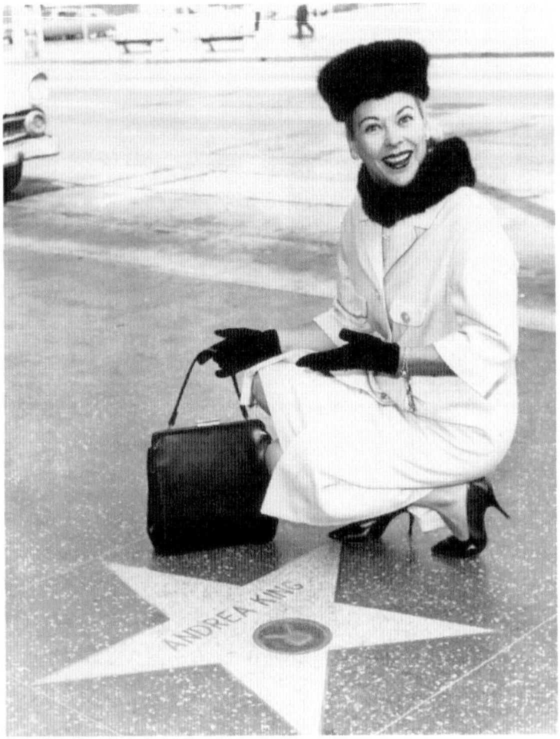

Andrea King

The prominent stage, film, and television actress Andrea King (1919–2003), also known as Georgette McKee, lived in Forest Hills from 1925 to 1940. In 1930, she graced the stage of the Community House in a dance benefit featuring "Alice in Wonderland." Her daughter, Deb Callahan, said "If her audience reads her story, 'More Than Tongue Can Tell' by Paul Miles Schneider and Andrea King, they will realize that she was a woman of many talents including acting and writing."

Successfully acting into her 70s, her proudest accomplishments were starring on Broadway in *Growing Pains* at 14, being signed by Warner Bros. in 1944, and receiving her star on the Hollywood Walk of Fame in 1960. Warner Bros. photographers voted her the most photogenic actress in 1945. Some film and television appearances include *Ride the Pink Horse*, *The Lemon Drop Kid*, *Perry Mason*, and *Maverick*. (Courtesy of Deb Callahan.)

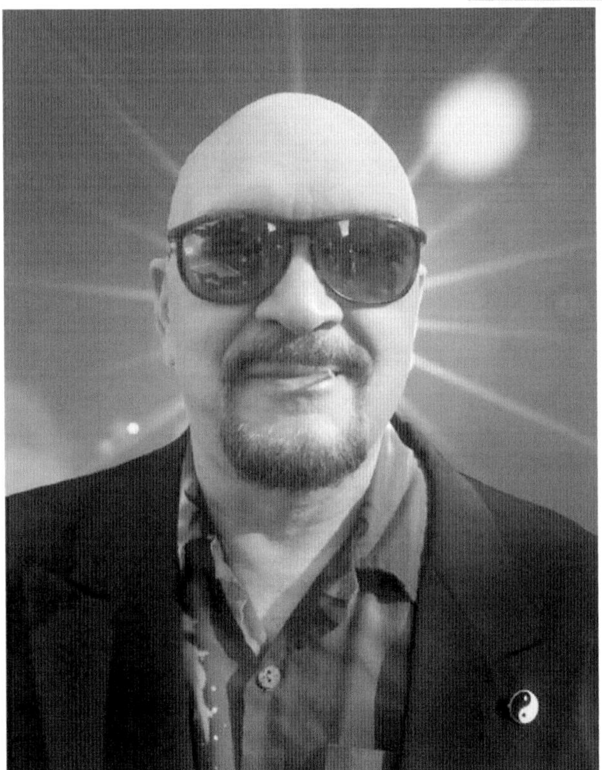

Chris Rush

Comedian, actor, writer, and radio personality Chris Rush (born 1948) of Forest Hills performed at The Metro comedy club on Metropolitan Avenue. In 2009, he launched *Bliss: An Evening of Laughter with Chris Rush.* "This one-man show merging intense laughter, quantum physics, and Eastern mysticism, backed by my mentor George Carlin, was my proudest accomplishment," said Rush. He has had numerous gigs at The Bottom Line, alongside comic legends Dick Shawn, The Firesign Theatre, and Elayne Boosler, and also opened for musicians Meat Loaf, B.B. King, and Talking Heads. His national television appearances were on *Comedy Tonight* and HBO. (Courtesy of Bill Kates.)

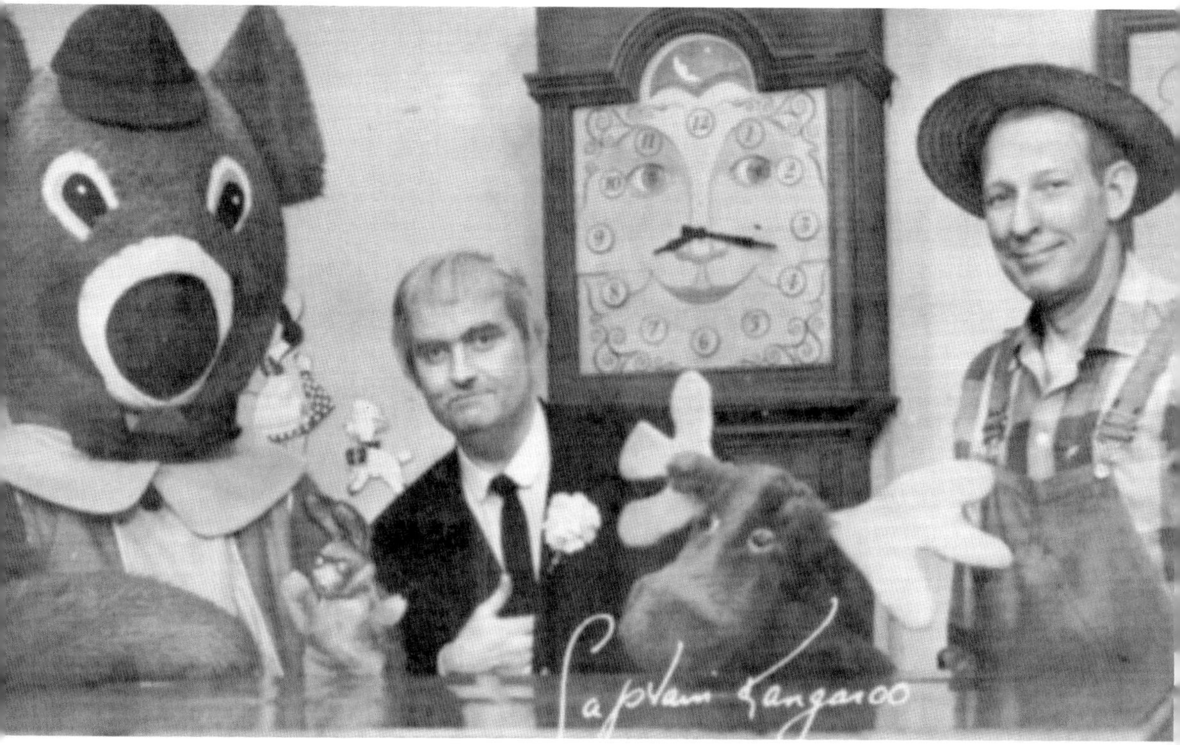

Bob Keeshan

Shortly after World War II, television programs debuted. Among the earliest was *Howdy Doody* on NBC in 1947, where Bob Keeshan (1927–2004) played Clarabell the Clown. He was deemed iconic for his portrayal of Captain Kangaroo on the self-titled children's show on CBS, which aired from 1955 to 1984. Audiences could sense his description of the show as "the warm relationship between grandparents and children." Memorable characters included Mister Green Jeans, Mister Moose, Bunny Rabbit, Dancing Bear, and Grandfather Clock.

Raised in a quaint home situated at 75-42 113th Street, Keeshan often described his childhood as "delightfully free from worries or insecurities."

Keeshan felt children's television shows were no grounds for violence. He was a strong proponent of reinforcing values, manners, and good behavior through his character and in real life, and also advocated for the safety and well-being of children, as an author and lecturer. "Parents are the ultimate role model for children," said Keeshan. One of his books was *Growing Up Happy: Captain Kangaroo Tells Yesterday's Children How to Nurture Their Own*. This 1945 Forest Hills High School graduate achieved success with six Emmys, three Gabriels, and three Peabody Awards. (Author's collection.)

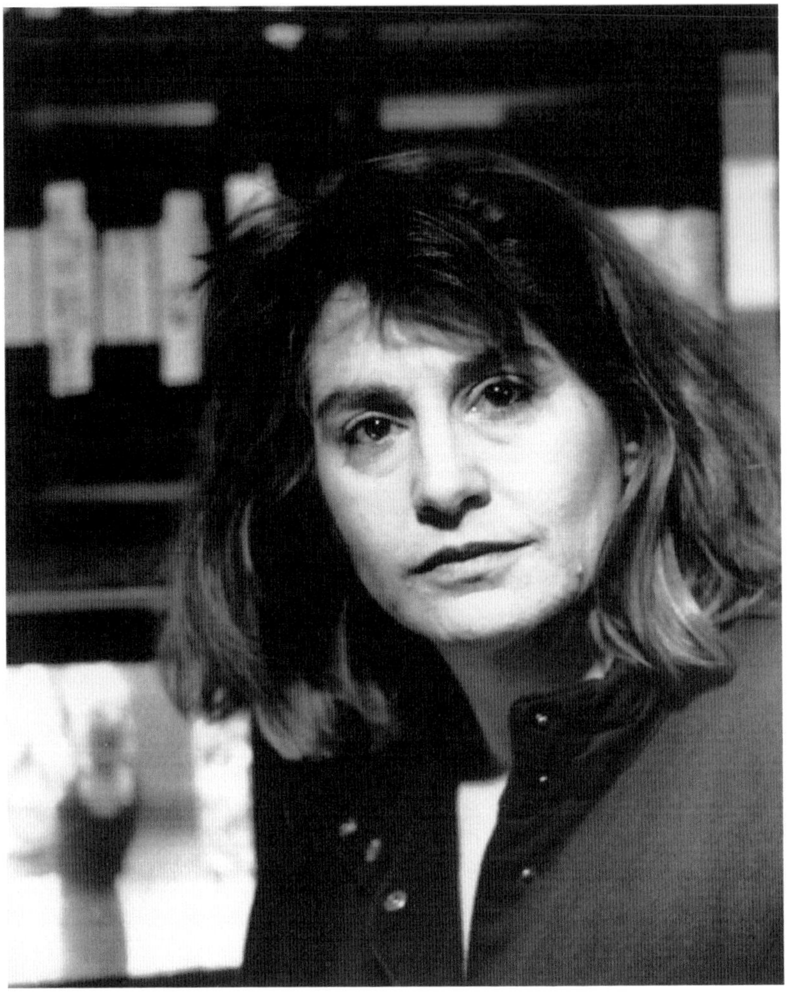

Dara Birnbaum

The internationally recognized artist and independent producer Dara Birnbaum (born 1946) was raised in the Howard Apartments in Forest Hills, and is the daughter of notable architect Philip Birnbaum. The Yale University School of Art explained, "Her work addresses the ideological and aesthetic character of mass-media imagery. Her installations and videotapes have examined and challenged how women have been portrayed historically within Western European culture." As a master of reconstructing television imagery, her work entails repetitive images with interspersed music and text. One of her most prominent works is the 1978 video "Technology/Transformation: Wonder Woman."

Birnbaum is the recipient of numerous awards, including the Carnegie Mellon University Alumni Achievement Award, Louis XIII de Remy Martin Award of Excellence, and the Certificate in Recognition of Service and Contribution to the Arts by Harvard University. Her work resides in permanent collections at museums including the Museum of Modern Art and the Whitney Museum of American Art in New York City, Museum of Contemporary Art in Barcelona, and the Israel Museum in Jerusalem. She is a faculty member of the School of Visual Arts in New York, and the senior critic at the Yale University School of Art. The Dara Gardens apartment complex in Kew Gardens Hills, designed in 1952 by her father, is named after her.

Dara Birnbaum is pictured around 1987 at Studio in Soho, New York City. (Photograph by Peter Downsbrough, courtesy of Dara Birnbaum and the Marian Goodman Gallery, New York City.)

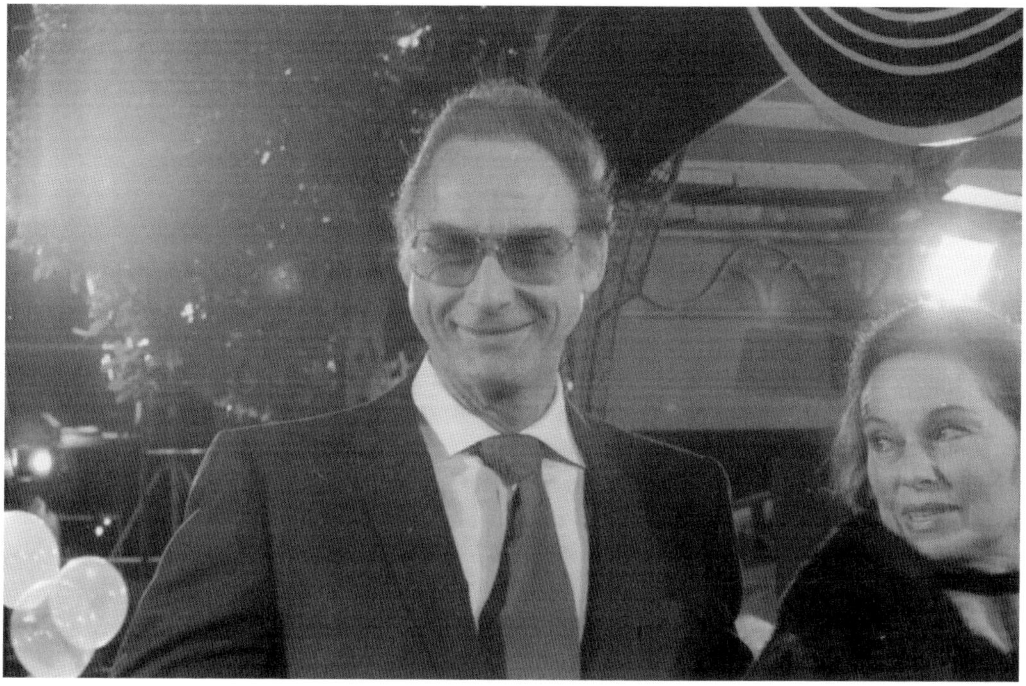

Sid Caesar

Comedian, actor, composer, and saxophonist Sid Caesar (1922–2014), born Isaac Sidney Caesar, lived in Walden Terrace at 98-10 64th Avenue in Rego Park and was spotted shopping on Queens Boulevard in the 1950s. At that time, he and Imogene Coca were pioneers of live television with a 90-minute NBC weekly series, *Your Show of Shows*, which featured movie parodies and monologues. That resulted in a Best Comedy Team win in 1953. His memorable film roles include *It's a Mad, Mad, Mad, Mad World* (1963), *Silent Movie* (1976), and Coach Calhoun in *Grease* (1978). Caesar earned a star on the Hollywood Walk of Fame in 1960, and was a Television Academy Hall of Fame inductee in 1985. (Photograph by Alan Light.)

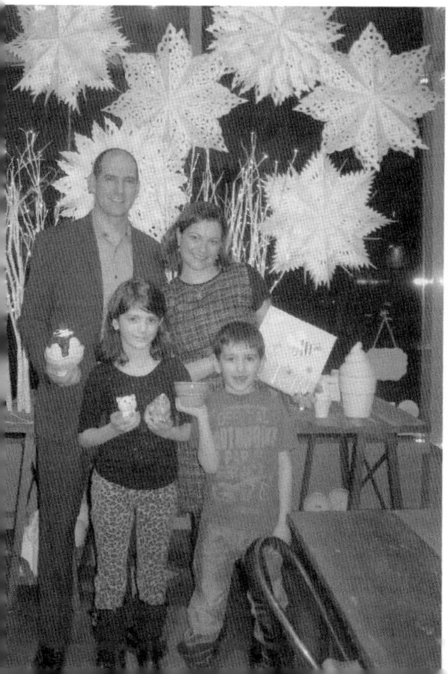

The Mandells of Ololi Studio

Sandra and Matthew Mandell and their children Eva and Oliver opened Oliloli Studio at 103-23 Metropolitan Avenue in 2012, and brought a novelty touch to Forest Hills. "Oliloli is a community space where families and friends unplug from the digital world, get creative, and connect with neighbors," said Sandra. Patrons can paint pottery or canvas, fuse glass, build eco-friendly dollhouses, and participate in workshops, festive art celebrations, and summer camp activities. (Photograph by Michael H. Perlman.)

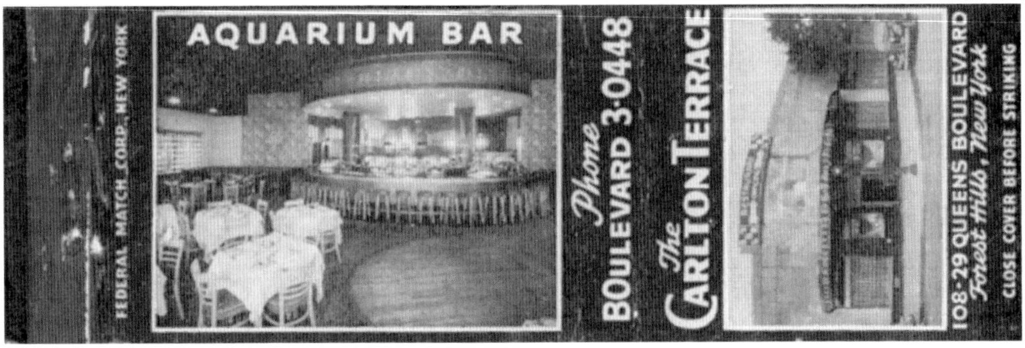

The Carlton Terrace and the Stratton

On opposite corners of 71st Road were two famous nightspots, known as Stratton Restaurant & Bar at 108-36 Queens Boulevard (operated from about 1949 through 1986) and the Carlton Terrace at 108-29 Queens Boulevard (from about 1940 to the early 1970s). This was the scene for musical acts, banquets, weddings, and dinner dances.

Patrons entered the Carlton Terrace's streamlined Art Deco front, bounded by glass block and a stainless steel marquee, and came upon the specially lit Aquarium Bar with its waterfall and tropical fish. In 1940, $2.50 was the admission to a New Year's Eve party, followed by a New Year's Day dinner for $1. A luncheon cost from 50¢ and a dinner from 85¢. With no cover, patrons enjoyed a revue and danced nightly to acts such as Gaspare Barbie's Orchestra, Johnny Black, and Bob Ryan and the Twins. Steaks, chops, and seafood were on the menu.

The Stratton was advertised as "Joe Vogel's popular Boulevard spot" and "Queens' most distinguished restaurant." Early on, the Stratton Retail Shop offered hors d'oeuvres, table delicacies, and baked goods. In its later years, patrons sat in a sidewalk café and enjoyed fine American and Continental cuisine. Dishes ranged from omelets to charcoal-broiled chicken to lamb chops. Many locals recall the sounds of Tito Puente and The Drifters, and reflect upon their dates during Latin and disco nights. (Above, author's collection; below, courtesy of Queens Chamber of Commerce.)

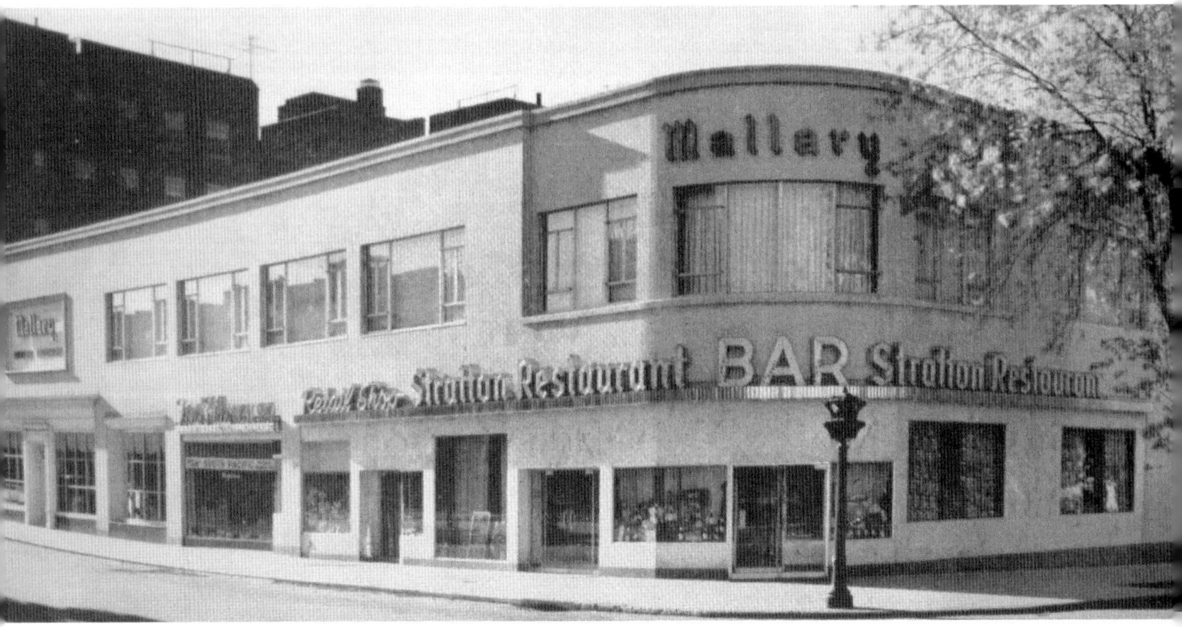

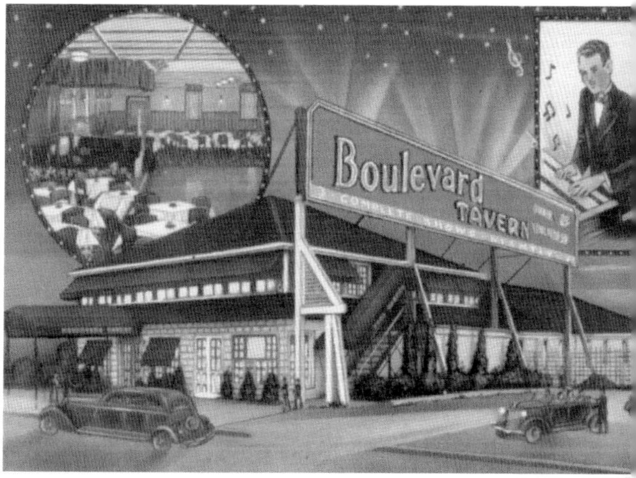

Boulevard Tavern

A large Queens Boulevard billboard for the Boulevard Tavern read, "Dine, Dance, And Be Merry." Situated at 94-05 Queens Boulevard, Boulevard Tavern was later renamed The Boulevard and was Rego Park's "in-place" from the 1930s through the 1960s. It hosted three shows nightly, wedding receptions, bachelor dinners, and banquets. An audience of up to 800 surrounded an elevated dance floor, a bandstand, and an electric organ. Singer Patti Page was among the notables who would pose for photographs with fans. Other performers included singers Harry Belafonte, Connie Haines, Norma Sykes (Sabrina), and Jan Fredric's Orchestra. (Author's collection.)

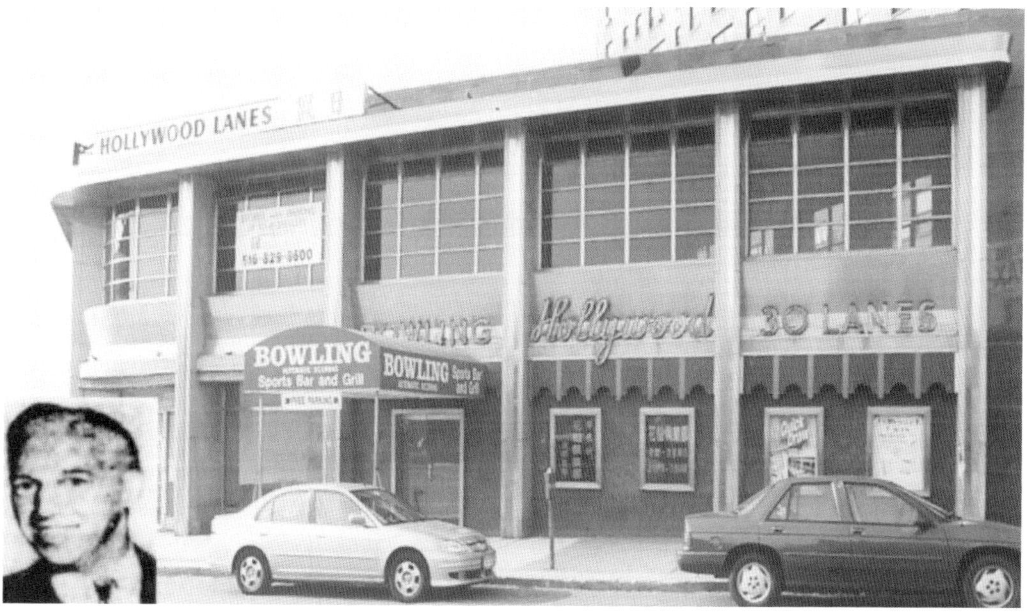

Hollywood Lanes and Mannie Rose

Opened on November 8, 1952, at 99-23 Queens Boulevard in Forest Hills and built at a cost of $400,000, the popular Hollywood Lanes housed 30 lanes and offered lunch, dinner, a cocktail lounge, and a snack bar. General manager Mannie Rose envisioned grand tournaments. Open daily, it remained in operation until 2002. The opening ceremony's special guest was Dick Hoover of Akron, Ohio, who was the youngest bowler to win the All-Star tournament at age 21. Hollywood Lanes accommodated professional bowlers, championships, open bowling, and birthday parties. By 1990, New York City had 44 bowling alleys, in comparison to approximately 160 in the 1960s, but Hollywood Lanes remained a major establishment. (Photograph by Michael H. Perlman.)

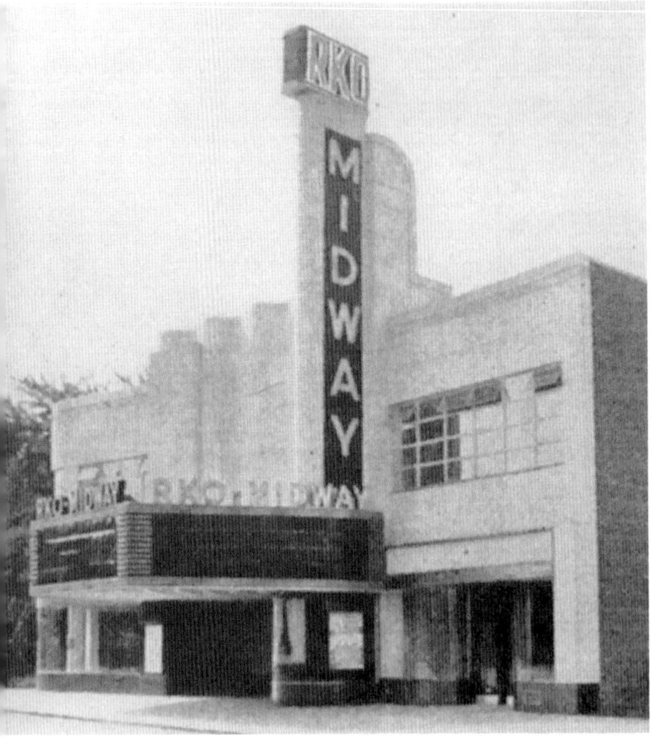

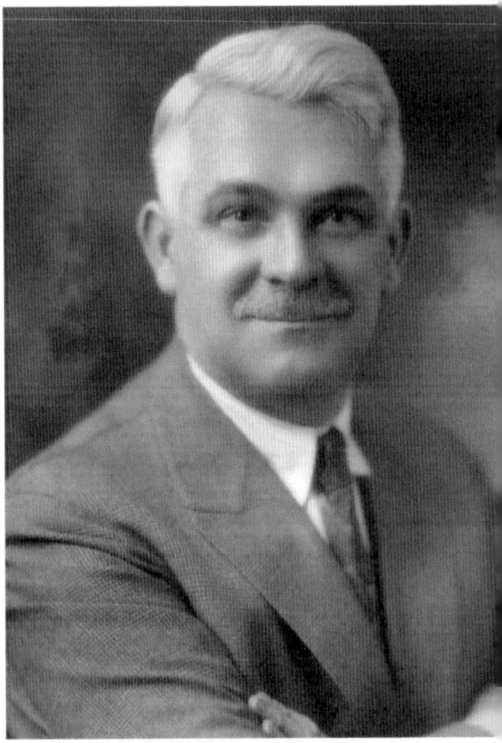

Midway Theatre and Thomas Lamb

America's foremost theater architect, Thomas White Lamb (1871–1942) designed over 300 US theaters. The Art Moderne–style Midway Theatre at 108-22 Queens Boulevard in Forest Hills was designed in 1942. A lobby mural once paid homage to the courageous Americans on Midway Island during World War II's Battle of Midway. Patrons would vote for Outstanding Star of the Year, and photographs of Bob Hope, Bette Davis, Fred Astaire, Ginger Rogers, Jack Benny, and Humphrey Bogart were displayed.

Lamb's great-grandson Tom Andrew Lamb stated, "Lamb lived the American dream, and understood it was within him to create that. Regardless of one's social status, he created community spaces where beauty is valued. Everyone could walk into his theaters and feel like they belong. Great architecture lifts the mind and spirit."

A stone curtain-like accordion exists above the marquee and accompanies a curved corner with a streamlined band conveying harmony. An accentuated vertical beacon reads "Midway" in neon lights, which adds a Jazz Age touch on Queens Boulevard.

The oval grand foyer features a 30-foot ceiling with domes and a South Beach color scheme. A whimsical winding staircase leads to the mezzanine promenade with its definitive picture window, which enables an abundance of natural light. Movie-going was fashionable in the 1940s, and one can visualize how a woman's dress would conform to the sweeping staircase.

Opening attractions were *The Pied Piper*, *Just Off Broadway*, and the U.S. Navy's Technicolor short subject *The Battle of Midway*. The Midway screened first-run entertainment, Walt Disney cartoons, and up-to-the-minute news.

Today, the Midway offers nine screens with first-run features and state-of-the-art digital projection, and remains a community cornerstone. For the theater's 70th anniversary in 2012, president Leslie Brown and treasurer Steve Melnick of the Forest Hills Chamber of Commerce partnered with Regal Entertainment to screen Alfred Hitchcock's 1954 classic *Rear Window*, and the proceeds benefited the New York City Chapter of the Alzheimer's Association. (Left, author's collection; right, courtesy of Tom Andrew Lamb.)

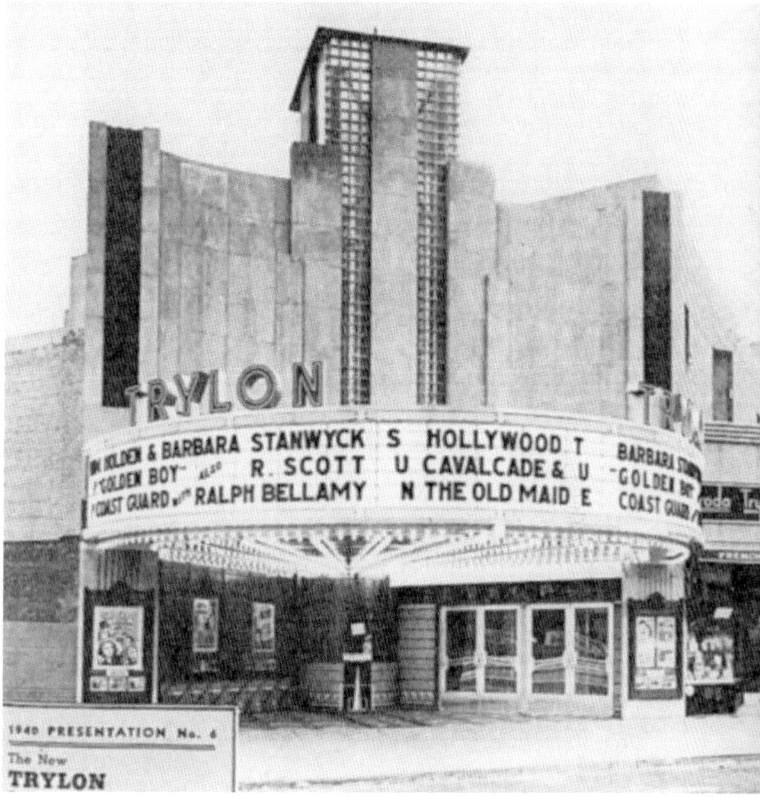

Trylon Theater and Joseph Unger

With the advent of the 1939 World's Fair, Joseph Unger (1896–1996), a notable New York architect, designed the Trylon Theater at 98-81 Queens Boulevard in Forest Hills to reflect the Fair's technological innovations and respond to a booming population. This Art Deco neighborhood theater was named after the Fair's symbolic monument, the Trylon, which was alongside the Perisphere. Analogous to the Fair's theme, "The World of Tomorrow," the theater was "The Theater of Tomorrow," and memorialized the Trylon in its mosaic-tile ticket booth, terrazzo floor, and fountain, and also featured thematic murals alongside the proscenium. In operation until 1999, the elliptical marquee once boasted classics such as *The Wizard of Oz*, *Gone with the Wind*, and *The Ghost Breakers*, starring Bob Hope. (Author's collection.)

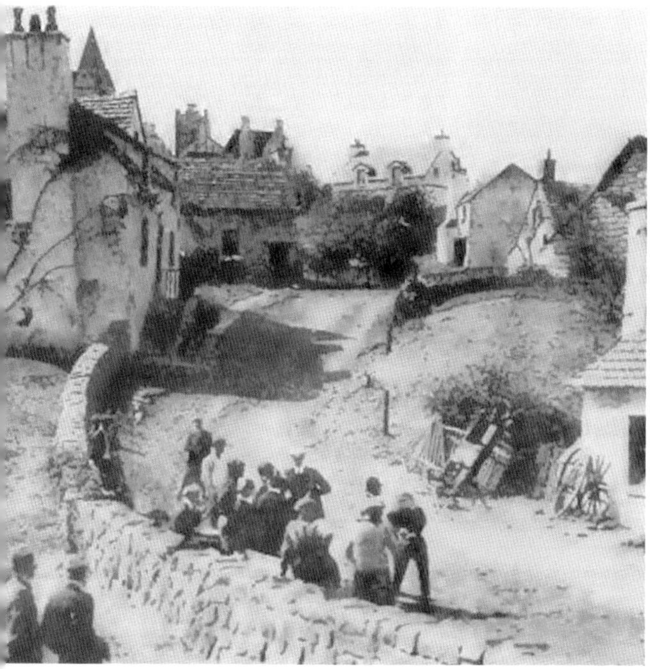

Sentimental Tommy

The rural, steep hill along 66th Road between 102nd Street and 110th Street grabbed the attention of Astoria Studios, which erected a set depicting a Scottish village for *Sentimental Tommy*, a silent film from 1921. Scottish-born Tommy was a needy boy with a rich imagination, who proved to Grizel that he loved her for who she was, and not on the basis of pity. Two years prior, the same spot accommodated a replica of a Civil War–era American village for Augustus Thomas's play *The Copperhead*. Architect Robert M. Haas, chair of the art and decoration department of the Famous Players–Lasky Corporation, designed both sets. This same forested hill, where children would tend to their sleds, was nicknamed "the green jungle," and in the 1960s, Birchwood Towers was erected here. (Author's collection.)

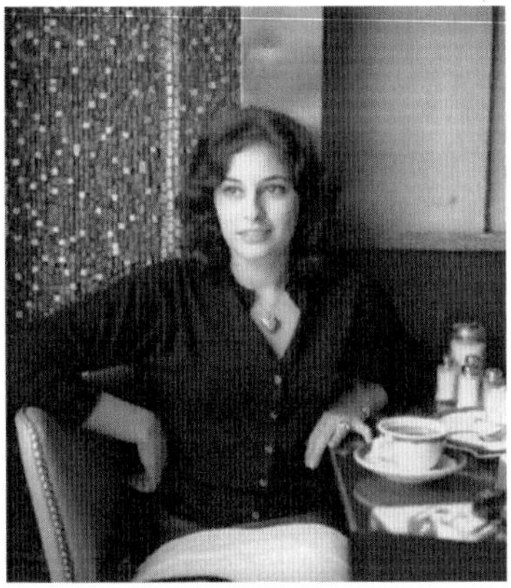

Ina Balin

Actress Ina Balin (1937–1990) won a Golden Globe for *From the Terrace* starring Paul Newman. She co-starred with Elvis Presley in *Charro!* Her brother Richard Balin explained, "A proud moment was Forest Hills' Trylon Theater screening her film *The Black Orchid* and coordinating a red carpet affair. Adopting her three Vietnamese daughters, evacuating hundreds of orphans from the An Lac orphanage in Saigon, and her film *The Children of An Lac* were her proudest accomplishments."

She guest-starred in *Bonanza, The Dick Van Dyke Show*, and *Quincy, M.E.* Balin lived in The California at 64-20 Saunders Street and Walden Terrace, and was a Forest Hills High School graduate. (Courtesy of Richard Balin.)

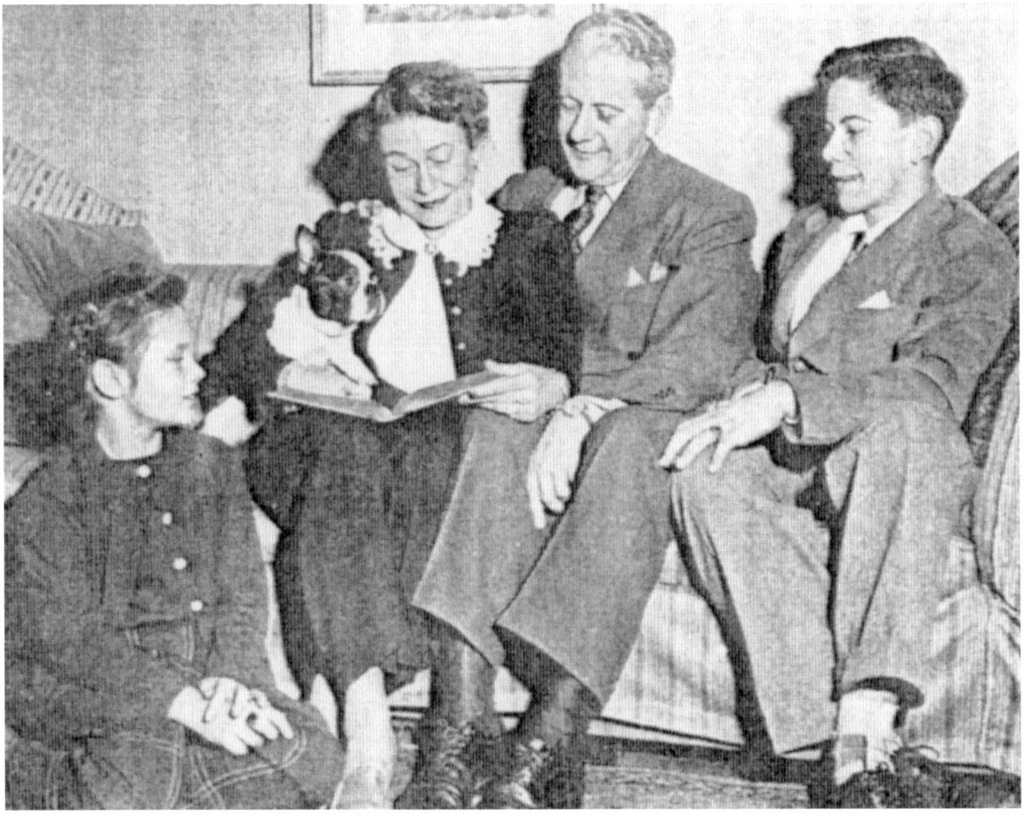

Thelma Ritter

Actress Thelma Ritter (1902–1969) of 65 Greenway Terrace in the Forest Hills Gardens won a Tony Award for Best Leading Actress in a Musical for her role in *New Girl in Town* (1957). She was highly recognized for her comedic roles and New York accent, and was a recipient of six Academy Award nominations for Best Supporting Actress. She appeared in classic films such as *Miracle on 34th Street* (1947), *All About Eve* (1950), *Titanic* (1953), *Rear Window* (1954), *Pillow Talk* (1959), and *Birdman of Alcatraz* (1962). Her dramatic television series appearances included *Alfred Hitchcock Presents* and *The United States Steel Hour.* As of 1952, Ritter and her family became parishioners of the Church-in-the-Gardens. Here, Ritter is reading a script to Monica, Beany the dog, Joe, and Anthony around 1952. (Courtesy of Church-in-the Gardens.)

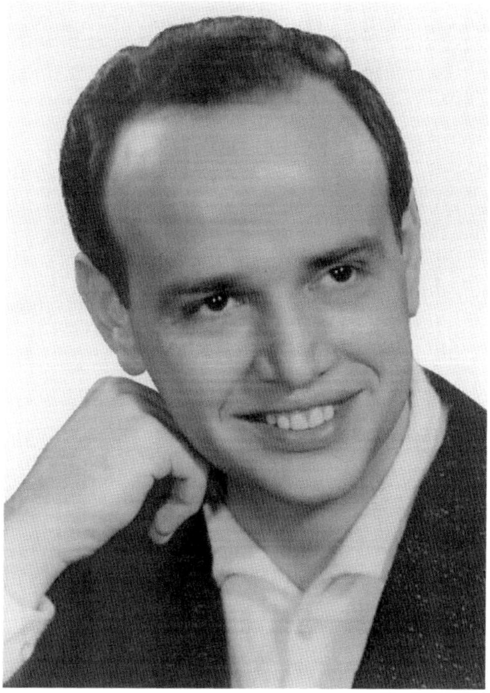

Roger Williams

On January 25, 1971, Roger Williams, the pianist who recorded "Autumn Leaves" and "Born Free," played at the Forest Hills Theatre at 107-16 Continental Avenue, signed autographs, and introduced a computerized method of teaching piano and organ. This helped promote the newly opened Roger Williams International Music Center at 71-30 Austin Street. Williams was born as Louis Wertz (1924–2011), resided in Rego Park, and tickled the ivories at the Forest Hills Inn.

Williams knew 10,000 songs by heart, performed for nine presidents beginning with Harry Truman, and achieved 21 gold and platinum records. He was the first pianist to receive a star on the Hollywood Walk of Fame, a recipient of the Lifetime Achievement Award from Steinway & Sons, and a 2010 inductee into the Hit Parade Hall of Fame when "Autumn Leaves" was considered the best-selling piano solo record of all time. (Photograph by Stan Greeson of Music Corporation of America, courtesy of Pete Greeson.)

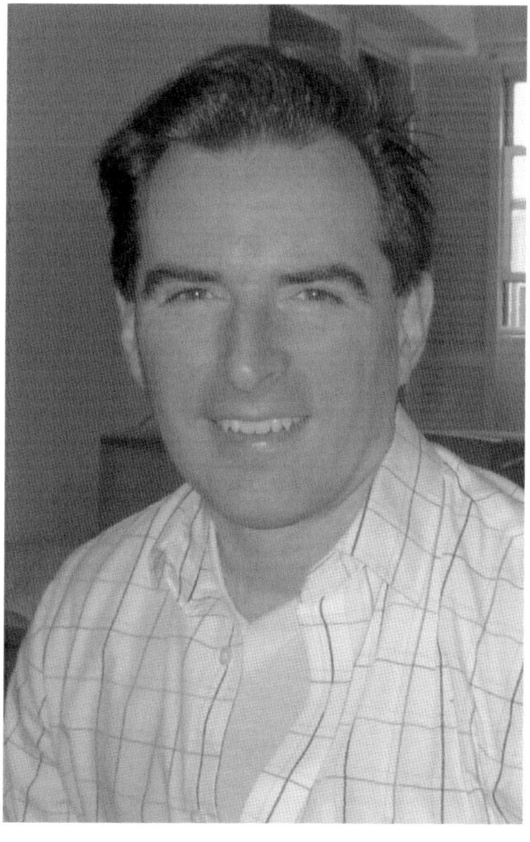

John Stanisci

John Stanisci, a professional comic book artist who designed comics for Marvel and DC Comics ranging from Batman to Superman to Spiderman, has landed in Forest Hills. He is an inker, penciller, and writer. His graphic novel *Batman Beyond: Hush Beyond* was a *New York Times* bestseller. At IDW Publishing, his achievements include *Judge Dredd* and *The X-Files*. Comparing himself to a film director, he said, "Comic book art is a medium where you create six to eight images per page which work together, are visually interesting, and communicate clearly what the writer of the story intended. That is almost unnatural in the order of art." As an actor, he starred opposite Tovah Feldshuh in the Broadway play *Irena's Vow*. (Courtesy of John Stanisci.)

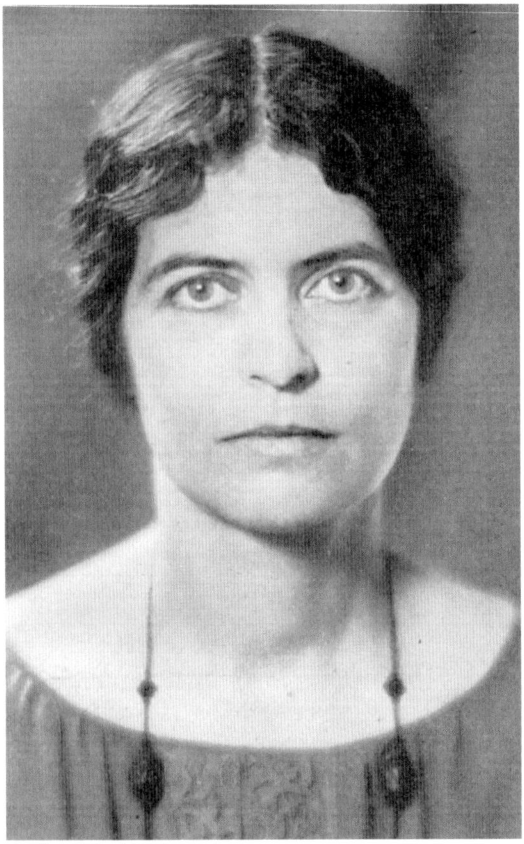

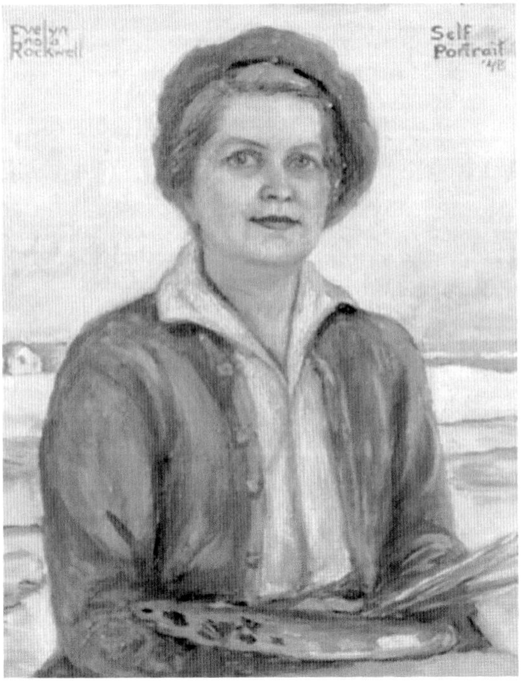

Evelyn Enola Rockwell

Evelyn Enola Rockwell (1887–1955) of 40 Deepdene Road in the Forest Hills Gardens was skillful with oil paint and pastel crayons for her portraits of children and adults, as well as seascapes. Rockwell particularly took pride in her portraits of over 500 children, most of whom were from prominent social families. That came in handy in 1926 when half of her work's proceeds benefited the new Church-in-the-Gardens Community House. Their publication read, "Miss Rockwell's recognition in the art world has come through her ability to portray a subject with pleasing exactness and yet marked with individuality. In spite of chubby faces, sailor collars or curls, it is startling to find wee personalities peering at you from the finished portraits."

She studied at the Art Students League in Manhattan, and exhibited at the Ainslie and Ehrich Galleries and the MacDowell Club. Her sister Elizabeth Rockwell (1896–1977) would direct children's fairytale plays in their home's basement studio and coordinate productions at the Community House and local schools. Both sisters worked where prominent typeface designer Frederick W. Goudy (1865–1947) once had his studio. Today, Evelyn's great-nephew Al Rockwell preserves their legacy. (Top, courtesy of Church-in-the-Gardens; bottom, courtesy of Al Rockwell.)

Sid and Ron Ramin

Sid Ramin (born around 1919, pictured at left below) is a multi-talented musician and Academy, Emmy, and Grammy Award winner. From 1949 to 1968, he lived in Rego Park and in the Howard Apartments at 99-32 66th Road in Forest Hills. That was when he orchestrated the most successful Broadway musicals, including *West Side Story*, *Gypsy*, and *A Funny Thing Happened on the Way to the Forum*. He composed music for *The Patty Duke Show*, was music director for *Candid Camera*, and wrote some well-known jingles during the "Mad Men" period of advertising. In 1966, "Music to Watch Girls By" was written for Diet Pepsi and became one of the most successful instrumentals of the era.

Sid's fond Forest Hills memories feature the Boulevard Delicatessen, Topsy's fried chicken dinners, his son playing at the Forest Hills Little League on Fleet Street, Forest Hills Jewish Center, and the Midway and Trylon Theaters.

His son Ron Ramin (born 1953, at right) composed music for 20 primetime television series and 30 movies/miniseries for television. He received an Emmy nomination in 1994 for the pilot of *Christy* on CBS and won a CableAce Award for Best Original Score for *Rent-A-Kid* in 1996. Known for his dramatic orchestral scores, his works have been featured on major networks.

Ron also lived in the Howard Apartments from 1953 to 1968. He reminisced, "From my window on 66th Road, I could see the bright lights at Shea Stadium and the nightly fireworks display at the 1964 World's Fair. My favorite activities were Saturday morning bowling league at Hollywood Lanes and spring baseball through the Forest Hills Little League. The hot dogs at Ben's Best, the milkshakes at Addie Vallins, and shopping at the Eliot Shop outfitters (72-08 Austin Street) will never be forgotten." He was Bar Mitzvah'd at Forest Hills Jewish Center in 1966. (Courtesy of Ron Ramin.)

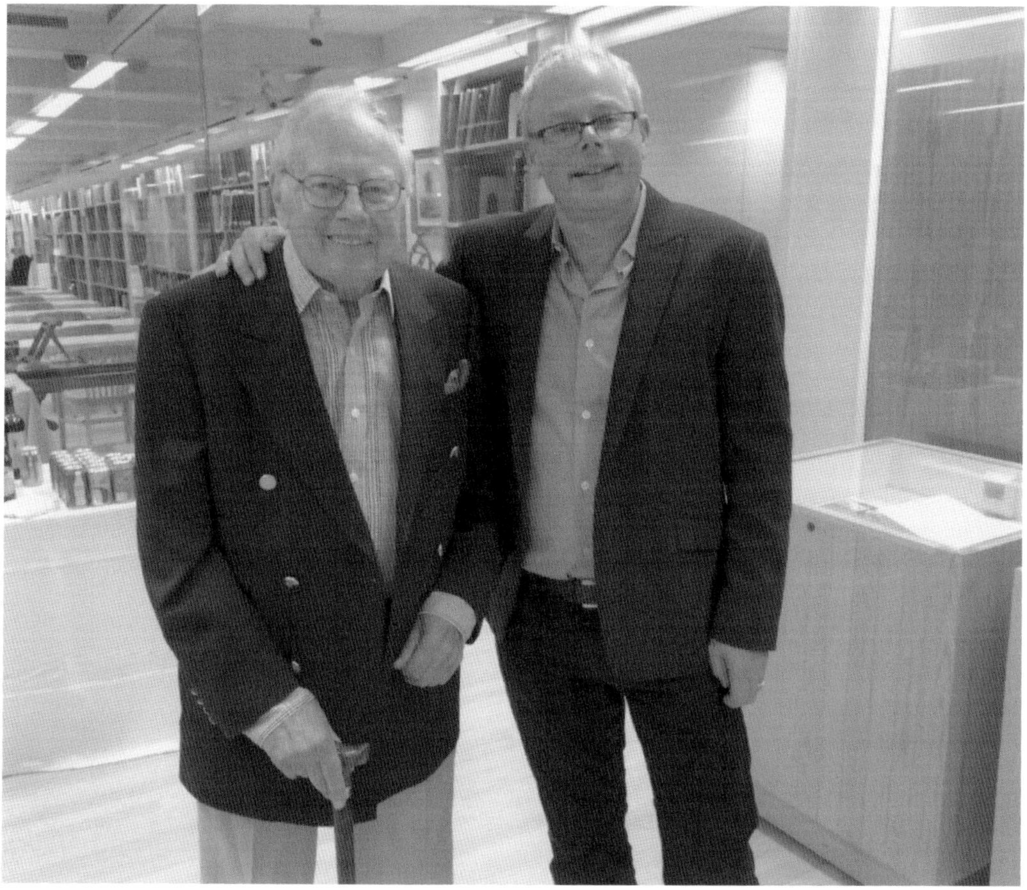

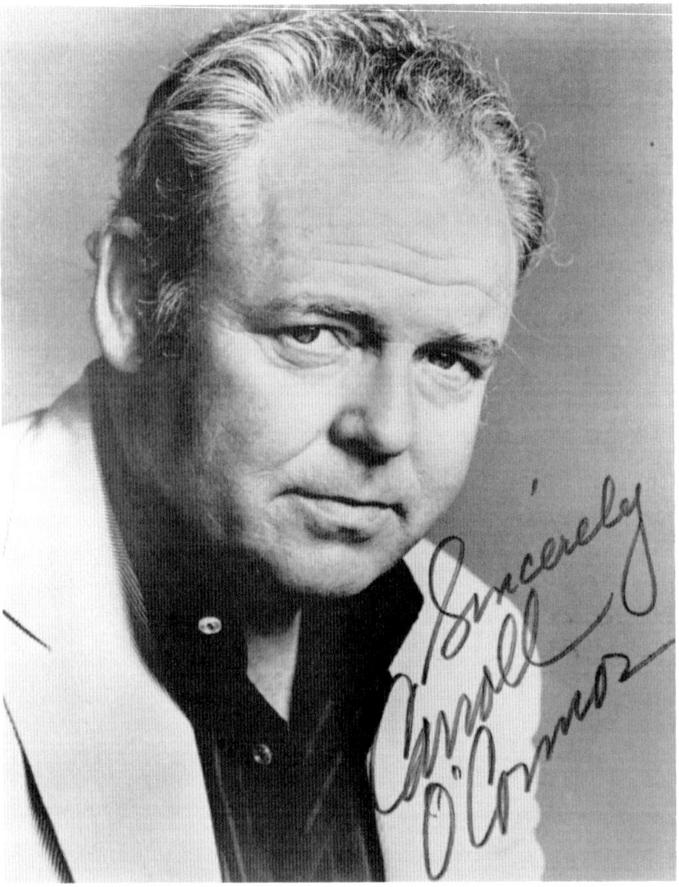

Carroll O'Connor

Carroll O'Connor (1924–2001) was raised at 69-41 112th Street in Forest Hills and graduated from Public School 3. Acting, directing, and producing distinguished his four-decade career. Generations were entertained with his most memorable role of Archie Bunker in the sitcom *All in the Family* (1971), which consisted of 307 episodes over 12 years. He also starred in the crime drama *In the Heat of the Night* (1988). Earlier in his career, O'Connor pursued an Off-Broadway production, *Ulysses in Nighttown*, and was an understudy in the Broadway show *God and Kate Murphy.* At the Juilliard School of Fine Arts, he was an acting and dialogue professor. (Courtesy of Queens Community Board 6.)

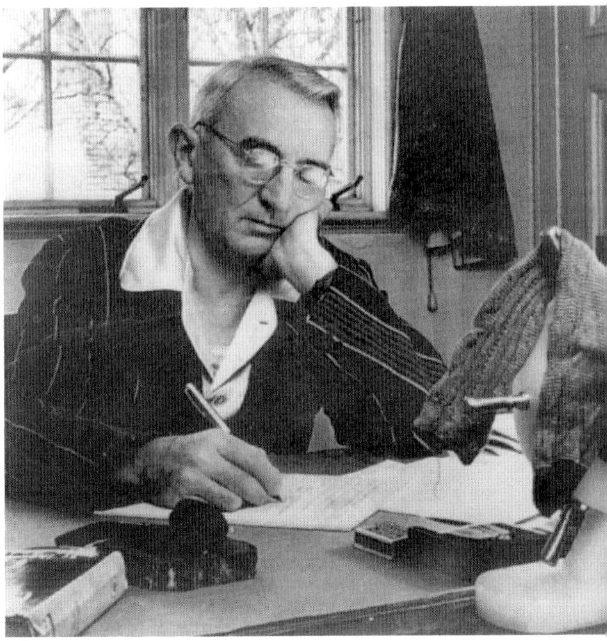

Dale Carnegie

"Forget yourself; do things for others" and "Cooperate with the inevitable" were the thought-inspiring words of Dale Carnegie (1888–1955), a lecturer and writer who developed courses in public speaking, self-improvement, corporate training, and salesmanship. He lived at 27 Wendover Road in Forest Hills. *How to Win Friends and Influence People* (1936) was his signature book. An underlying theme of his books was that there is potential for changing other people's behavior by changing one's behavior toward them. He founded the Dale Carnegie Institute, which expanded into 750 American cities and 15 countries. Today, it operates as a business training firm in 75 countries. (Courtesy of Queens Community Board 6.)

Robert Lipsyte

Sports journalist, author, and ESPN Ombudsman Robert Lipsyte (born 1938) was raised in Norwich Hall at 96-11 65th Road in Rego Park, and was a Halsey Junior High School 157 and Forest Hills High School graduate. By the fourth grade, he dreamed of becoming a writer. He reminisced, "I was a fat kid, and only in my fiction could I control the world. How else could I wow those hot girls?" Hosting *The Eleventh Hour*, a nightly PBS public affairs show, resulted in an Emmy in 1990. Other awards were Columbia University's Mike Berger Award for distinguished reporting in 1966 and 1996, and the American Library Association's Margaret Edwards Award for lifetime achievement in young adult literature in 2001, including such novels as *The Contender* and One Fat Summer. (Photograph by Sara Krulwich, *The New York Times*.)

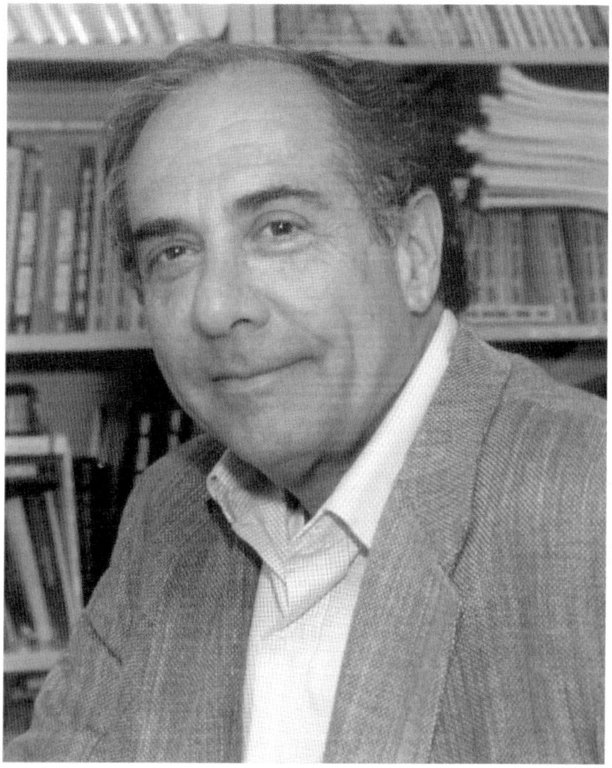

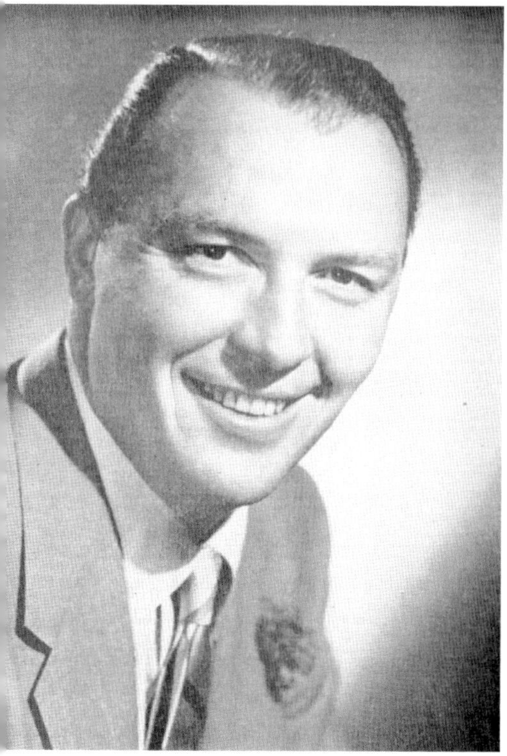

Ed Herlihy

NBC's longtime radio and television announcer was Forest Hills resident Ed Herlihy (1909–1999), who lived in Forest Close at 111-19 76th Avenue. He hosted *The Horn and Hardart Children's Hour* and narrated Sid Caesar's *Your Show of Shows*. For Universal-International, he narrated newsreels such as Pres. Franklin Delano Roosevelt's death, the attack on Pearl Harbor, and the initial American newsreel on Sputnik's launch. From the 1940s through the 1980s, he was the memorable voice behind Kraft Foods commercials. (*Radio Annual Television Yearbook*, 1959, author's collection.)

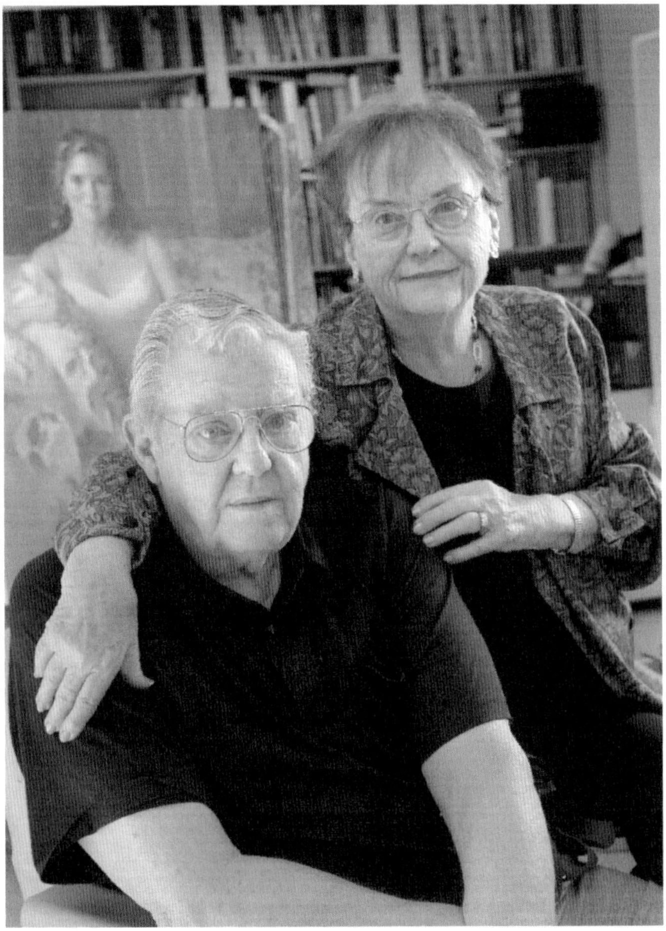

Joseph Bowler Jr.
Artist and illustrator Joseph Bowler Jr. (born 1928) was raised near the Forest Hills Tennis Stadium and began drawing as early as age three. His first illustration was published in *Cosmopolitan* at 19. After the Artists' Guild of New York named him Artist of the Year in 1967, magazines commissioned him to create portraits of notables. That included eight presidential candidates' wives for *McCall's* in 1968, Rose Kennedy on the *Ladies' Home Journal* cover in August 1971, and Julie and David Eisenhower on *The Saturday Evening Post* cover. By 1992, he was inducted into the Society of Illustrators Hall of Fame. In 2014, he was presented with the Portrait Society of America's Gold Medal. Joseph Bowler Jr. and his wife, Marilyn Carscallen Crang Bowler, are pictured in 2007. (Photograph by Mark Staff, courtesy of Jolyn L Bowler.)

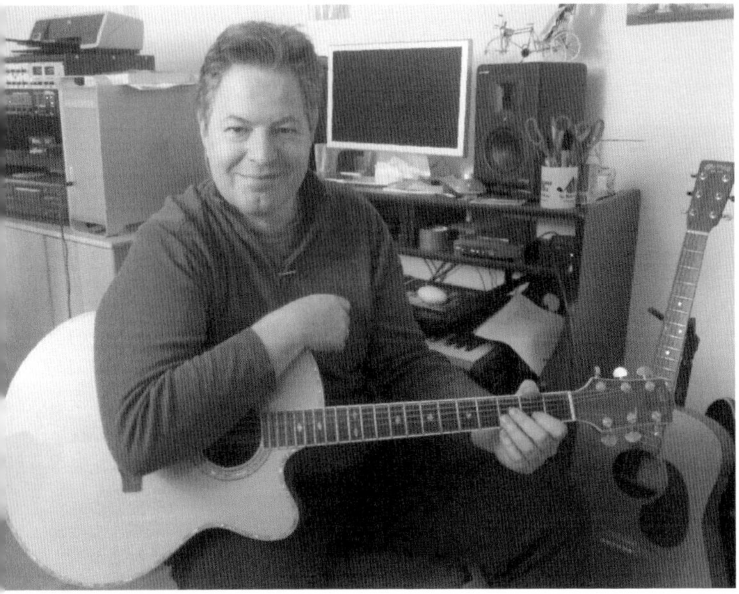

John Beltzer
Forest Hills musician John Beltzer's epiphany led to his creation of the Songs of Love Foundation, a national nonprofit founded in 1996. National songwriters compose personalized songs to inspire children experiencing life-threatening illnesses. Beltzer explained, "We use songs as tools of healing on a mass scale. A typical story involves a child hearing their song during chemotherapy. This helps alleviate pain, fear, and trauma, and builds self-esteem." As of September 2014, a total of 24,764 children received their Song of Love. (Photograph by Michael H. Perlman.)

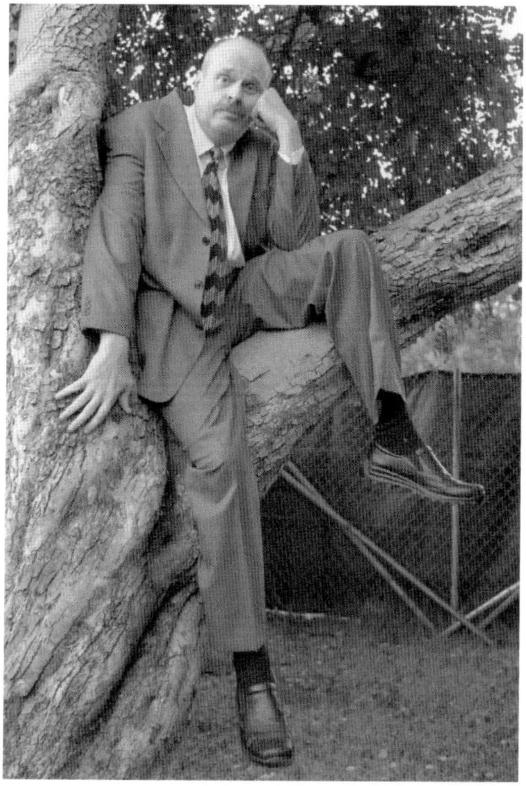

Rick Overton

Screenwriter, actor, and comedian Rick Overton (born 1954) was raised in The Grover Cleveland at 67-38 108th Street in Forest Hills, a block away from Devil's Hill (now Yellowstone Park). "It was the spot to take your sled to have dirt bomb fights," he reminisced, and also mentioned "The White Castle slider burgers around the corner from the Midway Theatre before seeing *A Hard Day's Night*.

His father, Hal Overton, was Thelonious Monk's big band arranger. Rick said, "Coming out to see my dad play in a jazz club in the early 1960s afforded me the chance to see standup comedians. In the early 1970s, I formed a comedy team, and was hooked on the laugh."

Among Overton's proudest accomplishments are winning an Emmy as a writer for HBO's *Dennis Miller Live* series and portraying Terry Wilson in the 2009 film *The Informant!* Numerous film appearances include roles on *Mrs. Doubtfire* and *Groundhog Day.* He appeared in *Seinfeld* and starred in HBO and Showtime specials. (Photograph by Dan Dion.)

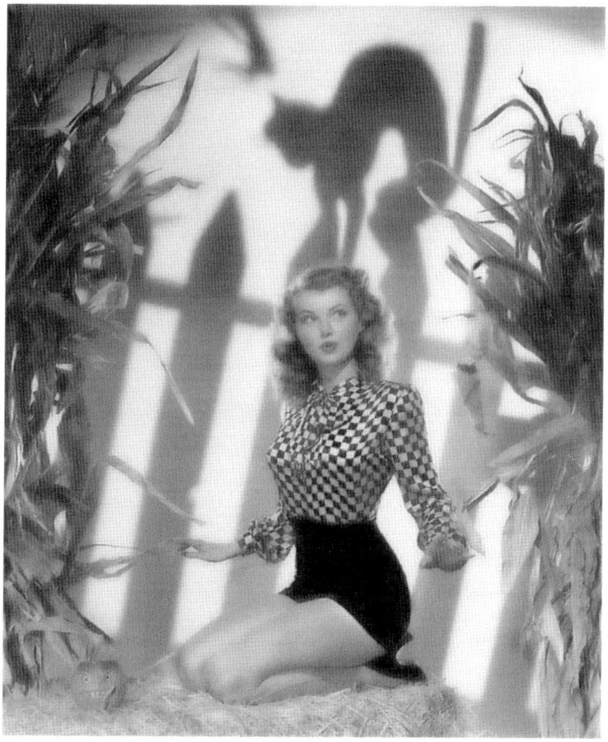

Lillian Wells

Model and actress Lillian Wells (1927–1977) was born in Forest Hills. In 1947, she was featured in six films, which include *Down To Earth*, *Dead Reckoning*, and *Framed*. Her modeling days spanned the 1950s and 1960s. She was known as a Halloween pin-up girl. (Courtesy of Pierre Tourigny.)

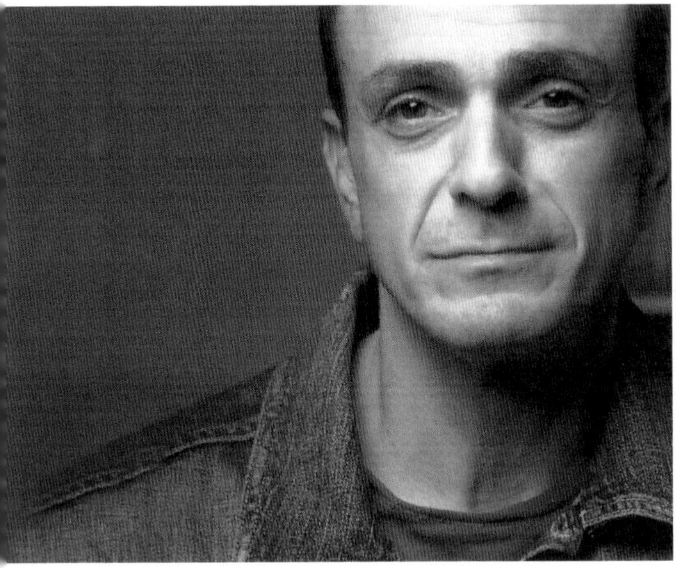

Hank Azaria

Forest Hills native Hank Azaria (born 1964) is a television, film, stage and voice actor, as well as a director, producer, and comedian. He rose to fame in 1989 as the voice behind Moe Szyslak on the animated Fox television show *The Simpsons*, and won three Emmys for Outstanding Voice-Over Performance. For his role in *Tuesdays with Morrie*, he won an Emmy for Outstanding Supporting Actor in a Miniseries or a Movie. He appeared on television shows such as *Friends* and *Mad About You*, films including *Pretty Woman*, *The Birdcage*, *Godzilla*, and *The Smurfs*, and in the Broadway musical *Spamalot*. (Courtesy of John Ales.)

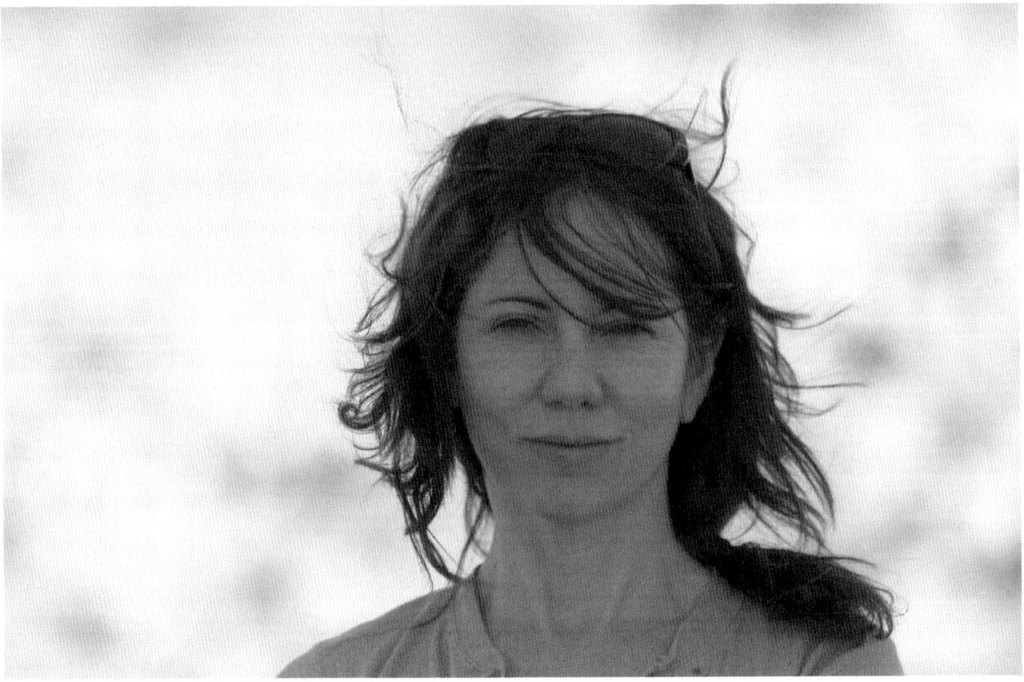

Leslie Urdang

Producer Leslie Urdang (born 1956) takes pride in her films, such as *Beginners*, *Rabbit Hole*, and *A Midsummer Night's Dream*, as well as the theater company she co-founded, New York Stage and Film. "Dedicated to the development and production of new works by established and emerging artists, it has made important contributions to our national culture for 30 years," said Urdang. Her dream was cultivated by her work in dance and theater at Forest Hills High School's *SING!*, the University of Pennsylvania, and the Yale School of Drama. "Dancing with the New York City Ballet and George Balanchine powerfully informed my esthetic, taught me rigor and discipline, and offered a first glimpse of the divine in art." (Courtesy of Olympus Pics.)

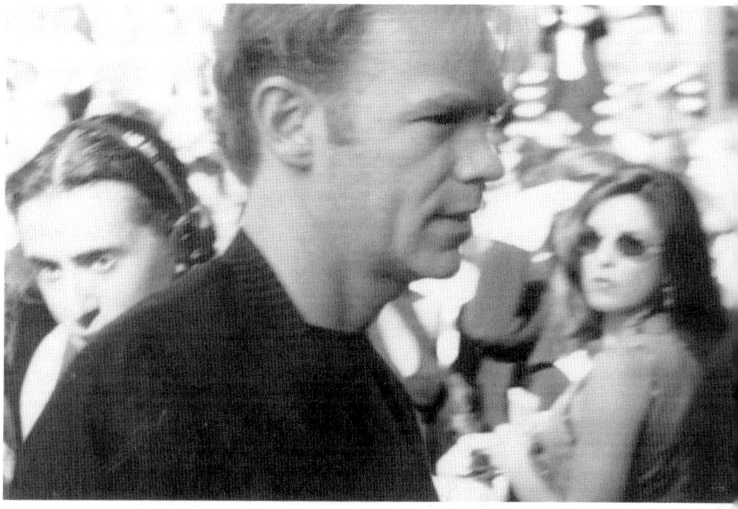

David Caruso
Actor and producer David Caruso (born 1956), a former resident of 56 Ingram Street in the Forest Hills Gardens, appeared in films such as *An Officer and a Gentleman* (1982), *Jade* (1995), and *Proof of Life* (2000). He portrayed Detective John Kelly on *NYPD Blue*, for which he won the Golden Globe for best actor, and also played Lt. Horatio Caine on *CSI: Miami*. (Photograph by Alan Light.)

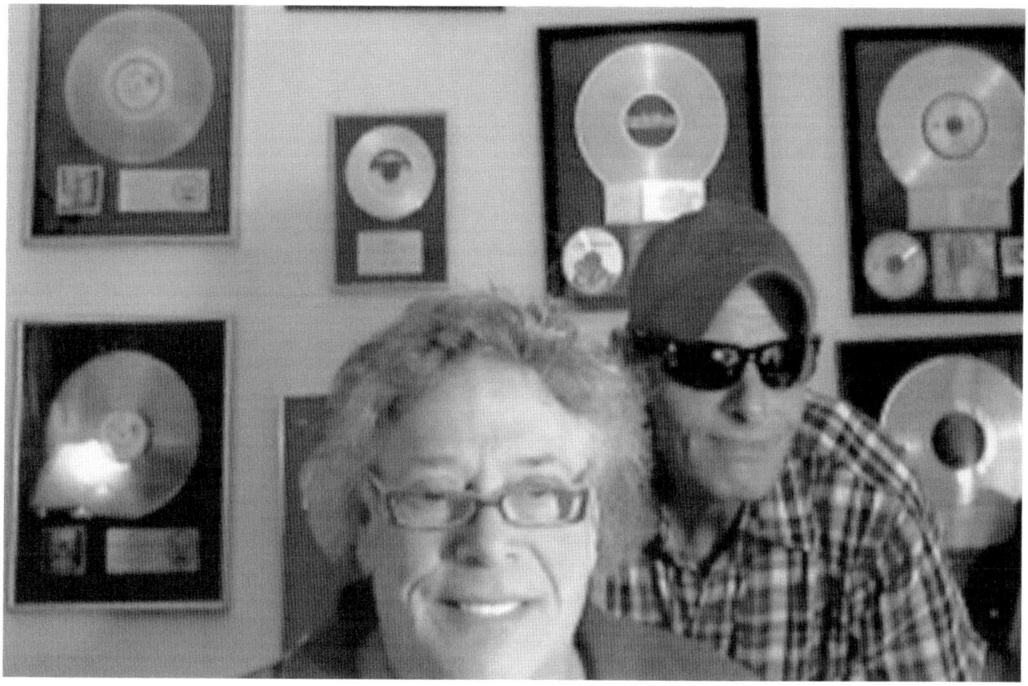

Leslie West and Larry West
Brothers Leslie West (born 1945, left) and Larry West Weinstein (born 1948, right) were raised in Forest Hills. Leslie lived at Saxon Hall at 62-60 99th Street. In the 1960s, bass guitarist and vocalist Larry founded The Vagrants, an R&B/blue-eyed soul rock band, which also featured Leslie on guitar and vocals. "We would practice at the Cameo Bowling Alley (Austin Street and Continental Avenue) and anywhere we could plug in," said Larry.

By 1969, Leslie launched hard rock band Mountain, where his unique guitar sound captivated audiences. Mountain was chronicled on VH1's *100 Greatest Artists of Hard Rock*, and Leslie was inducted into the Long Island Music Hall of Fame. Songs titles such as "Mississippi Queen" and "Nantucket Sleighride," and "For Yasgur's Farm" contribute to rock music's legacy. Leslie has recorded or played alongside rock icons including The Who, Mick Jagger, and Billy Joel. (Courtesy of Larry West Weinstein.)

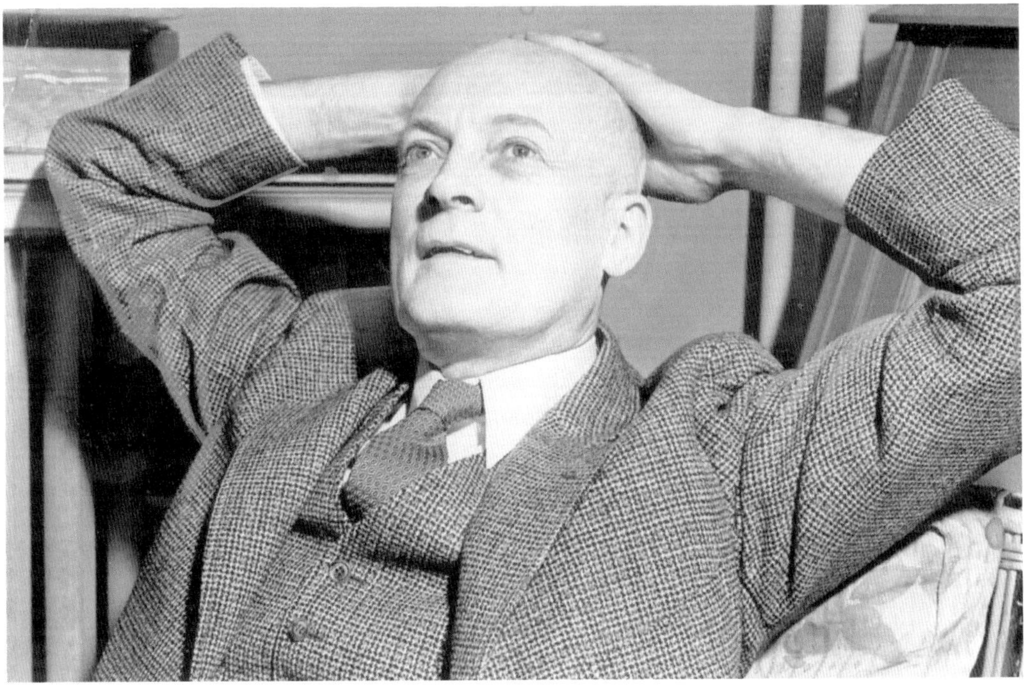

Homer Croy

Homer Croy (1883–1965) of 10 Standish Road in Forest Hills was an author, screenwriter, and humorist. He was the son of American pioneers who immigrated to Missouri in a covered wagon. As a child farmer, he studied the dictionary and began submitting articles to journals, which marked his humble beginnings. He was America's first student of journalism. He received compensation with postage stamps for his first novel, and was also first to pursue filming by touring the world. His novel *They Had to See Paris* (1926) became Will Rogers's first talking picture. He authored *Jesse James Was My Neighbor* and *Our Will Rogers*, and wrote for *The Saturday Evening Post.* (Courtesy of the Croy and Ebert family.)

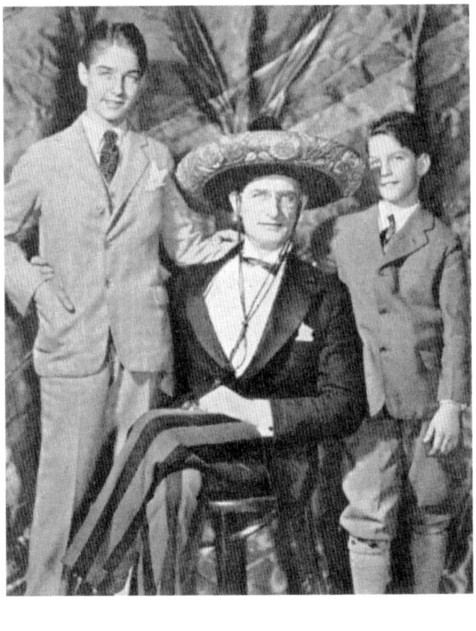

Julius Tannen

Forest Hills resident Julius Tannen (1880–1965, pictured at center) was one of the first vaudeville stand-up comedians. The use of props, costumes, or sets was not his style, but he became notable for his creative word games and clever improvisations. He took the stage of New York City's Palace Theatre, the premier vaudeville showcase. For 25 years, he appeared in films including *Stranded* and eight works directed by Preston Sturges. In *Singin' in the Rain*, he dramatized the technology of talking pictures. His stardom contributed to the careers of Milton Berle, Bob Hope, and Lucille Ball. He is pictured here with sons Charles (left) and Billy. (Courtesy of Church-in-the Gardens Community House.)

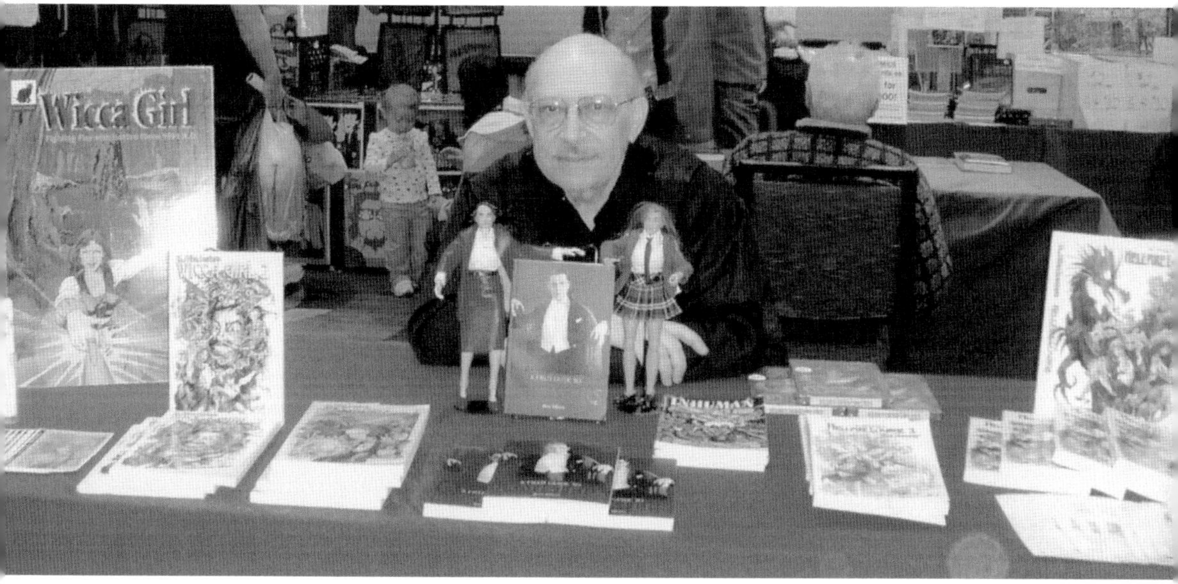

R. Allen Leider

Since the fourth grade, author and screenwriter R. Allen Leider (born 1944) had a gift for storytelling and writing. At Forest Hills High School (class of 1962), he wrote class competition *SING!* shows and the underground *Pseudo "I"* magazine. He became a copyboy for *CBS Evening News with Walter Cronkite* in 1970. In 1973, Alfred Hitchcock educated him about storyboards and screenplays during an interview. In 1985, he wrote the screenplay for *The Oracle*, a chiller. Creatively blending genres of fantasy, horror, mystery, and science fiction, in 2006, he authored the popular *Wicca Girl* trilogy and the *Hellfire Lounge* anthology series. He is the owner, editor, and film critic of The Black Cat Review online magazine, which is part of his Black Cat Media Associates business. Leider was raised at 110-56 and 110-20 71st Avenue. (Courtesy of Richard Allen Leider.)

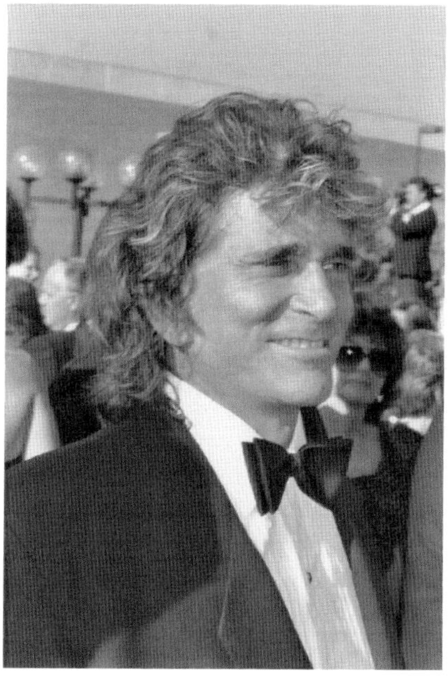

Michael Landon

Forest Hills native Michael Landon (1936–1991), born Eugene Maurice Orowitz, was an actor, writer, director, and producer. He is most remembered for his roles as Little Joe in the second longest running Western series, *Bonanza* (1959–1973), Charles Ingalls in *Little House on the Prairie* (1974–1983), and Jonathan Smith in *Highway to Heaven* (1984–1989). In 1984, he received a star on the Hollywood Walk of Fame. (Courtesy of Alan Light.)

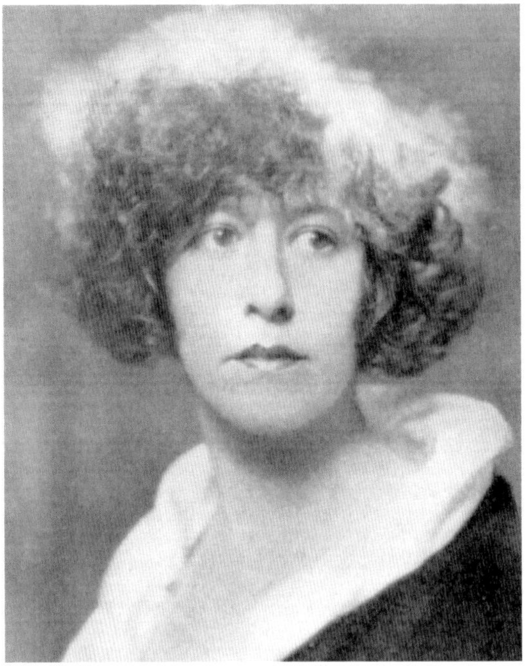

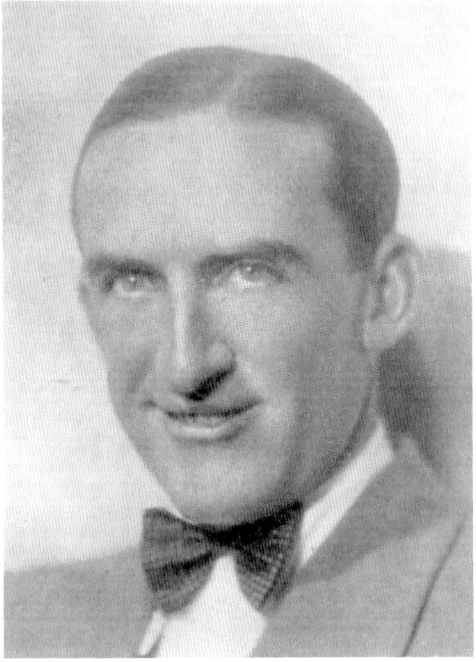

Frances Grant and Ted Wing

The famous dance duo Frances Grant and Ted Wing of Forest Hills performed at the 1926 opening of the Community House in the Forest Hills Gardens. They performed in Arthur Hammerstein's musical comedy *Tickle Me* at the Selwyn Theatre, among other Broadway shows. In August 1920, the *Brooklyn Standard Union* reported, "Novel and beautiful is the cascade of fluffy bubbles, and rising out of this artistic scenic gem, Frances Grant and Ted Wing glide into an eccentric dance, which gently fades away as the chorus of bathing beauties comes dashing into the soapy bath." (Courtesy of Church-in-the-Gardens Community House.)

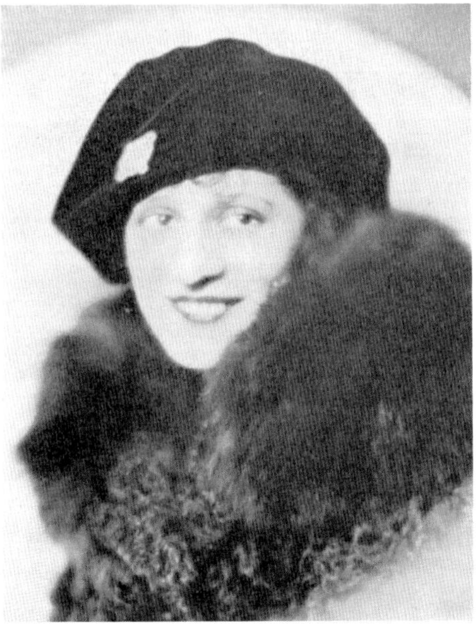

Gladys Rice

Gladys Rice (1890–1983) of Forest Hills was a recognized soprano of *Roxy and His Gang* at Manhattan's Roxy Theatre, the Capitol Theatre, and the Rivoli Theatre. At the Community House in the Forest Hills Gardens, she performed "Song Novelties" for its opening night program on August 12, 1926.

Samuel Lionel Rothafel, widely known as "Roxy," was among the first national radio stars through his broadcasts from the Capitol Theatre during the 1920s. *Roxy and His Gang* earned recognition on NBC and CBS radio shows of the 1920s and 1930s. Rice also recorded with one of the earliest labels, Edison Records. (Courtesy of Church-in-the-Gardens Community House.)

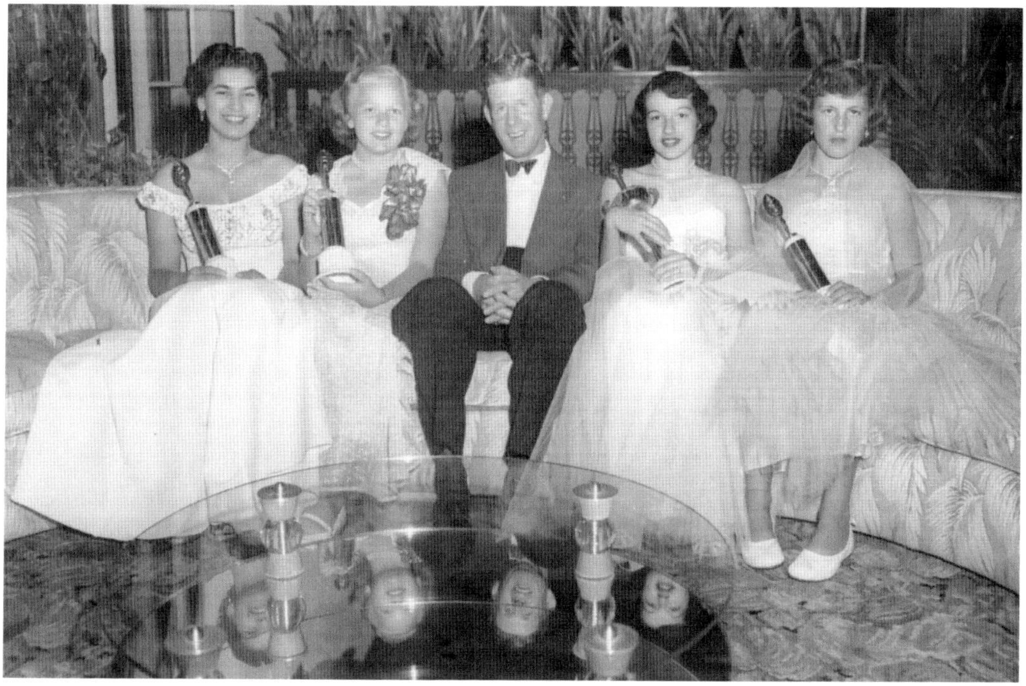

Rudy Vallée

Singer, saxophonist, bandleader, and actor Rudy Vallée once lived in Forest Hills, according to his widow, Eleanor Vallée. Born as Hubert Prior Vallée (1901–1986), he was a distinguished soft crooner whose voice was amplified by the use of a megaphone. Among his legendary recordings was "A Dream" (1921), "As Time Goes By" (1931), and "Brother, Can You Spare a Dime?" (1932). An audience of 200 million tuned in to *The Fleischmann Hour* (1928), which was the first radio talk show produced. As the Great Depression arrived, his music sales helped spare the sheet music industry. He starred in *How to Succeed in Business Without Really Trying* on Broadway (1961) and in the film (1967). Fans can pick up his autobiography, *Vagabond Dreams Come True*. (Courtesy of the Jeff Brodhead Collection.)

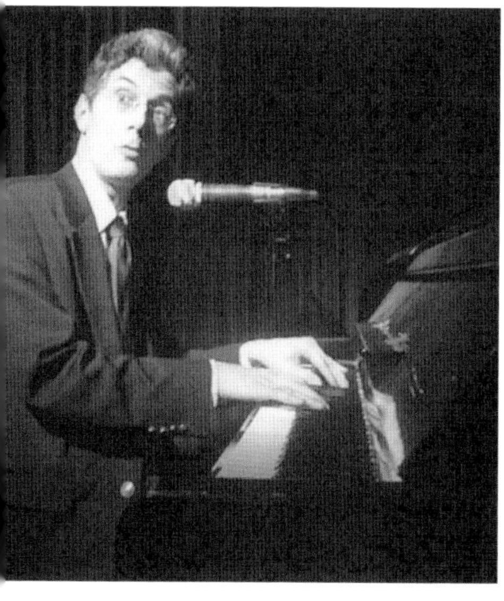

Peter Dizozza

Music composer, performer, pianist, photographer, filmmaker, writer, and lawyer Peter Dizozza (born 1958) grew up in Forest Hills. He composed over 200 songs and song settings for poems. As a music director, he provided scores for *The Great Enchanted Forest* and *Murder by Music* for the Women's Club of Forest Hills, and also directs at the Williamsburg Art and Historical Center. He serves as counsel at Cinema VII Entertainment Collective and is also chair of the New York City Bar Association's entertainment committee, which stages productions that honor legal luminaries including Chief Judge Jonathan Lippman. (Courtesy of Peter Dizozza.)

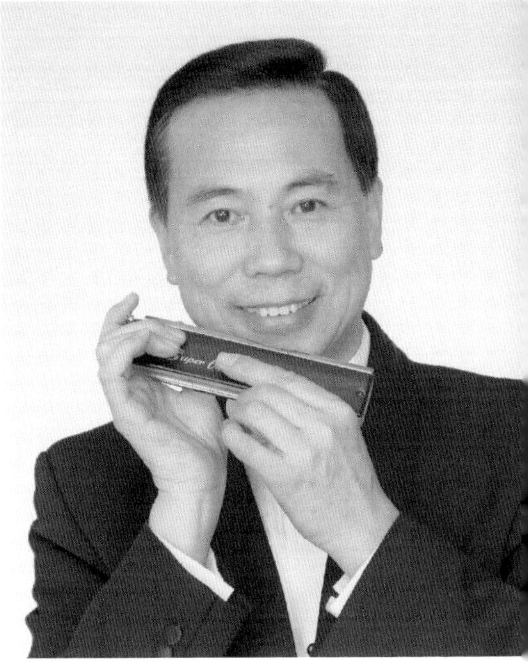

Jia-Yi He

Born in Beijing, China, in 1953, He called Forest Hills home in 2012. As a world-class harmonica virtuoso, concert performer, recording artist, and teacher, he makes his harmonica resemble a full orchestra. "Most harmonica players only play the harmonica, but I play the harmonica like other instruments," he said. He is a proud owner and master of more than 300 harmonicas.

He competed on *America's Got Talent*, taught Mayor Michael Bloomberg how to play the harmonica in Central Park, performed at the General Assembly Hall of the United Nations, soloed with the China National Symphony Orchestra and California Pops Orchestra, and is a regular throughout Asia and Europe. His May 2014 concert at the historic First Presbyterian Church of Newtown generated funds for its restoration. (Courtesy of Jia-Yi He.)

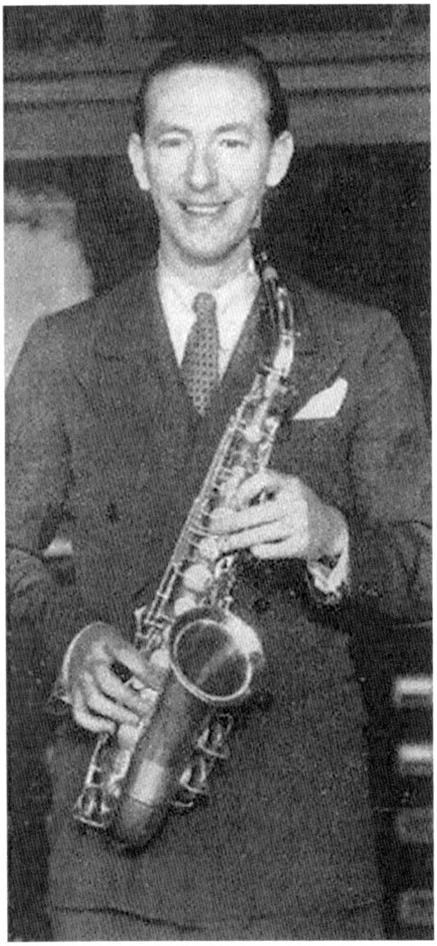

James Hal Kemp

Kemp (1904–1940), a jazz alto saxophonist, clarinetist, composer, arranger, and orchestra leader, resided at 53 Continental Avenue. In Forest Hills, he could be found practicing in a building adjacent to the T-Bone Diner. He founded Hal Kemp and His Orchestra and was among the most popular musicians of the 1930s. His recordings included "Lullaby of Broadway" and "Got a Date with an Angel." Some original compositions were "In Dutch with the Duchess" and "Blue Rhythm." He conducted at Hotel New Yorker, Hotel Pennsylvania, and the London Palladium. (Author's collection.)

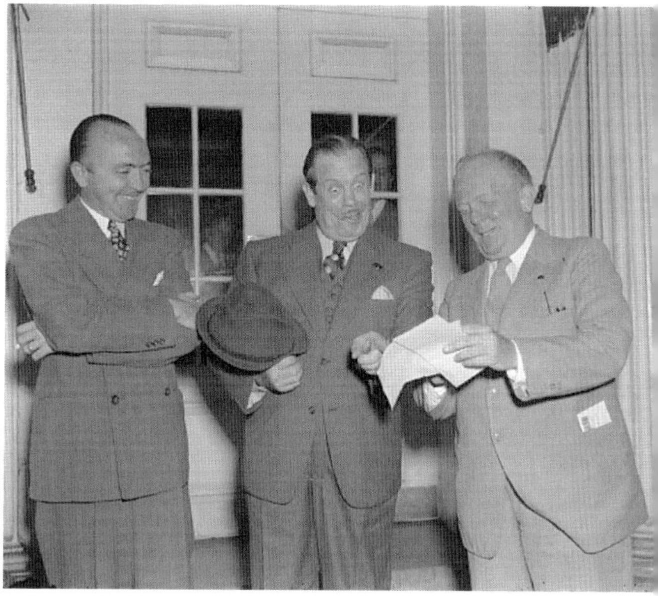

Lew Lehr

"Monkeys is the cwaziest people!" was among the humorous catchphrases of comedian Lew Lehr (1895–1950, pictured at center) of 90-05 63rd Avenue in Rego Park. He performed on the vaudeville and musical comedy stage and wrote for *Fox Movietone News*. He made movies of wrestling matches and football games, where his comments and flashes of him in deep thought with crossed eyes engaged audiences. His satires included *Lew Lehr's Unnatural History* and *Magic Carpet*. Lehr was caricatured in six Warner Bros. cartoons such as *Porky in Egypt* (1938). He is pictured here with George Durno and Karl Godwin around 1938. (Courtesy of Library of Congress.)

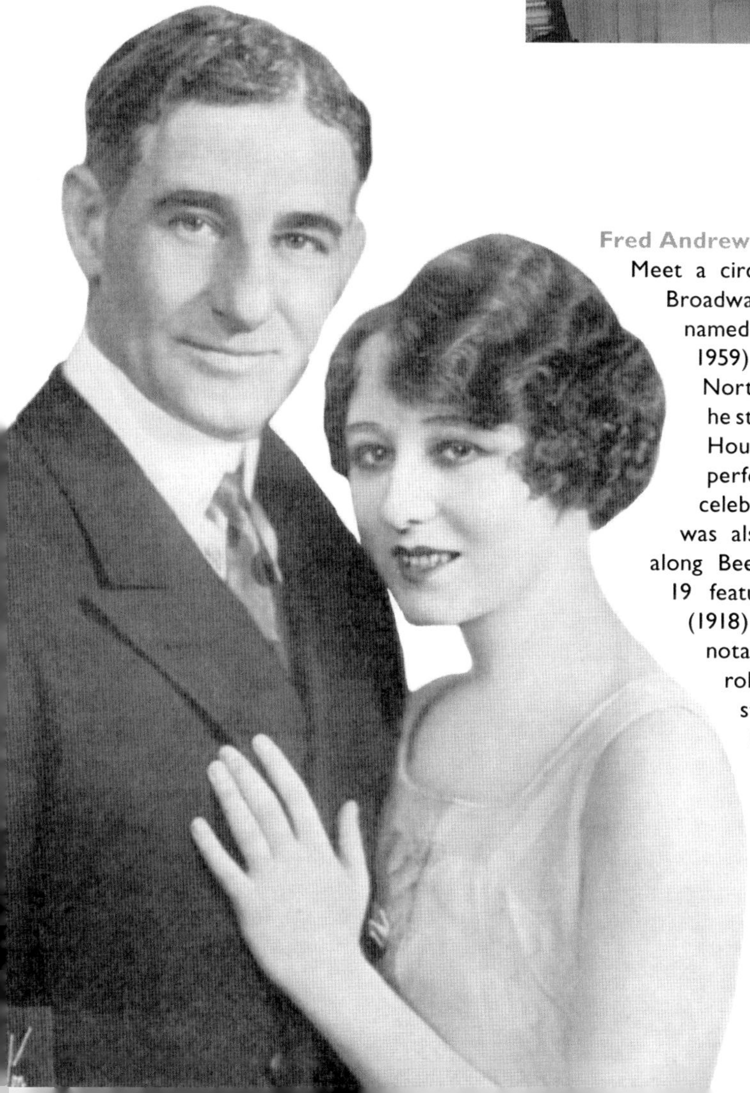

Fred Andrew Stone

Meet a circus performer, vaudeville star, Broadway performer, and film actor named Fred Andrew Stone (1873–1959), who resided at 150 Greenway North. In the Forest Hills Gardens, he starred in plays at the Community House with The Gardens Players, performed in Fourth of July celebrations in Station Square, and was also spotted riding his unicycle along Beechknoll Road. He starred in 19 feature films including *The Goat* (1918) and *Alice Adams* (1935). Most notably, Stone played the Scarecrow role in *The Wizard of Oz*, a 1902 stage production. His daughter, Dorothy Stone (right), joined him in the portrayal of Raggedy Ann and Raggedy Andy in the 1923 musical *Stepping Stones*. (Courtesy of Church-in-the Gardens Community House.)

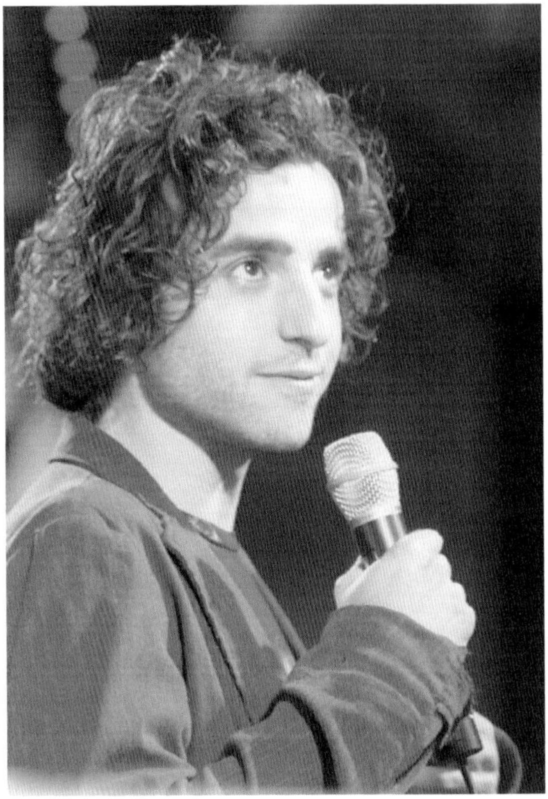

David Krumholtz
Actor David Krumholtz (born 1978) attended Halsey Junior High School 157. Since the early 1990s, he appeared in a wide range of films, such as *The Santa Clause* (1994) and its sequel, *10 Things I Hate about You* (1999), *Harold & Kumar Go to White Castle* (2004) and its two sequels, and *Serenity* (2005). He is best known for portraying Charlie Eppes in the CBS drama series *Numb3rs* from 2005 to 2010. "I genuinely believe Forest Hills is a magical place; a breeding ground for an acutely unique perspective that provides the foundation for a creative and artistic life," said Krumholtz, who once co-owned The Melting Pot restaurant at 1 Station Square. (Courtesy of Raven Underwood.)

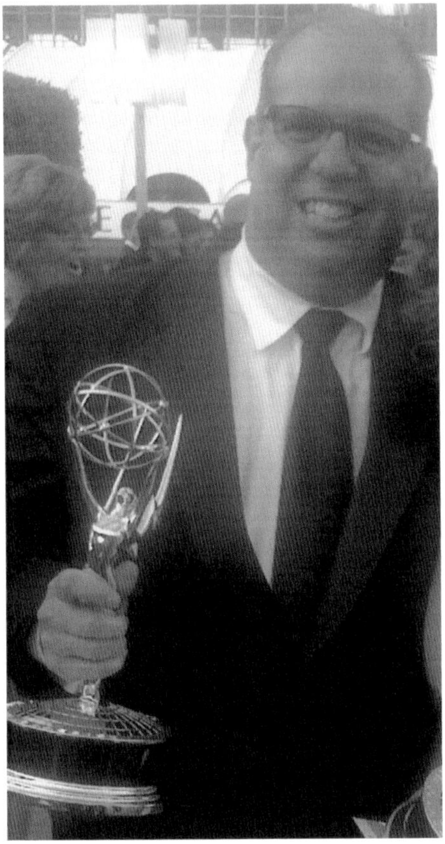

Ross Meyerson
Forest Hills native Ross Meyerson is a casting director who won a 2008 Emmy for *Damages* in the Outstanding Casting for a Drama Series category. Some shows that he cast are *Nurse Jackie* and *The Affair* on Showtime, *The Following* on Fox, and *White Collar* on USA. In January 2015, *The Affair* won a Golden Globe for Best Television Series—Drama, and for Best Actress. His casting for film pilots includes *Homeland* and *Dexter* on Showtime, *True Blood* on HBO, and *Jezebel James* on FOX. His movie credits are *One for the Money* and *Man on a Ledge*. His casting work for *Rescue Me*, *Damages*, and *Homeland* earned him the prestigious Artios Award from the Casting Society of America. (Courtesy of Ross Meyerson.)

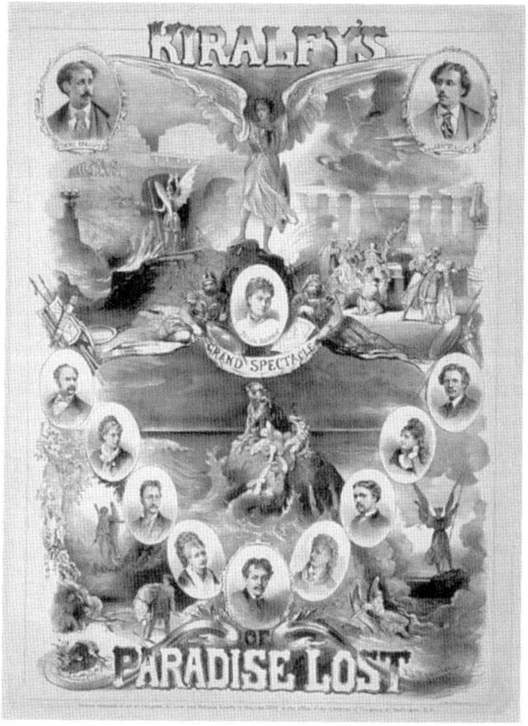

Kiralfy Brothers

Imry (pictured in inset at upper left) and Bolossy Kiralfy (upper right) were burlesque and spectacle producers in America and Europe during the latter part of the 19th century. Their musicals include *Around the World in Eighty Days* at the New York Academy of Music. Bolossy said their goal was to "convert American theatre audiences into enthusiasts for the French style of musical spectacle." Imre produced an illuminated aquatic festivity known as *Venice–The Bride of the Sea* at Olympia. Bolossy's grand Parisian production was *Dolores*. (Courtesy of Church-in-the-Gardens Community House.)

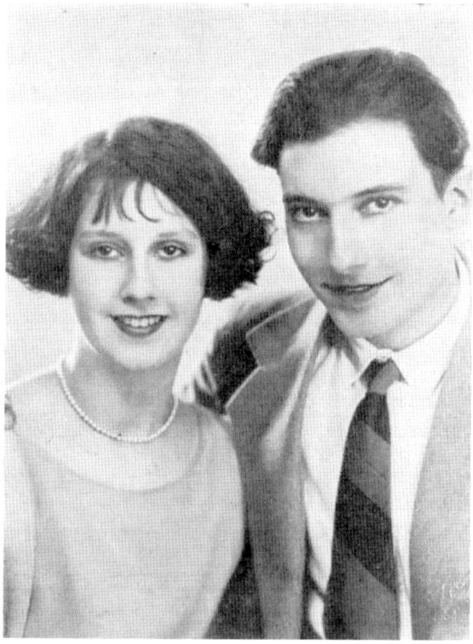

Kiralfy Kids

Bolossy Kiralfy's children, Verona (left) and Calvin Kiralfy (right), performed an act, "Feet, Fiddle and Foolishness" for the opening of the Community House in the Forest Hills Gardens in 1926. Earlier, they were famous performers in many countries under the Kiralfy Kids title. They performed for Pres. Woodrow Wilson and King George. (Courtesy of Church-in-the-Gardens Community House.)

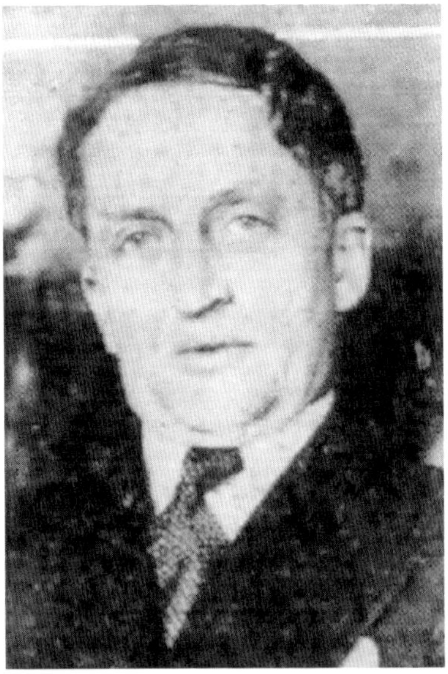

Lyman Beecher Stowe

Stowe (1880–1963) was an author, lecturer, and civic leader who resided at 275 Greenway South. His lectures included "How Uncle Tom's Cabin Was Built," "Mark Twain: Self-Appointed Instructor of the Public," and "This World of Ours: The Struggle Between Communism, Fascism and Democracy." As the grandson of the *Uncle Tom's Cabin* author Harriet Beecher Stowe, he wrote *Harriet Beecher Stowe: The Story of Her Life* and *Citizens Made and Remade: An Interpretation of the Significance and Influence of George Junior Republics*. When Col. Theodore Roosevelt arrived at Station Square on July 4, 1917, for his "One Hundred Percent American" speech, Stowe was an official greeter. From 1927 to 1929, Stowe was president of the Forest Hills Gardens Corporation. (Courtesy of Church-in-the-Gardens.)

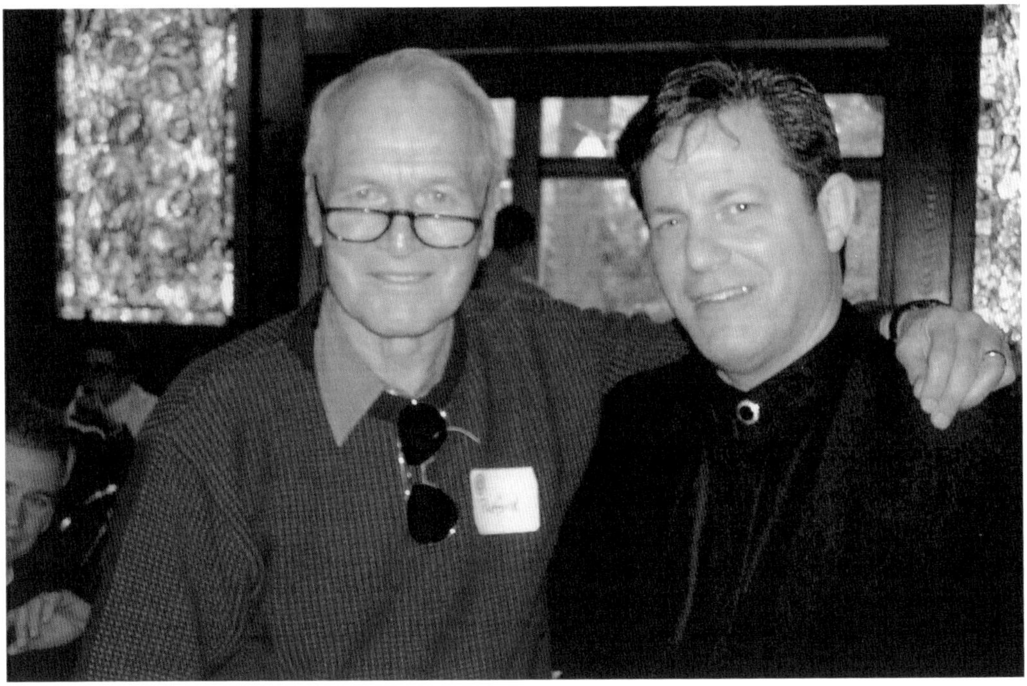

Michael Chaut

New Yorkers are spellbound by Michael Chaut (pictured on the right with Paul Newman), a professional magician, mentalist, magic advisor, entertainment consultant, and a Forest Hills High School graduate. He performs New York's longest-running off-Broadway magic show, *Monday Night Magic*, at the Players Theatre in Greenwich Village, and performed *Magical Nights* at the former Feinstein's at Loews Regency. "Think about how powerful it is to help people experience the feeling of magic," said Chaut. Paul Newman, Michael Douglas, Mayor Rudy Giuliani, and Julia Roberts are among the notables who witnessed his acts. His television appearances include *Good Morning America* and NBC's *Today Show*. (Courtesy of Michael Chaut.)

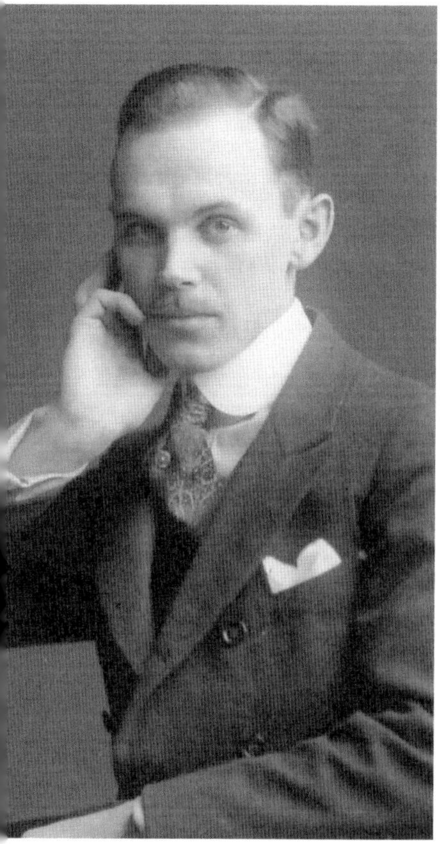

Malthe M. Hasselriis

The Duchess of Windsor, Eleanor Roosevelt, Pres. John F. Kennedy, Madame Chiang Kai-shek, and Pearl Buck were some notables who posed for Danish-native Malthe Hasselriis (1888–1970), a self-taught miniature painter who resided at 116 Ascan Avenue and 52 Seasongood Road. He painted portraits on ivory, illustrated for *McCall's* and *Woman's Home Companion*, and used watercolors for children's books such as *The Ugly Duckling* and *Tales of a Chinese Godmother.* Hasselriis was one of the few masters of the ancient art of Chinese painting on silk. (Courtesy of Floyd Hasselriis.)

Marty Ingels

Class of 1954 Forest Hills High School graduate Marty Ingels (born Martin Ingerman in 1936) is an actor, comedian, theatrical agent, and voice-over artist for cartoons and commercials. He was raised at Princeton Gardens at 88-04 63rd Drive in Rego Park. When asked about his proudest accomplishments, he responded, "My 38-year relationship with my wife, [actress and singer] Shirley Jones, and my ABC television series, *I'm Dickens, He's Fenster* in 1963." He appeared in the 1969 film *If It's Tuesday, This Must Be Belgium*, and also guest-starred on *The Love Boat* and *The Dick Van Dyke Show.* Ingels and Jones are the administrators of California's only 9/11 memorial park, Fawn Park. Marty Ingels is shown with his wife, Shirley Jones. (Courtesy of Marty Ingels.)

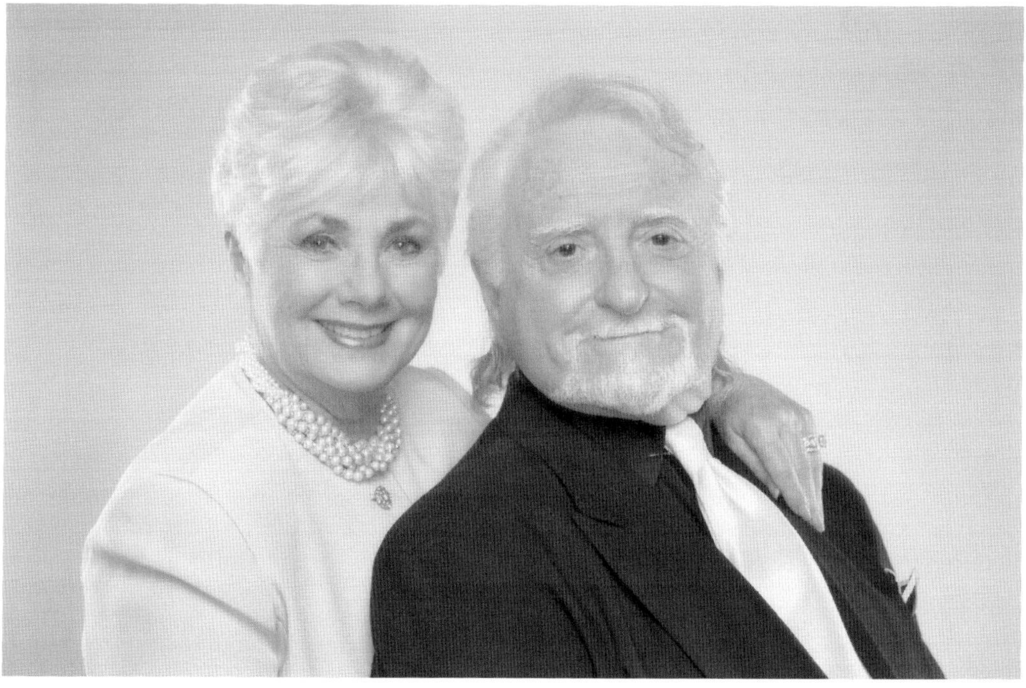

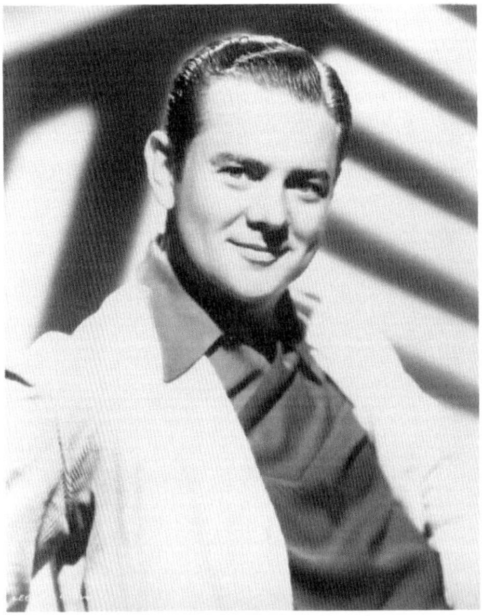

Lee Sullivan

Nightclub and radio singer, film actor, and Broadway star Lee Sullivan (1911–1981) of 111-19 75th Road at Arbor Close was also the entertainment chairman of the Community House in the Forest Hills Gardens. On Broadway, he appeared in *Brigadoon*, *Let Freedom Sing*, and *Walk with Music*. Telecast from Tavern on the Green for WNBC, Sullivan and Ed Herlihy co-hosted the popular morning show *Date in Manhattan*. Among his popular films was *The Great John L.* (1945). Along with his wife, Anne Sullivan, they opened Hill and Dale Travel at 71-58 Austin Street in Forest Hills, which served some of the most influential figures in rock music, including The Rolling Stones, Bruce Springsteen, Cyndi Lauper, Hall & Oates, Supertramp, The Allman Brothers Band, and Tommy Mottola. (Courtesy of Church-in-the-Gardens.)

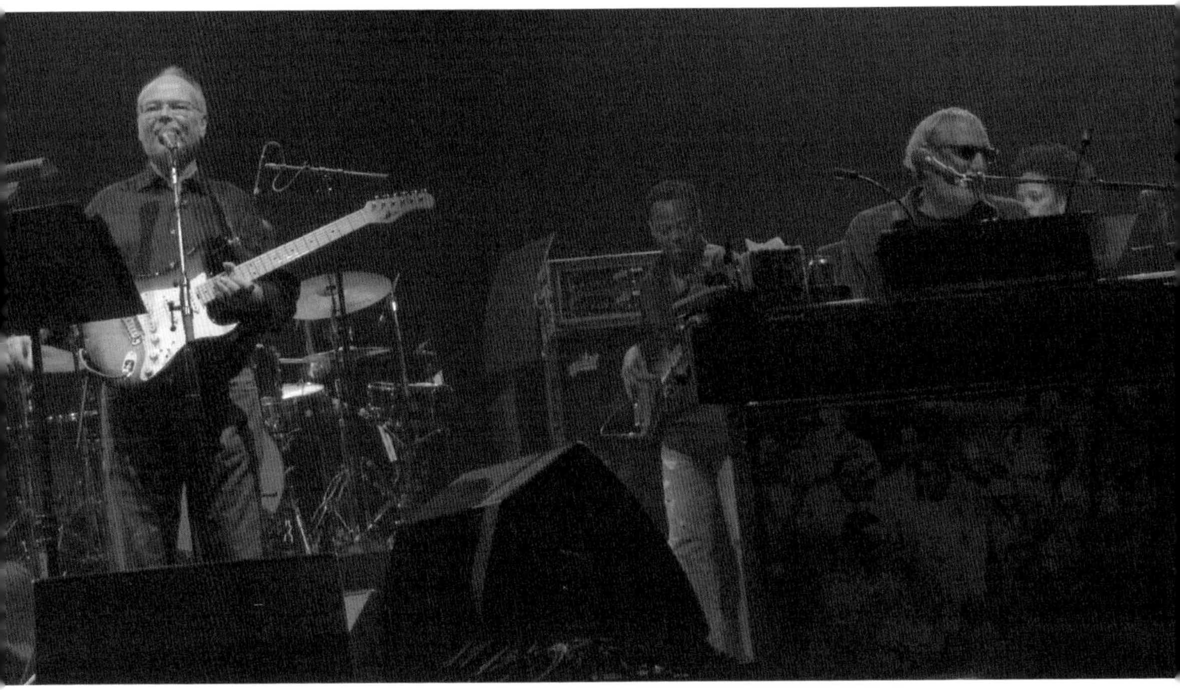

Walter Carl Becker

Forest Hills native Walter Carl Becker (born 1950, pictured on the left) is a guitarist, bassist, and co-songwriter of the jazz-rock band Steely Dan. In 1967, he befriended Donald Fagen (born 1948), the band's lead singer. Their first album *Can't Buy a Thrill* was released in 1972 under the name Steely Dan, and they toured the United States and Britain in 1973. In 1981 they disbanded, but reunited in 1993 and 2000. *Two Against Nature* won four Grammys in 2001, and Becker and Fagen were inducted into the Rock & Roll Hall of Fame. Some well-known hits are "Do It Again" and "Rikki Don't Lose That Number." (Photograph by Randy Reichardt.)

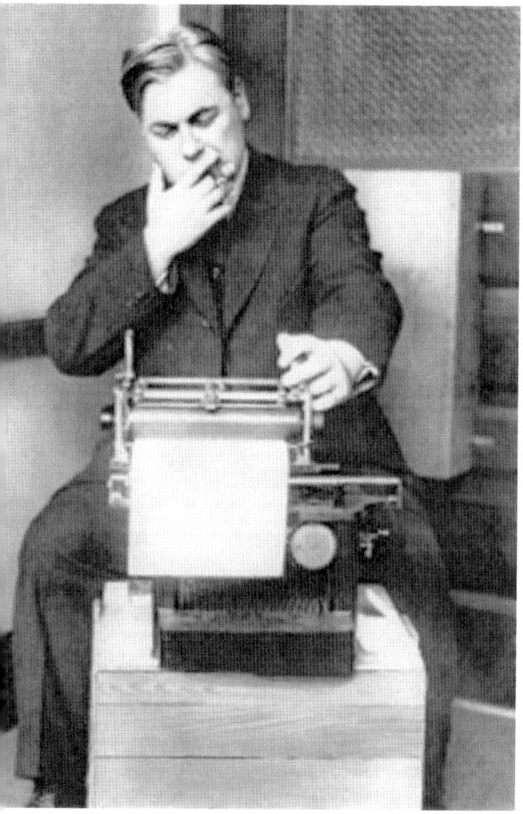

Don Marquis
Don Marquis (1878–1937) of 51 Wendover Road in the Forest Hills Gardens had a range of occupations, including humorist, novelist, columnist, playwright, and poet. As a playwright, he wrote the humorous Broadway hit *The Old Soak* in 1922. As a columnist, he created the characters "Archy the Cockroach" and "Mehitabel the Cat." He wrote for *The Evening Sun* and the *New York Tribune*. "Danny's Own Story" was his first book, which resulted in critics comparing him to Mark Twain. In the 1920s, he was one of the most quoted writers in Manhattan. (Photograph by Paul Thompson, courtesy of John Batteiger.)

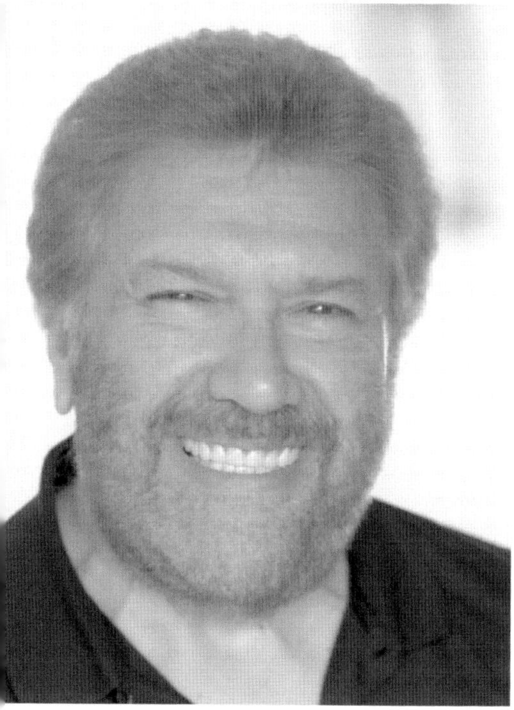

Doug Leblang
Forest Hills resident Doug Leblang is a commercial designer, illustrator, and art director who completed over 200 paintings utilizing pastels, colored pencils, collages, and the computer. Fans can become nature enthusiasts by discovering his *Central Park Rainbow*, observe his vision of *Theodore Bikel* who played Tevye in *Fiddler on the Roof*, encounter Forest Hills Tennis Stadium performer *Bob Dylan*, or step back in time to *Eddie's Sweet Shop* in Forest Hills.

As a humanitarian, lecturer, and teacher, Leblang applies his touch citywide. In addition, he is the One Man Klezmer Band and plays the clarinet, accordion, keyboard, and sings and does comedy. (Courtesy of Doug Leblang.)

Richard Haas

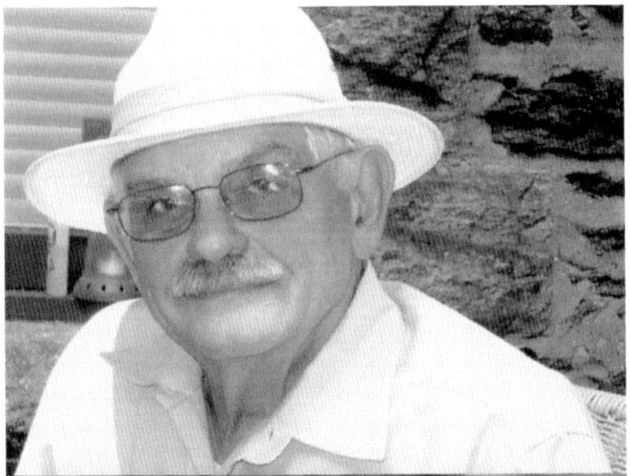

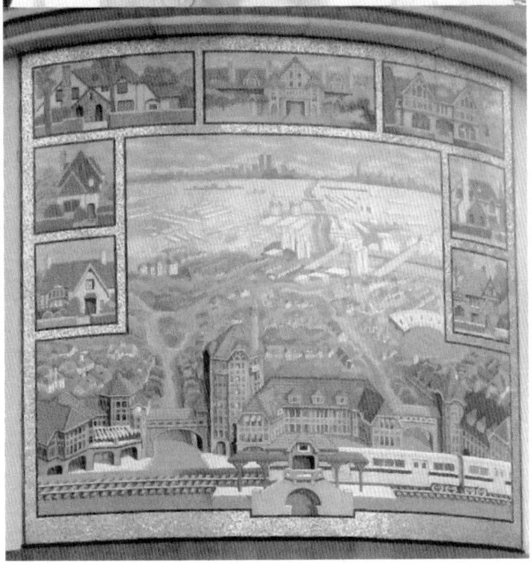

In 1989, architectural muralist Richard Haas (born 1936) designed a mosaic mural for the Home Savings Bank of America's facade at 108-36 Queens Boulevard, which depicts a birds-eye view of the Forest Hills Tennis Stadium, Station Square, and Tudor homes of the Forest Hills Gardens, with a backdrop of the Manhattan skyline featuring the Twin Towers. "It was executed in Spilimbergo, Italy by professional craftsmen under Mr. Trasavenuto's leadership, and installed by Mr. Cravato. I was taken by the history of Forest Hills as a planned community, based more on English precedents," said Haas. Since 1975, he has painted outdoor murals across America and redefined the trompe l'oeil technique. He creates an optical illusion by adding architectural detail and dimension to an otherwise blank canvas. (Top, courtesy of Richard Haas; bottom, photograph by Michael H. Perlman.)

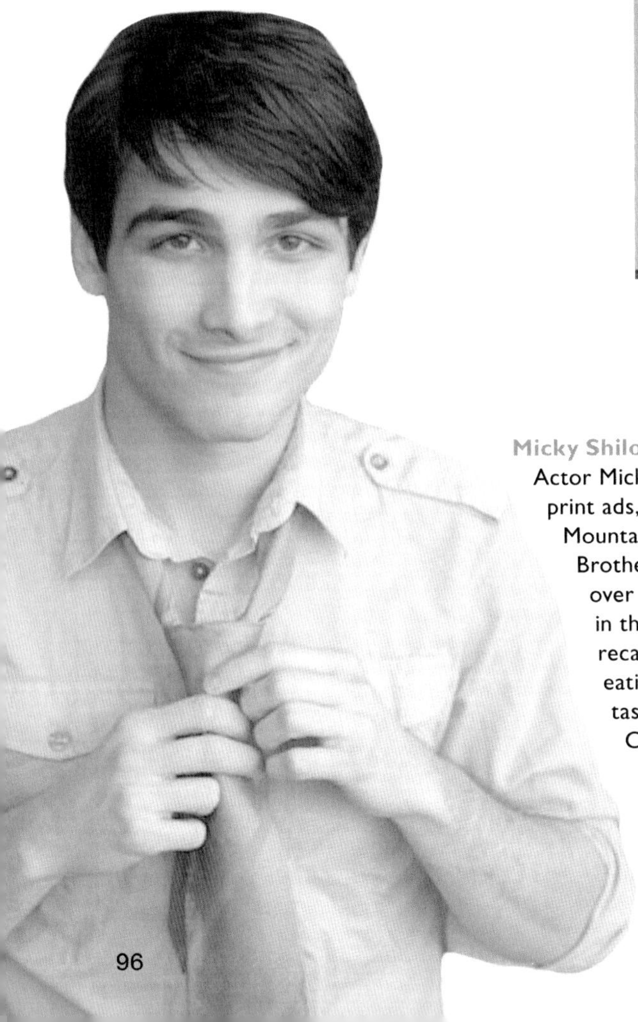

Micky Shiloah

Actor Micky Shiloah (born 1984) appeared in music videos, print ads, and commercials for Acura, Sony, Best Buy, and Mountain Dew. He landed a television spot for Robbins Brothers Engagement Rings, a television/radio voice-over for 5-Hour Energy, and starred with Kathy Baker in the 2012 independent film *The Party Is Over.* Shiloah recalled childhood moments in Forest Hills such as eating at the Forest Diner on 108th Street or the taste of the pickles and hummus at the longtime shop Carmel. (Courtesy of Micky Shiloah.)

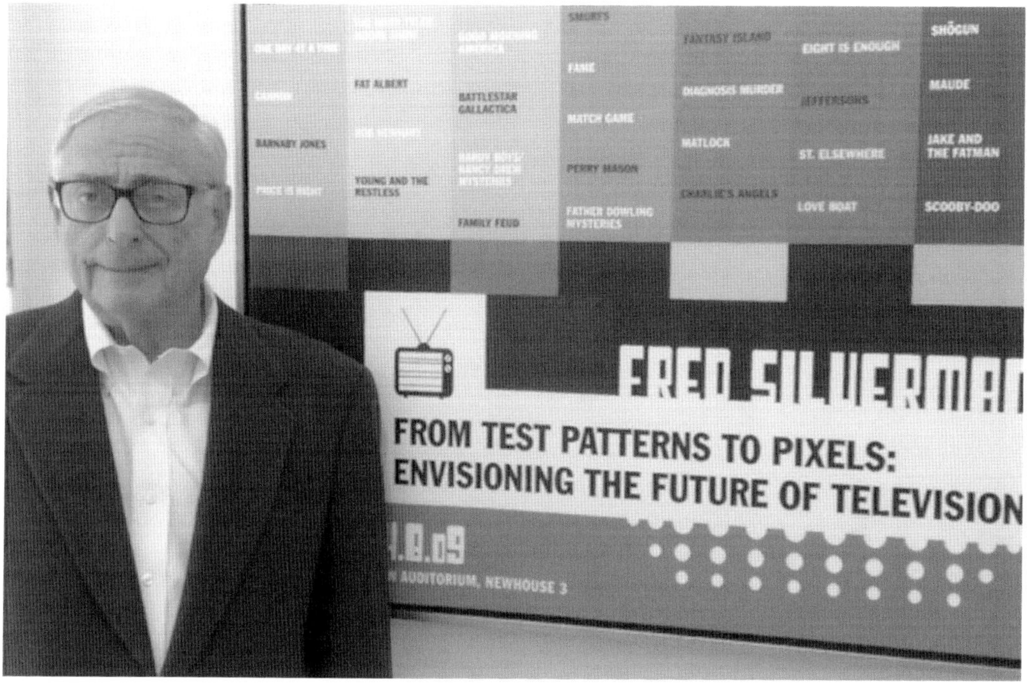

Fred Silverman

One of television's most influential producers grew up at 89-11 63rd Drive (Princeton Gardens complex) in Rego Park. Fred Silverman (born 1937) served as the head of programming for ABC and CBS, and president of NBC from 1978 to 1981. In the 1970s, he programmed *Mary Tyler Moore*, *All in the Family*, *M*A*S*H*, *The Jeffersons*, *Charlie's Angels*, and *The Sonny and Cher Show*. Other favorites that he developed include *The Love Boat* and *Laverne & Shirley*. After founding The Fred Silverman Company, he began producing more household favorites, such as *Matlock* and *Jake and the Fatman* in the 1980s. (Courtesy of the Fred Silverman Company.)

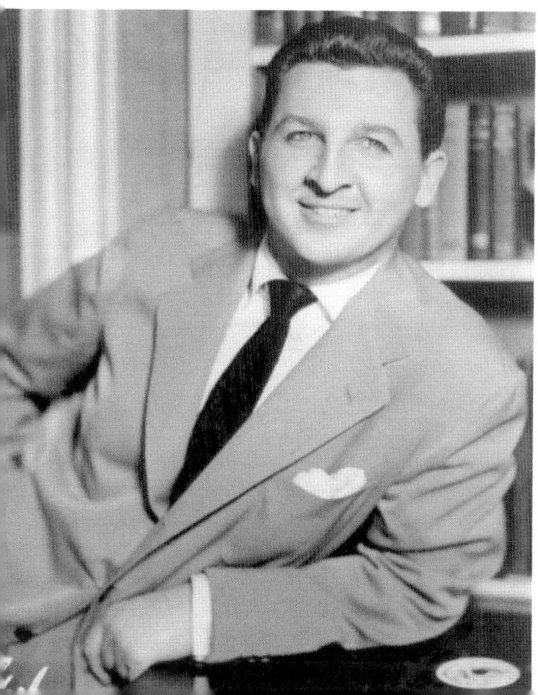

Eddie Bracken

Film actor and Broadway performer Eddie Bracken (1915–2002) of 88-12 63rd Avenue in Rego Park earned a star on the Hollywood Walk of Fame. At age nine, he managed to get inside a Manhattan motion picture studio, and his audition resulted in leading roles in films. Since the 1940s, his numerous films included *We're Not Married*, *Too Many Girls*, *The Miracle of Morgan's Creek*, *Hail the Conquering Hero*, and *Two Tickets to Broadway*. He was often spotted in shows including *The Odd Couple*, *Hello, Dolly!*, *Show Boat*, and *Carousel*. *The Eddie Bracken Show* was his popular radio series. (Author's collection.)

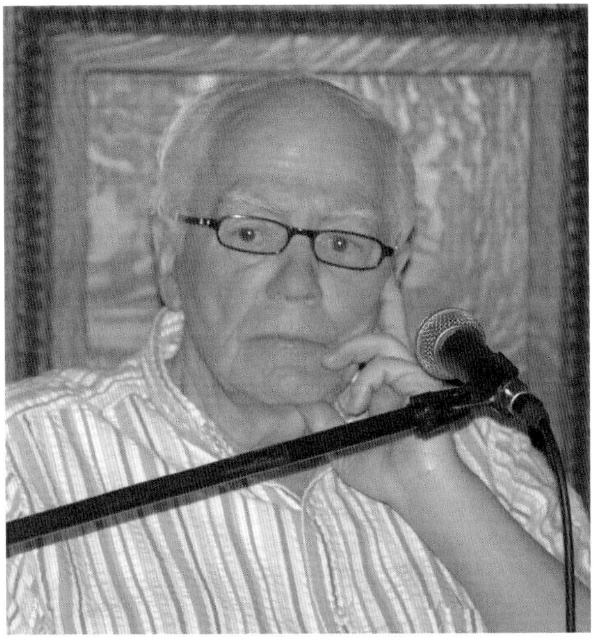

Jimmy Breslin

Known as a Pulitzer Prize–winning novelist, investigative journalist, playwright, screenwriter, and actor, Jimmy Breslin (born 1930) lived at 52 Deepdene Road in Forest Hills. As a columnist, he worked with the *Daily News*, *Newsday*, and the *New York Herald Tribune*. Some of his most noteworthy works are "A Death in Emergency Room One," which captured the hospital scene following President Kennedy's assassination, and "Digging JFK Grave Was His Honor," where he chronicled the burial from the gravedigger's perspective. His novels include *Damon Runyon* and *Branch Rickey*. (Courtesy of David Shankbone.)

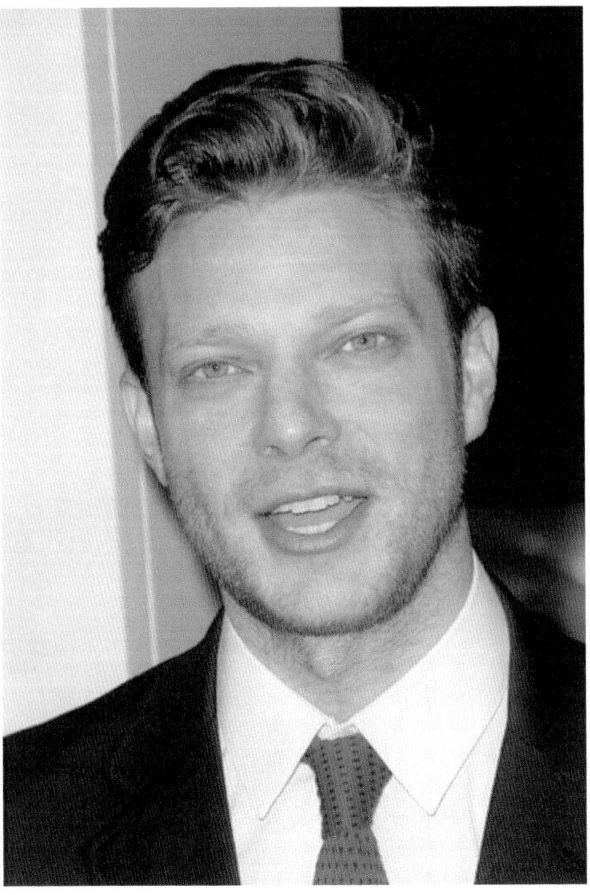

Todd Strauss-Schulson

Director, writer, and editor Todd Strauss-Schulson (born 1980), a Kew-Forest School graduate, always spotted new film titles on the Midway Theatre marquee across from his Park Briar apartment window (110-45 Queens Boulevard), and knew he wanted to become a director. "After months of relentless pestering, my grandfather bought me a giant VHS Sylvania video camera for my Bar Mitzvah, and I spent the next seven years making a movie a day after school," he said. His proudest accomplishment was *A Very Harold & Kumar 3-D Christmas* (2011). The scene where Kumar and Adrian are driving to Harold's house is shot in Forest Hills, with views of Austin Street and Ascan Avenue. He also directed commercials for the Oscars and Emmys, and some clients include Pepsi and Microsoft. (Courtesy of Todd Strauss-Schulson.)

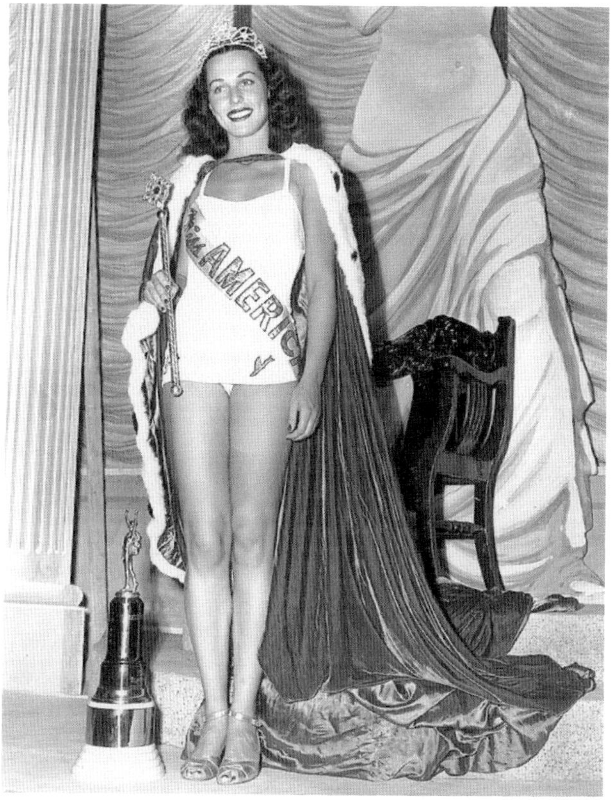

Bess Myerson
Bess Myerson (1924–2014), who was known as Miss New York, became the first Jewish Miss America in 1945. Pageant head Lenora Slaughter asked her to change her name, thinking it would make her win, but she refused. When organizations rejected her public appearances, she was determined to place a damper on anti-Semitism and traveled countrywide to speak on behalf of the Anti-Defamation League of B'nai B'rith. In the 1950s, she lectured at Rego Park Jewish Center. She was a panelist on the *I've Got a Secret* game show and a co-host of *Candid Camera*. Under Mayor John V. Lindsay, she was New York City Consumer Affairs commissioner, and was chair of the Mayor's Urban Task Force of Community Problems in Forest Hills, Rego Park, and Kew Gardens. She once lived in Park City Estates at 61-55 98th Street in Rego Park. (Author's collection.)

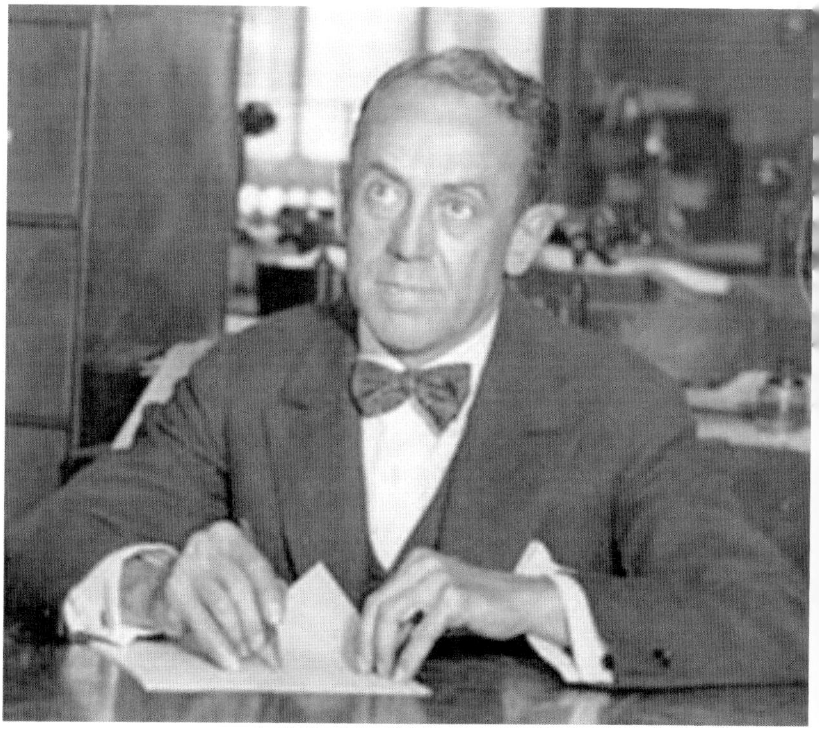

Burns Mantle
Burns Mantle (1873–1948) was a drama critic, writer, and producer who resided at 44 Seasongood Road in the Forest Hills Gardens. He founded *The Best Plays Theater Yearbook* in 1920, and through 1947, edited a series that became known as a significant contribution to the American stage. He also wrote for the *New York Evening Mail*, and by 1922, earned the title of drama critic for the *New York Daily News*. He was the author of *American Playwrights of Today* in 1929. (Courtesy of Jeffrey Eric Jenkins, *The Best Plays Theater Yearbook*.)

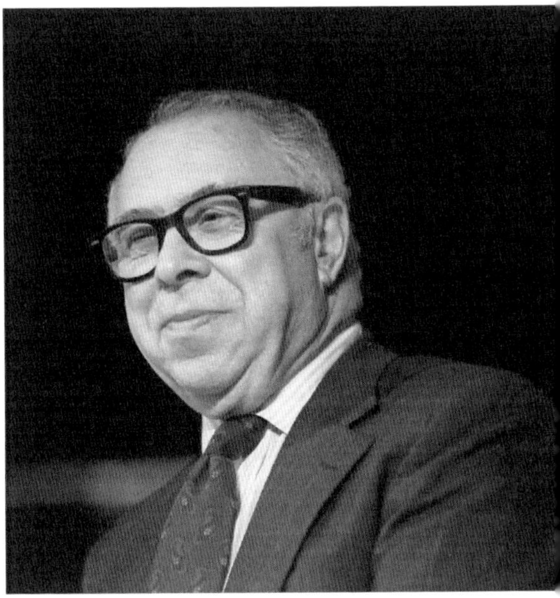

Art Buchwald

Humor columnist, author, and actor Art Buchwald (1925–2007) once resided in Forest Hills. He was highly regarded for his long-running column in *The Washington Post*, and in 1982, won a Pulitzer Prize for Outstanding Commentary. His syndicated column appeared in over 550 newspapers. Backtracking, he launched his first column in the *Herald Tribune* in Paris, where his noted work explained Thanksgiving to the French. An author of over 30 books, his best-selling memoir was *Leaving Home*, and a worthy novel was *A Gift from the Boys*. His stage comedy *Sheep on the Runway* had a Broadway run.

He maintained his humor, continued writing, and survived long after doctors gave him weeks to live. *Too Soon to Say Goodbye* (2006) documents his experience in a hospice. (Courtesy of Miami Dade College archives.)

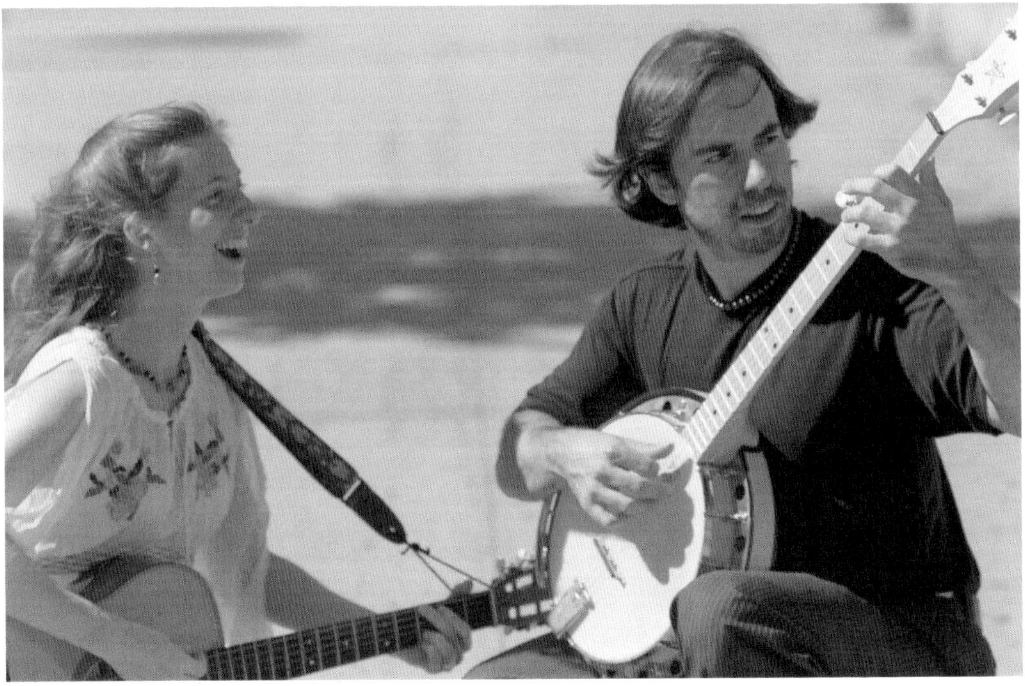

Betina Hershey Russo

"I was born singing and dancing," said Forest Hills resident Betina Hershey Russo (left), who is a singer, songwriter, guitarist, dancer, and poet. She often performs with her husband, Nick Russo (right). The Garden Players musical theater program has been a Forest Hills staple for over 50 years, and since 2002, Hershey serves as director. It encourages creativity, individuality, and confidence, with children learning singing, acting, and improvisation. Her recent musical, *Space Pirates!* is co-written with award-winning composer, writer, and arts educator Denver Casado and Gwynne Watkins. Another proud achievement was her role as Meg Giry in *The Phantom of the Opera*'s national tour. (Courtesy of Betina Hershey Russo.)

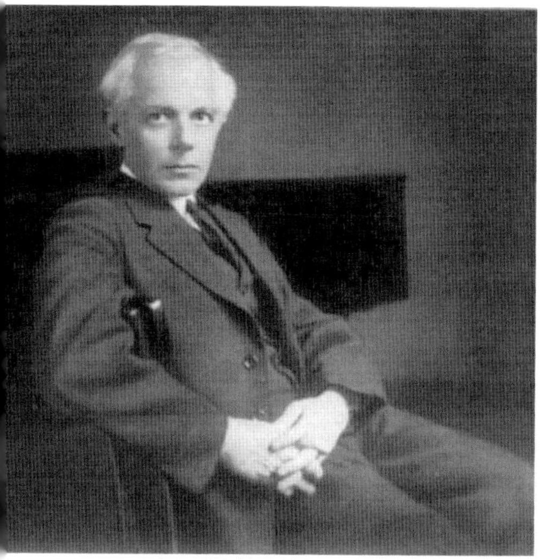

Béla Bartók

Béla Bartók (1886–1945), born in Hungary and later residing at the New Hampshire Apartments at 110-31 73rd Road in Forest Hills, was one of the most significant 20th-century composers. He was noted for his blend of late Romanticism, Eastern European folk music, and Debussy. In 1927, he debuted in America with the Philharmonic Orchestra in Carnegie Hall with *Rhapsodie Op. 1*. His stage works include *Prince Bluebeard's Castle*, *The Wooden Prince*, and *The Miraculous Mandarin*. Compositions include a *Dance Suite*, *Two Portraits*, *Two Pictures*, and *Music for Strings, Percussion and Celesta*. Sad themes can be heard in *String Quartet No. 6*, which was his response to World War II. He also composed songs based on Hungarian folk melodies and piano music. (Courtesy of Queens Community Board 6.)

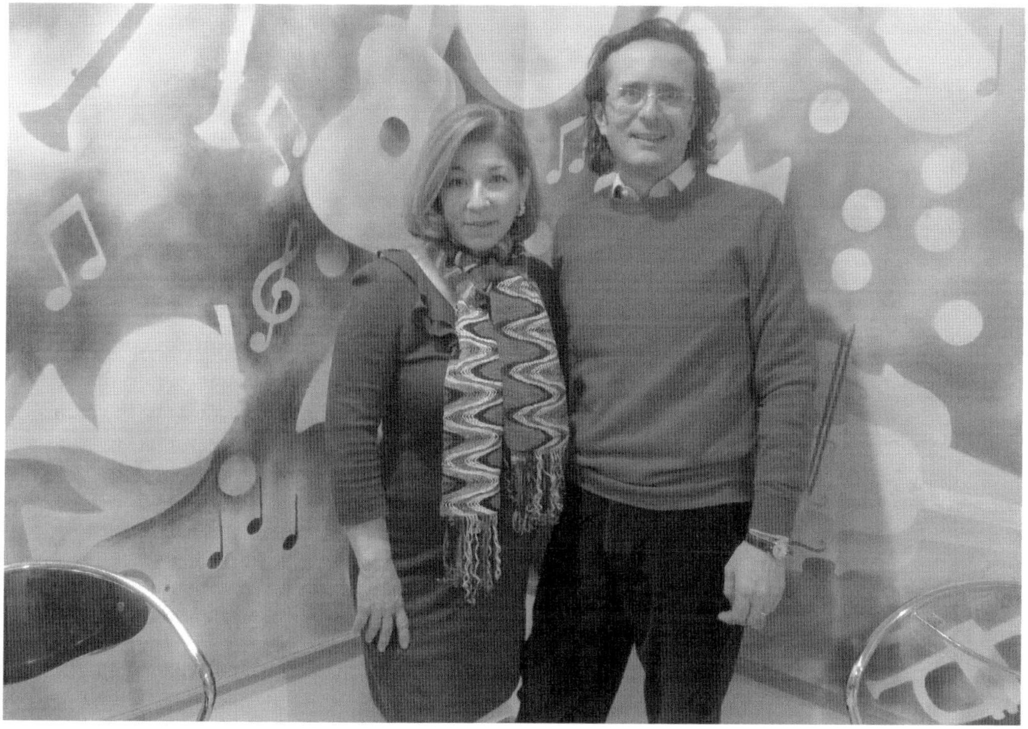

Belle Arti Center for the Arts

Rome native and Classical pianist Massimiliano Facchini and Dominican pianist Claudette Munné founded Belle Arti at 108-10 72nd Avenue in July 2007, which became Forest Hills's only boutique-like music school of European heritage. From private to group settings, students discover and refine their talents. Courses include voice, piano, violin, cello, guitar, flute, recorder, music theory, Musical Aurora, and most recently, Early Bird Rock, Italian Language, and Create Your Own Comic Book Workshop. At Carnegie Hall and in Rome's Parco della Musica, Munné and Facchini made history premiering merengues on two pianos. They perform solo, with orchestras, and in chamber groups. (Photograph by Michael H. Perlman.)

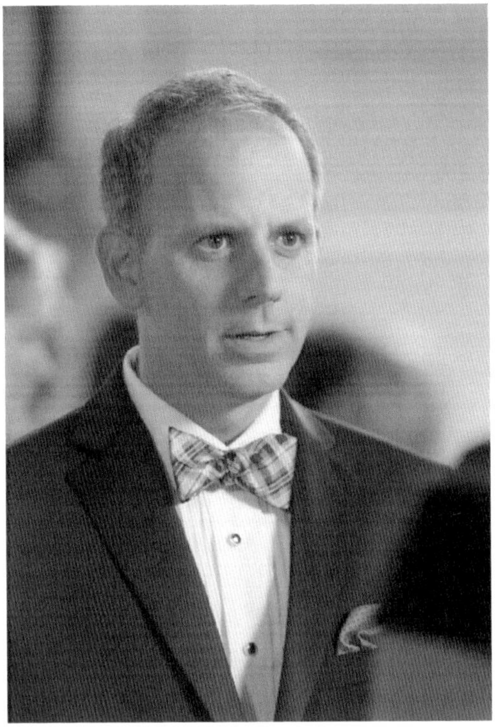

Emil Beheshti

Actor Emil Beheshti (born 1971) was raised at 170 Puritan Avenue in the Forest Hills Gardens. He holds cherished memories of Children's Day at Flagpole Park and sledding at Deepdene Park. His career was motivated by visits to the Cinemart and Midway theaters, and roles in plays at Russell Sage Junior High School.

Presently, he works in television, film, and commercials. He guest-starred or recurred in over 30 television shows including *Castle*, *Grey's Anatomy*, *24*, *Will and Grace*, *CSI: Miami*, and *The King of Queens*, as well as over 40 commercials. He appeared in *Big Momma's House 2*, *Prom*, and *Puppy Love*. (Courtesy of Emil Beheshti.)

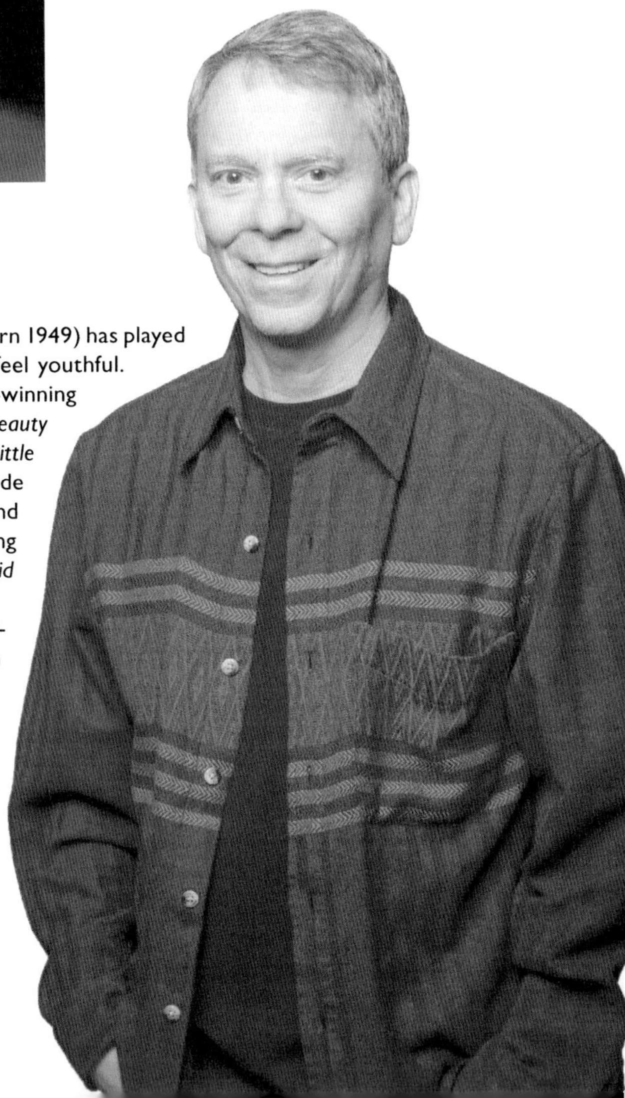

Danny Troob

Orchestrator and arranger Danny Troob (born 1949) has played a dominant role in making any generation feel youthful. He orchestrated Alan Menken's Oscar-winning scores for films and Broadway, such as *Beauty and the Beast*, *Aladdin*, *Pocahontas*, and *The Little Mermaid*. His other popular credits include *Shrek the Musical*, *Newsies*, *Enchanted*, and *Tangled*. His proudest moment was composing the underscore for Disney's *The Little Mermaid II*, which he orchestrated in 10 days.

He was raised in The Beaverbrook at 77-35 113th Street in the Forest Hills South development. "My PS 196 music teacher asked me to create arrangements for our elementary school recorder group, which led to other school performances," said Troob.

A graduate of Forest Hills High School, Troob returned 48 years later as the class of 2014 commencement speaker. (Courtesy of Danny Troob.)

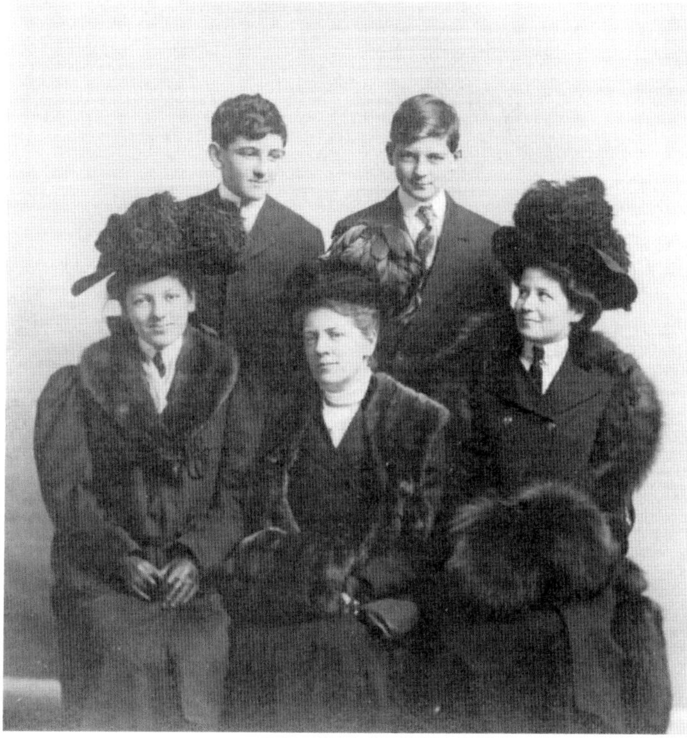

Alrick Hubbell Man Jr.
Alrick Hubbell Man Jr. (1892–1975) of 4 Dartmouth Street was the captain of the USTA Davis Cup Committee from 1947 to 1950. He also founded the International Club, which promoted tennis. His father, Alrick Man, developed Kew Gardens, and his grandfather Albon Man founded Richmond Hill. Pictured from left to right in Coney Island are (first row) Elizabeth Man, Lucy Russell Man, and Jean Moir; (second row) Alrick Man Jr. and Duncan Moir. (Courtesy of Richmond Hill Historical Society.)

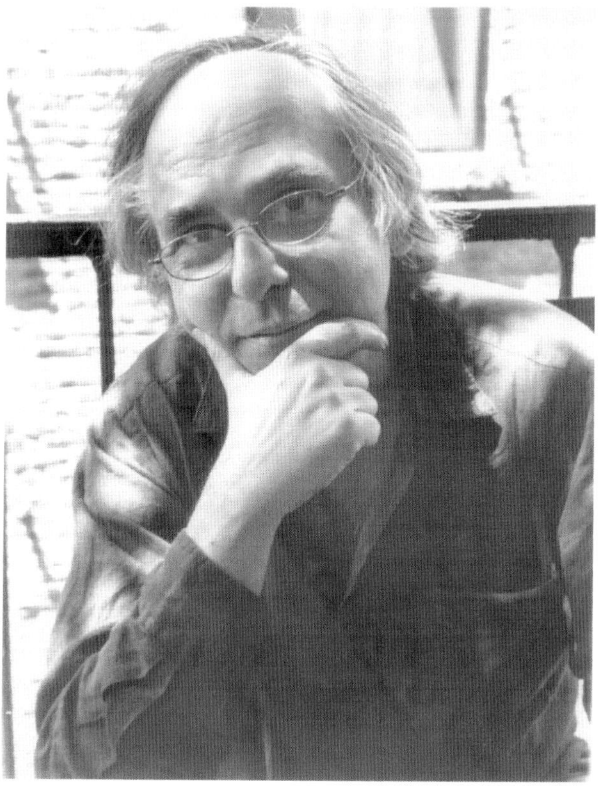

Art Spiegelman
Rego Park native Art Spiegelman (born 1948) is a cartoonist, comics advocate, and editor who won a Pulitzer Prize in 1992 for his Holocaust comic novel *Maus*. It portrayed human races as distinct animals, and was influenced by interviews with his father, a Polish Jew and Holocaust survivor. He published the avant-garde comics magazine *RAW*, drew "Bazooka Joe" comic strips accompanying Bazooka bubble gum, drew caricatures of sports figures, and designed famed magazine covers for *The New Yorker*.

"At age 12, I began drawing comics and looking at comics on racks at a neighborhood luncheonette and the Rego Park Library," said Spiegelman. His illustrations were featured in his Russell Sage Junior High School yearbook. Around 1960, the *Long Island Post* published an article that referred to him as a budding artist. He lived at 63-12 Carlton Street. (Courtesy of Nadja Spiegelman.)

Paul Noble

Five-time Emmy Award recipient and television producer Paul Noble lived in the Chatwick Gardens at 68-49 Burns Street and graduated from Forest Hills High School. He produced Eleanor Roosevelt's television series, and with Metromedia and Fox, he produced successful series such as *The Bishop Sheen Show* and *Dr. Ruth*. He was vice president of Lifetime TV, and helped bring the cable network to number one. Noble is the past president of the New York Chapter of the National Academy of Television Arts & Sciences, which distributes Emmy Awards. Other notables that he worked with were Pres. John F. Kennedy, Marvin Hamlisch, and Marc Chagall. Now in Florida, he is active on television, film, and theater boards, and is a film studies educator. (Courtesy of Paul Noble.)

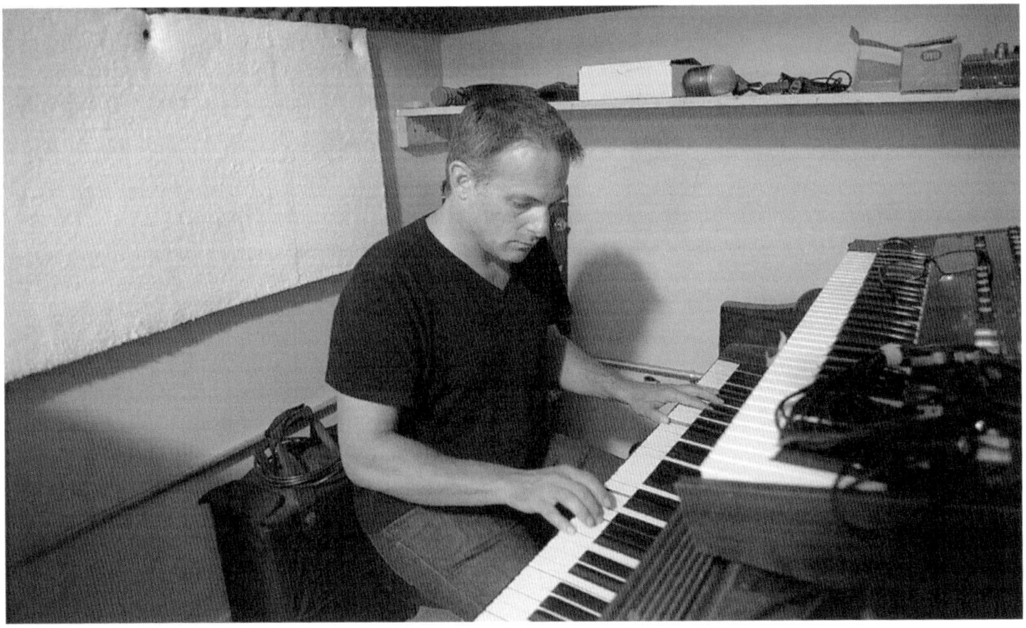

Perry Serpa

Talented singer, songwriter, and pianist Perry Serpa (born 1965), formerly a resident of Arbor Close in Forest Hills, takes the lead in the chamber pop collective The Sharp Things, which originated in the late 1990s. In 2009, Serpa was among the performers at Autumn Lights, which rejuvenated the musical vitality of the Forest Hills Gardens during its centennial. The band is recognized for a collaboration of strings, horns, woodwinds, keyboards, and vocals. Their popular single "Here Comes the Sharp Things" uniquely explores genres including British folk, classical, jazz, and 1970s radio pop. (Photograph by Alex Brown.)

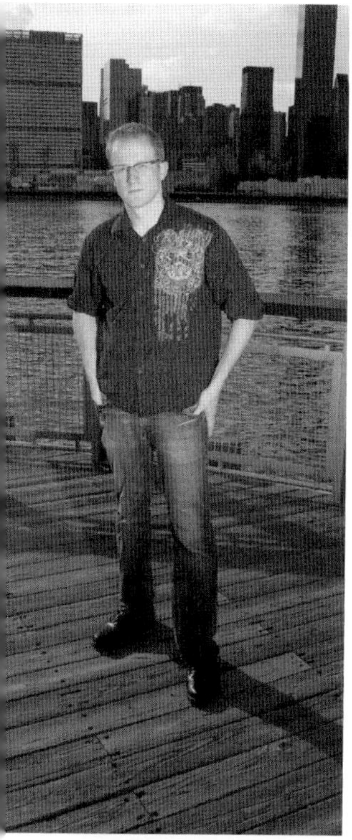

Steve Hofstetter

Born in 1979, Steve Hofstetter is often called "The hardest working man in show business." He is a comedian, author, and columnist who lived in Parker Towers in Forest Hills. He is the host and executive producer of *Laughs*, a standup comedy show on Fox Network, and hosted the *National Lampoon Sports Minute (Or So)*, which aired on over 170 radio stations. Formerly he was a *Sports Illustrated* and *NHL* weekly columnist, as well as a segment producer for Fox's *Dish Nation*. He also appeared on CBS, ABC, ESPN, CNN, VH1, and E!, among others. (Photograph by Adam Teixiera.)

Todd Wolfe

Blues/rock guitarist and singer/songwriter Todd Wolfe (born 1957) performed at the Battle of the Bands at Halsey Junior High School 157, and with his band Aerborne at Forest Hills High School. Local establishments such as the Irish Cottage, Annie's at the Forest Hills Inn, and most recently Austin Public gastropub witnessed his talents. His proudest accomplishments were playing, writing, and recording with Sheryl Crow, opening for Bob Dylan and The Rolling Stones, and jamming with Eric Clapton. For a VH1 *Rock Honors* show, Steve Winwood joined them for a rendition of "The Weight." He co-wrote "Somebody Stand by Me" with Crow, which was covered by Stevie Nicks and Faith Hill. Wolfe released eight solo albums and has toured in the United States and Europe since 2001. He resided in The Fontaine, The Park Lane, Birchwood Towers, and the Howard Apartments. (Photograph by Bob Hakins.)

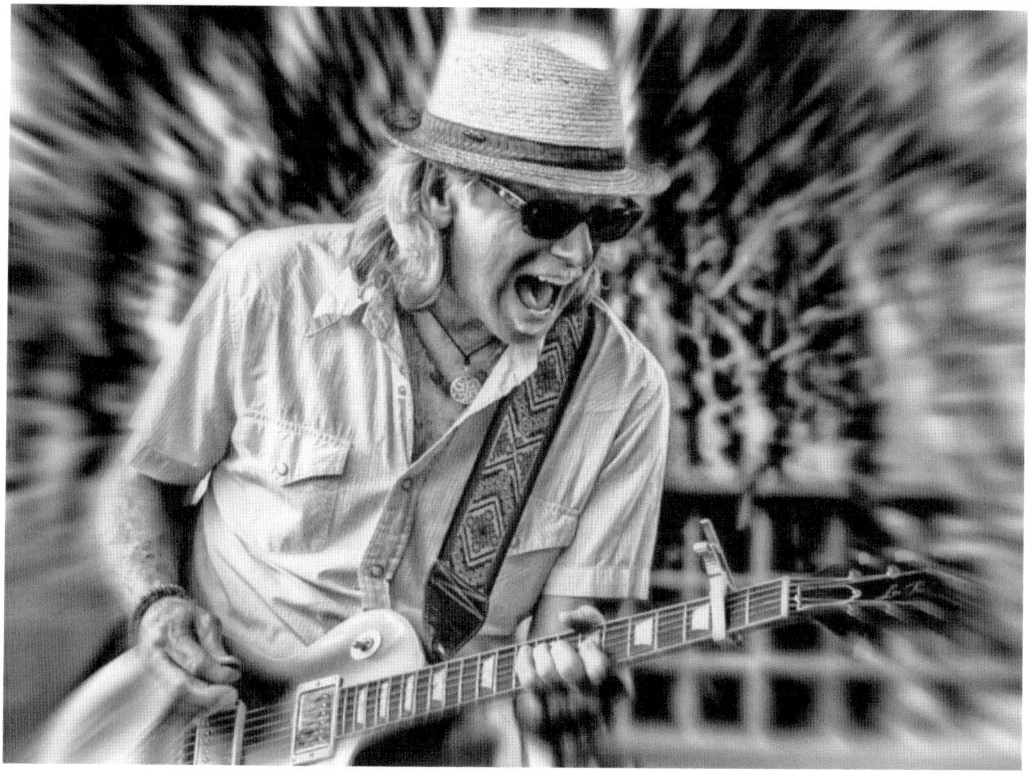

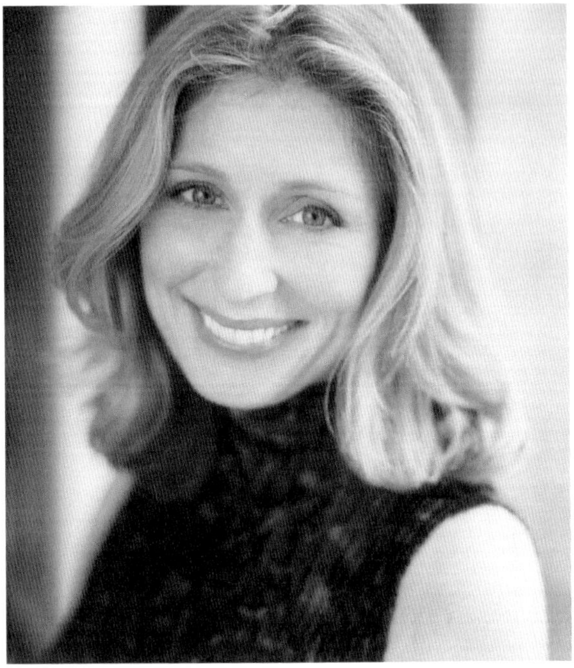

Ann Kittredge

"Creating from scratch is most rewarding," said Forest Hills Gardens resident Ann Kittredge, an accomplished actress and performer with numerous theater, film, and television credits. Her soprano voice is bell-like in its clarity and tone. In local schools, she voluntarily applies her theater skills to benefit students with curriculum-based plays, mini-concerts, and fundraising galas featuring neighborhood professional talents. Some of her proudest roles were in *Moon Over Buffalo* with Gavin MacLeod, *A Christmas Carol* with Roger Daltrey, *The Music Man* with Gregory Harrison, and playing Eleanor Roosevelt in *Eleanor*. (Photograph by Sabrina Reeves.)

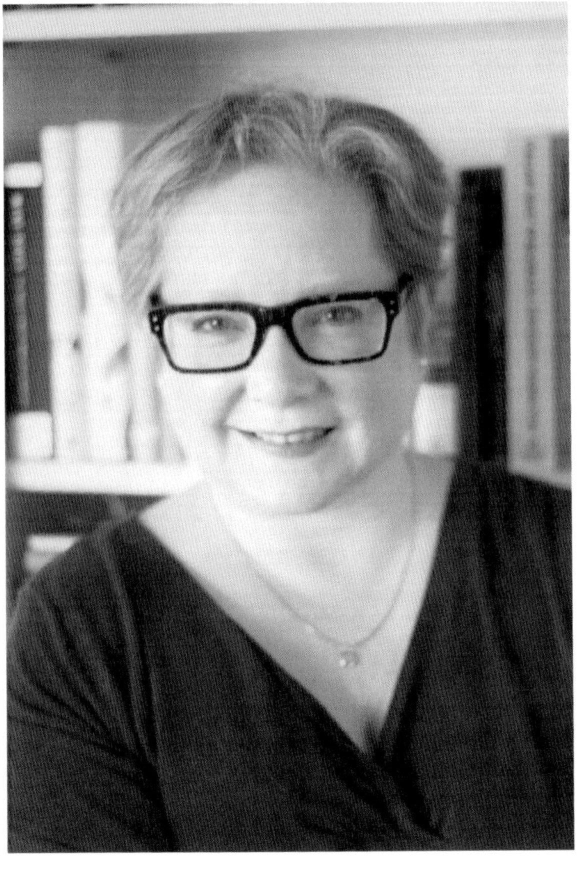

Elissa Altman

"As a food writer, my interest in food and cooking was jolted by the infamous 1973 Christmas Eve ice storm," said former Forest Hills resident Elissa Altman. Her father's surprise 50th birthday party called for catered food from Ben's Best Delicatessen, but instead, she reminisced, "I unearthed every package of salami from my mother's fridge, and prepared an artful platter of concentrically arranged meats, like a mandala."

In response to her first book, *Poor Man's Feast: A Love Story of Comfort, Desire, and the Art of Simple Cooking*, *The New York Times* called it "one of the finest food memoirs of recent years." She earned the James Beard Award for best individual food blog in 2012.

In 1967, Altman won the Greater Queens Shirley Temple Lookalike Contest. In the 1970s, she studied guitar with Eddie Simon, Paul Simon's brother. (Photograph by Susan Turner.)

CHAPTER THREE

Other Professional Pursuits

Forest Hills and Rego Park have bred architects, actors, and musicians among creative souls, and now the sequel calls for honoring other noteworthy professions. Have a look from orbit with the world's first paying space tourist, Dennis Tito. In the early evening, children and adults would be tempted by the sight of the personable "Al, the Good Humor Man" on 66th Road and 102nd Street in Forest Hills. Branch Rickey, president of the Brooklyn Dodgers, made history in 1945 when he signed African American player Jackie Robinson and broke Major League Baseball's color barrier.

A most courageous 20th-century individual was Helen Keller, an author and lecturer who resided at 71-11 112th Street in Forest Hills. Despite being blind and deaf, she was a revolutionary advocate for the removal of stigmas associated with sight and hearing disorders. Dr. Raymond Damadian, a Forest Hills Gardens resident, pioneered the use of nuclear magnetic resonance techniques to detect cancer and invented the MRI scanner.

Cross paths with award-winning science fiction writer Michael A. Burstein, a former Forest Hills resident. *I Remember the Future* features his award-nominated stories. He is president of the Society for the Advancement of Speculative Storytelling Inc. and the Society for the Preservation of Pluto as a Planet.

Reach into the freezer for Dr. Praeger Sensible Foods, invented by a "miracle worker" surgeon who established a popular American natural food company. Have an exclusive dining experience at one of Lidia Matticchio Bastianich's premier restaurants. This celebrity chef and restaurateur began with Buonavia in Forest Hills.

For a fashionable day out, take some design advice from world-recognized Donna Karan, another Forest Hills native.

Venture behind the scenes at the New York–based Kliegl Brothers Universal Stage Lighting Company, founded by John Kliegl and Anton Kliegl in 1896. Their Klieglight, introduced in 1911, was among the first carbon-arc lamps to offer a light intense enough for filming motion pictures indoors. A 2,000-watt wide-angle scenic projector and a remote color changer spotlight were among their other innovations. Their lighting proved beneficial at the 1939 World's Fair and Radio City Music Hall. When John died, his son Herbert Kliegl (1904–1968) of 35 Wendover Road in Forest Hills became president.

Finally, if up for the challenge, wrestle with the five-foot, three-inch "Jewish Tarzan" Abe Coleman, who once slammed the 465-pound Man Mountain Dean.

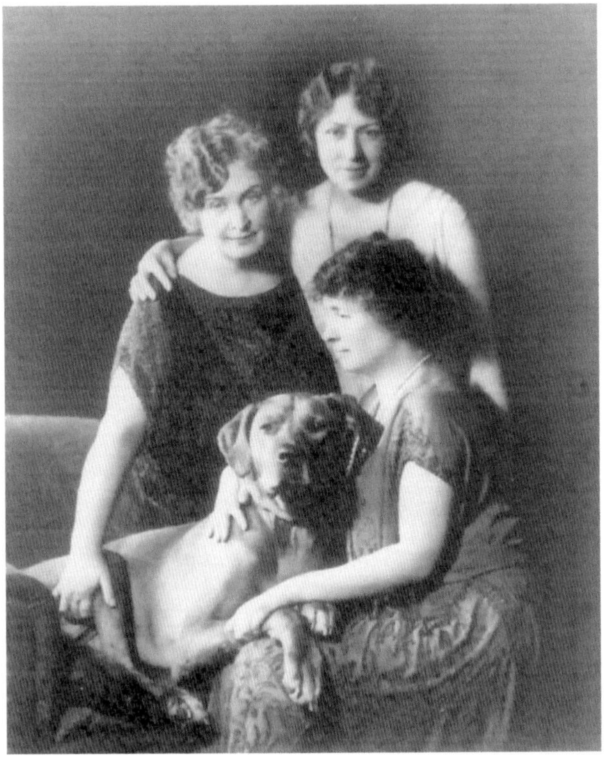

Helen Keller

Among the most courageous individuals of the 20th century was author, lecturer, and activist Helen Keller (1880–1968). From 1917 to 1938, her Forest Hills home was at 93 Seminole Avenue, later renumbered 71-11 112th Street. Keller became ill at 19 months, which resulted in blindness and deafness.

She was examined by Alexander Graham Bell, telephone inventor and pioneer speech teacher for the deaf, who referred her to the Perkins School for the Blind. At age seven, she met Anne Sullivan Macy (1866–1936), who was partially blind. "Miracle Worker" Macy moved in with Keller, becoming her teacher and closest companion.

Keller mastered the manual alphabet and learned to read Braille and print block letters. At age nine, she began to read lips and communicate. As a graduate of Radcliffe College in 1904 at age 24, Keller became the first deaf and blind individual to earn a bachelor of arts.

In 1913, she began lecturing on behalf of the American Foundation for the Blind, and her objective of removing the stigmas associated with sight and hearing disorders took her worldwide. She also campaigned for labor rights and women's suffrage. Keller's published works include *The Story of My Life* (1902), *The World I Live In* (1908), *Out of the Dark* (1913), and *Helen Keller's Journal* (1938).

Keller maintained an active lifestyle in Forest Hills. On her home's lawn, she celebrated her birthdays by coordinating large-scale parties for the blind, and held fundraising tours to benefit the American Foundation for the Blind. She also welcomed members of the Rainbow Division of the US Army in 1917, and then in Station Square, greeted 1,200 soldiers. She stated, "The Star Spangled Banner was more than 100 years ago dedicated as a symbol of freedom. We have since that time lived for that flag and for freedom, and I am proud to meet you, who are now ready to die, if need be for it, that there might be equal rights for all men and women alike."

Some of Keller's inspirational words were: "The best and most beautiful things in the world cannot be seen or even touched—they must be felt with the heart" and "The only thing worse than being blind is having sight but no vision." Helen Keller is pictured with her dog Sieglinde in the bottom row, and Anne Sullivan Macy and Polly Thomson are in the top row. (Courtesy of the Hof family.)

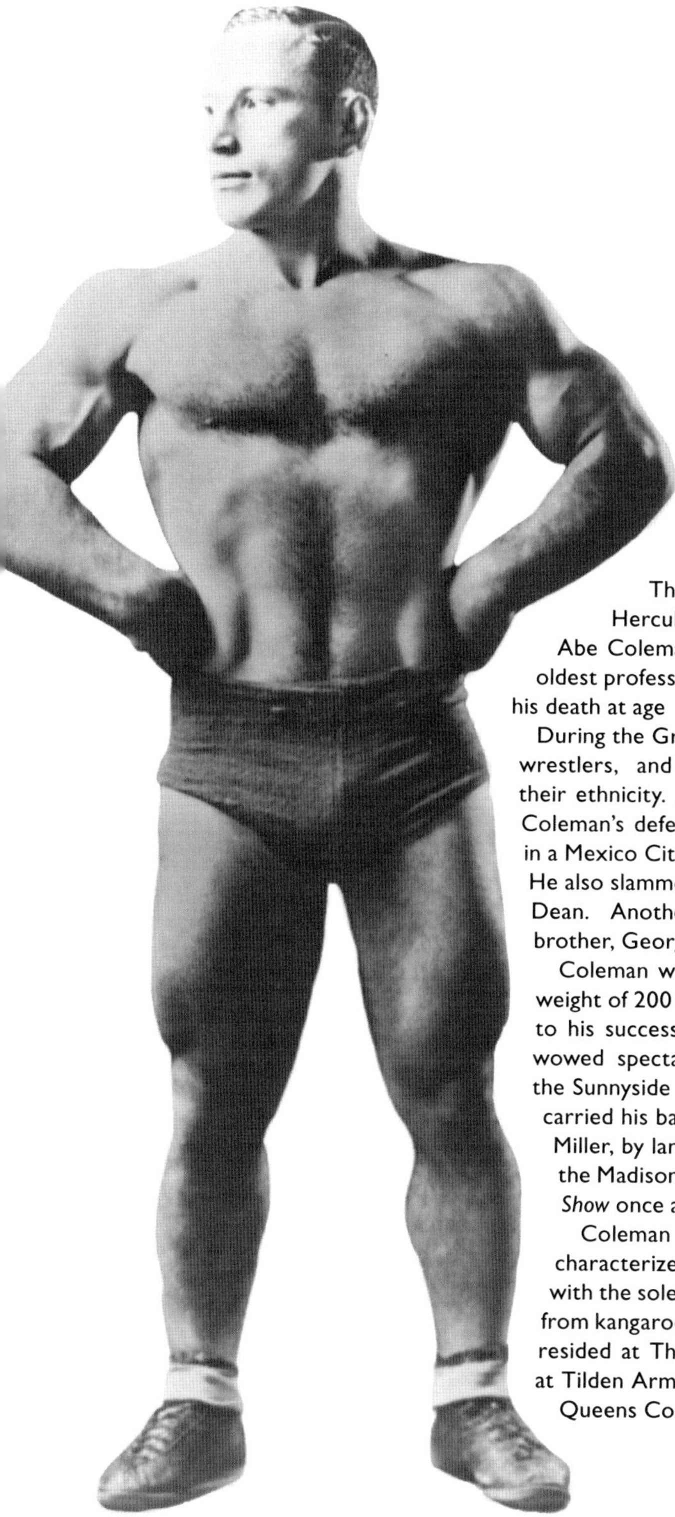

Abe Coleman

The "Jewish Tarzan" and the "Hebrew Hercules" is in the ring! Forest Hills resident Abe Coleman (1905–2007) was recognized as the oldest professional wrestler worldwide at the time of his death at age 101.

During the Great Depression, there were few Jewish wrestlers, and athletes were often promoted by their ethnicity. A wrestling highlight in the 1930s was Coleman's defeat of "the Golden Greek" Jim Londos in a Mexico City bullring in front of 60,000 spectators. He also slammed 465-pound opponent Man Mountain Dean. Another opponent was Shirley Temple's brother, George Temple.

Coleman was only five feet, three inches, but his weight of 200 pounds and 18-inch biceps contributed to his success in approximately 2,000 matches. He wowed spectators at Madison Square Garden and the Sunnyside Arena, and Mickey Rooney sometimes carried his bag. In 1936, he met his future wife, June Miller, by landing in her lap after being tossed from the Madison Square Garden ring. *The Jackie Gleason Show* once asked Coleman to appear.

Coleman coined the "dropkick," which is characterized by a wrestler kicking the opponent with the soles of both feet. His inspiration stemmed from kangaroos he spotted on an Australian tour. He resided at The Traymore at 110-34 73rd Road and at Tilden Arms at 73-20 Austin Street. (Courtesy of Queens Community Board 6.)

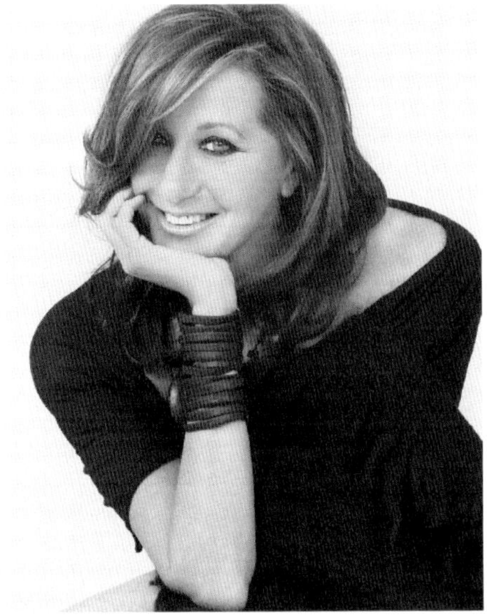

Donna Karan

Born in Forest Hills in 1948, Donna Karan rose to become a world-recognized fashion designer who produced the DKNY clothing label. Her outlook not only revolves around clothes, but also lifestyles. She applies a modern system of dressing, based on her "7 Easy Pieces" concept of interchangeable fashion items working in unison to create a wardrobe from day to evening, weekday to weekend, season to season.

She was the first American recipient of the Fashion Group International's Superstar Award and the recipient of the Council of Fashion Designers of America's Lifetime Achievement Award.
She founded the Urban Zen Foundation, which focuses on well-being, the empowering of children, and preserving cultures. (Photograph by Ruven Afanador.)

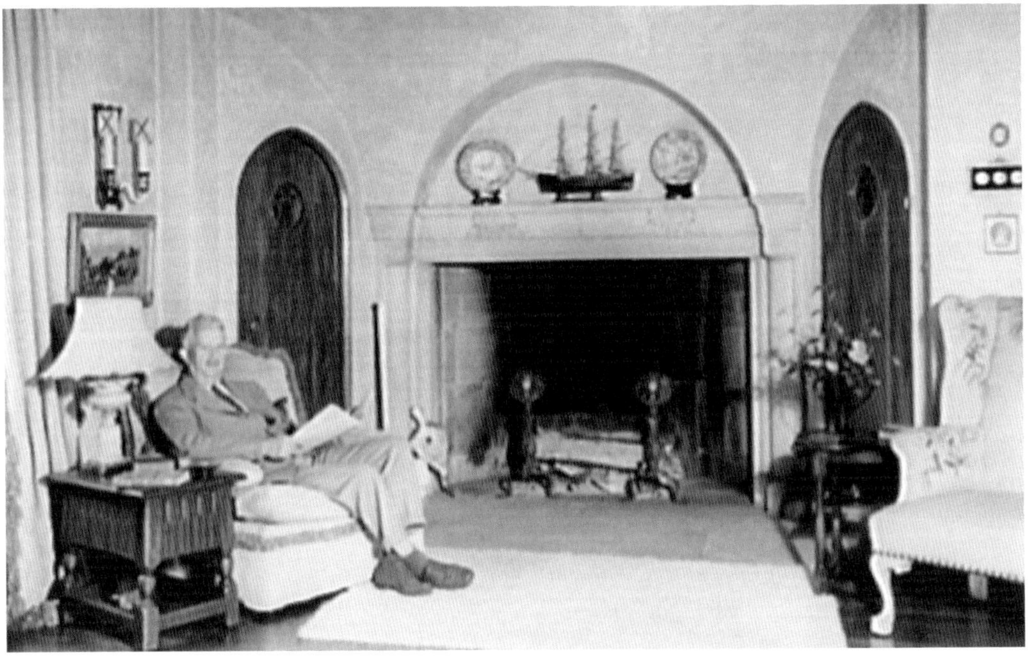

Albert Phelps Armour

Industrialist Albert Phelps Armour (born in 1882) wore many hats. During World War I, he supervised the construction of 188 airplanes, or one per day. Shortly after, Armour and partner Maurice Turner invented folding telephone booths and founded the Turner-Armour Company, which distributed 100 booths daily. He manufactured the battery for a submarine used by Theodore Roosevelt, and created the first ignition batteries for automobiles.

Armour supervised the construction of his Forest Hills Gardens mansion, Granston Tower at 123 Greenway North, which earned an architectural award from the Queens Chamber of Commerce in 1927. He later lived in The Livingston at 68-60 108th Street. Armour served as director of Boulevard Bank in Forest Hills, performed in musicals, and taught terpsichorean art. (Courtesy of Library of Congress.)

Ernie Grunfeld

Ernie Grunfeld (born 1955) is the president of the Washington Wizards and formerly was president of the New York Knicks. As a player, coach, executive, and broadcaster, he draws upon 35 years of experience with the National Basketball Association. He played professionally for the Milwaukee Bucks, Kansas City, and the New York Knicks. Once residing in The Essex House at 111-15 75th Avenue, he graduated from Russell Sage Junior High School and Forest Hills High School. (Courtesy of Queens Community Board 6.)

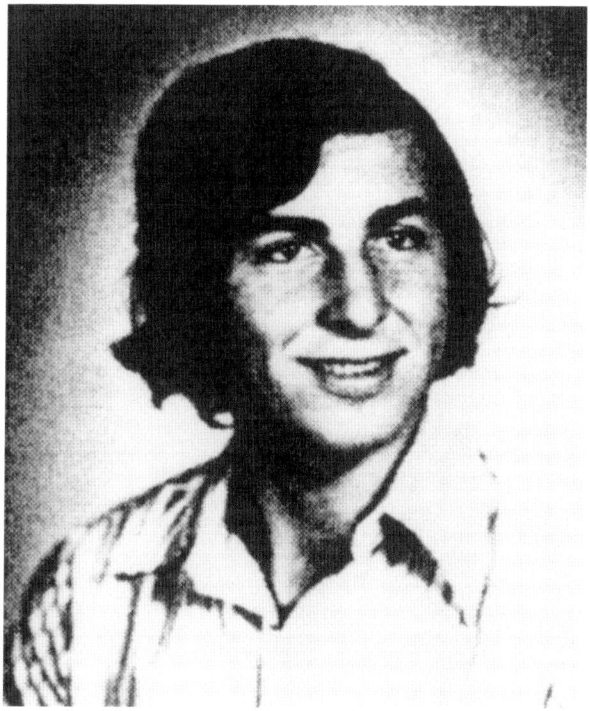

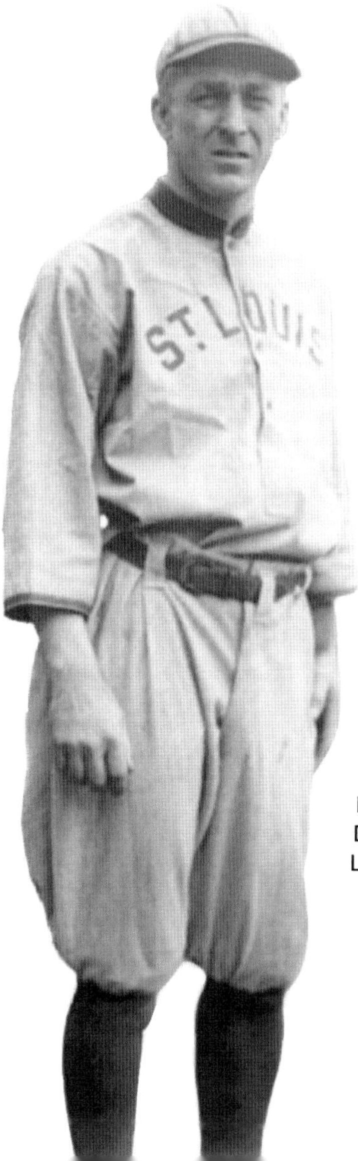

Branch Rickey

Branch Rickey (1881–1965) made his home at 34 Greenway South and was a member of the Church-in-the-Gardens. From 1906 to 1907, he was a catcher for the New York Yankees and the St. Louis Browns. He revolutionized Major League Baseball in 1919 by inventing the farm system, which trained and advanced players. By 1942, he was president and general manager of the Brooklyn Dodgers.

In 1945, he once again achieved a historic first by signing African American player Jackie Robinson and breaking Major League Baseball's color barrier. Shortly after, Rickey became a spokesman for civil rights. He was inducted into the Baseball Hall of Fame in 1967. The baseball careers of Joe Medwick and Dizzy and Paul Dean owed much to his influence. (Courtesy of Library of Congress.)

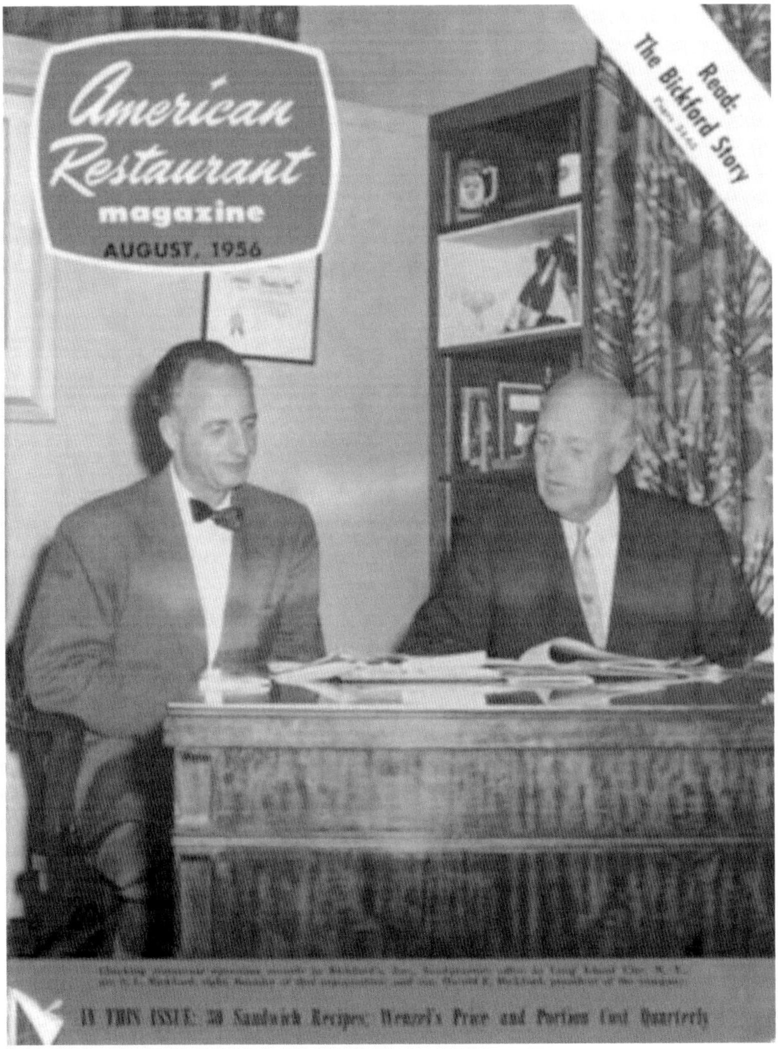

Bickford's

Bickford's, known for "Good Food, Quick Service," was a restaurant chain that had a successful run from 1921 to 1982. Its founder was Samuel Longley Bickford (1885–1959, pictured at right). His son Harold Evangeline Bickford (1910–1997, left) was president. Their Forest Hills Gardens address was 35 Wendover Road. A Bickford's diner was located on Woodhaven Boulevard in Rego Park. Before Starbucks, Americans enjoyed a cup of Bickford's Coffee. Bickford's even expanded nationally.

Bickford's had its own brand-name plane. "During Thanksgiving and Christmas, Bickford's would drop packages of food to lighthouse keepers along the New England coast," said Jeffrey S. Bickford, Harold's son.

The Bickford's culture was captured in Woody Allen's play *Death Knocks*, Alfred Hitchcock's film *The Wrong Man* featuring Henry Fonda, and in *The Seven Year Itch*, where Bickford's neon sign is in the background seconds before Marilyn Monroe stood over a subway vent with her skirt flying.

Jeffrey explained, "Beginning in the mid-1960s, Bickford's food and service was replaced by a competing menu of hamburger and French fries, served by part-time employees. With that change in America, away went a wider menu of healthy food, prepared by Bickford's, as if home cooked." (Courtesy of Jeffrey S. Bickford.)

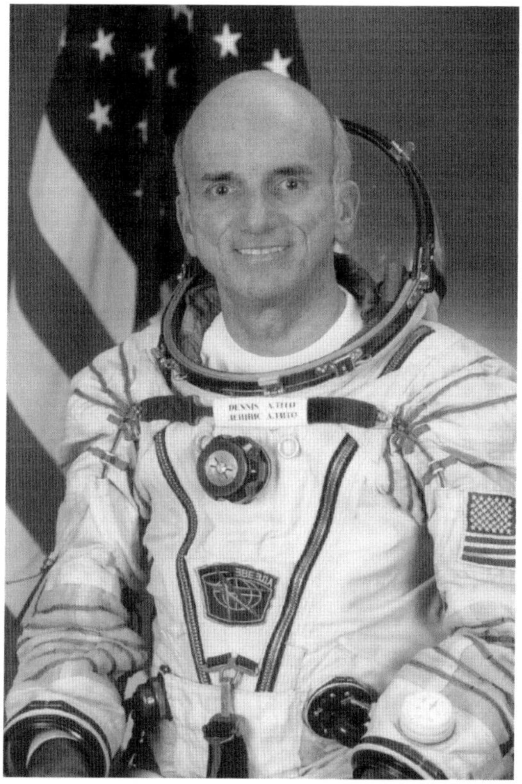

Dennis Tito

In 2001, Dennis Tito (born 1940) became the world's first paying space tourist when he flew aboard a Soyuz spacecraft to the International Space Station with a Russian crew.

Tito's career originated as a rocket scientist. While being employed by the Jet Propulsion Laboratory in the 1960s, he utilized computing technologies to plot the trajectories for the Mariner spacecraft mission to Mars.

Tito is the founder, chairman, and chief executive officer of Wilshire Associates. He launched the Wilshire 5000 Total Market Index, which is the broadest measure of the US securities markets, and assisted in the development of the quantitative investment analysis field. Raised at 94-05 Continental Avenue, Tito is a Forest Hills High School graduate. (Photograph by Marsel Gubaydullin.)

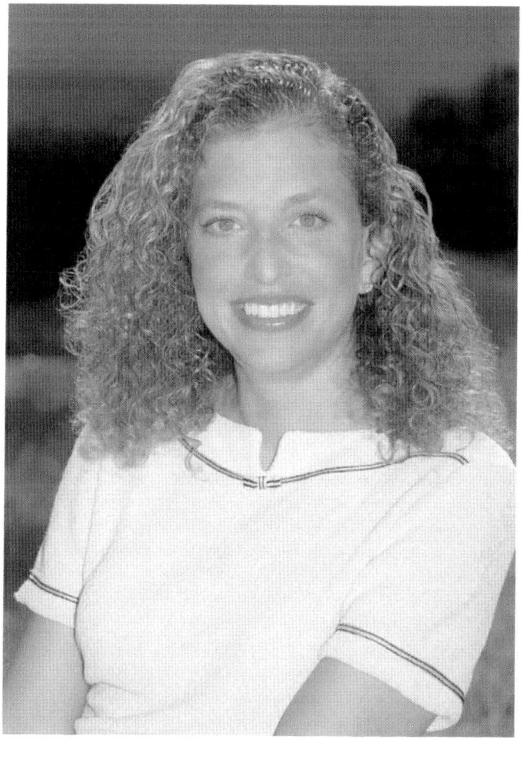

Debbie Wasserman Schultz

This Forest Hills native (born 1966) became the first Jewish congresswoman elected from Florida, representing the 23rd Congressional District. Schultz is a strong advocate for healthcare, Medicare, Social Security, children, education, women's rights, homeland security, and anti-Semitism. In 2005, *The Forward*, a national Jewish newspaper, named her one of the 50 most influential leaders in the American Jewish community. (Courtesy of the US Congress.)

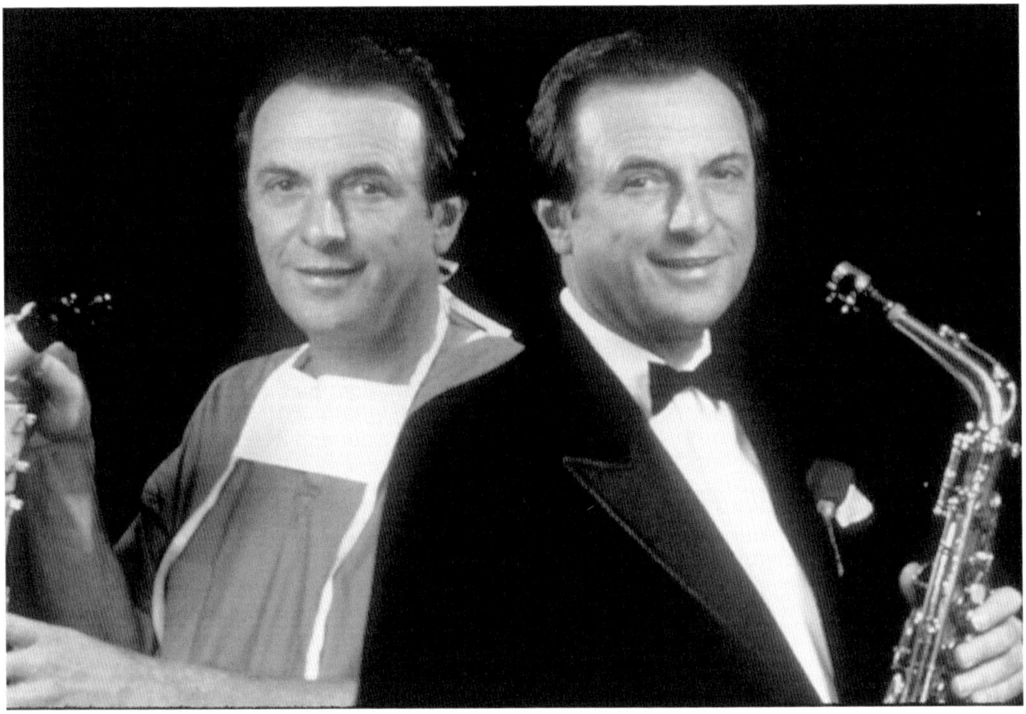

Dr. Charles D. Kelman

Dr. Charles D. Kelman (1930–2004) was a Forest Hills High School graduate who lived at 69-49 Groton Street. As an ophthalmologist, he revolutionized the removal of cataracts through Kelman phacoemulsification. It simplified the process from a 10-day hospital stay to today's outpatient procedure. By night, he was a singer, jazz saxophonist, and a clarinetist, also noted for stand-up. He played first clarinet with the Forest Hill High School orchestra, which was where he formed a band that played for dances and parties. Burt Bacharach was his pianist. Dr. Kelman took the stage at Carnegie Hall and on *The Tonight Show with Johnny Carson*. His awards include the National Medal of Technology from Pres. George H.W. Bush, the first Innovator's Award in Ophthalmology, and the Pisart Award from Lighthouse International. *Through My Eyes* (1985) is his autobiography. (Courtesy of the Dr. Charles and Ann Kelman Foundation.)

Cazzie Lee Russell

Cazzie Lee Russell (born 1944), a professional basketball player and coach, lived in Park City Estates at 61-25 98th Street. He spent five seasons with the New York Knicks from 1966 to 1971. He was voted one of the 100 Legends of the IHSA Boys Basketball Tournament in 2006. (Courtesy of the University of Michigan.)

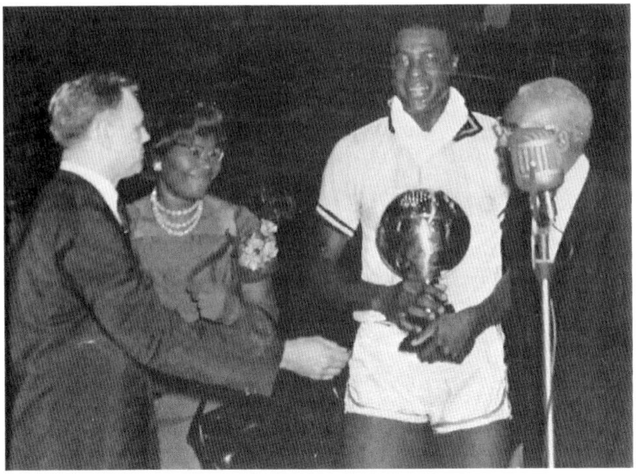

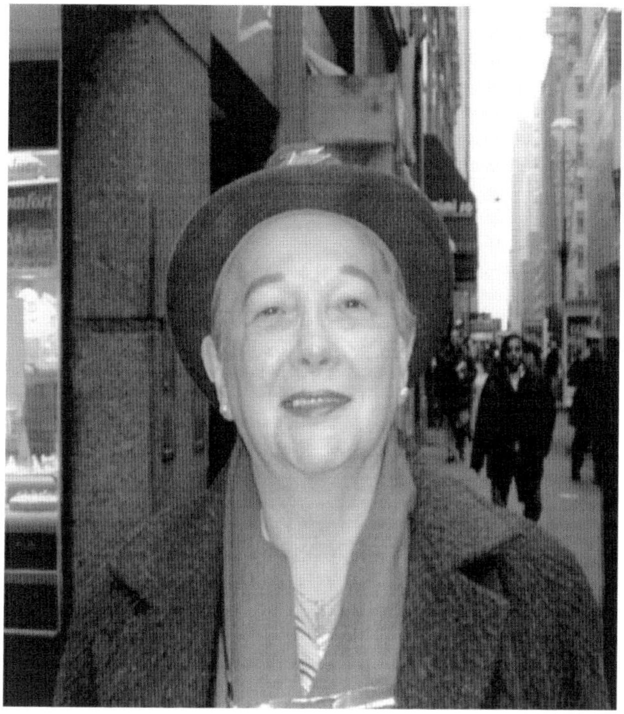

Ella Perlman Weisner
Great-aunt of author Michael H. Perlman and a former Forest Hills resident, Ella Perlman Weisner (1921–2002) was one of the earliest female diamond cutters, brokers, and Diamond Dealers Club members in a male-dominated industry in New York City's Diamond District. Her son Alan Weisner explained, "She arrived from Holland without a dime in her pocket, but as a hard worker who was diligent and persistent, she made a life for herself. She was incredibly skillful at evaluating stones, and could see their value very quickly." From the mid-1940s until her passing, she worked on 47th Street. (Courtesy of Alan Weisner.)

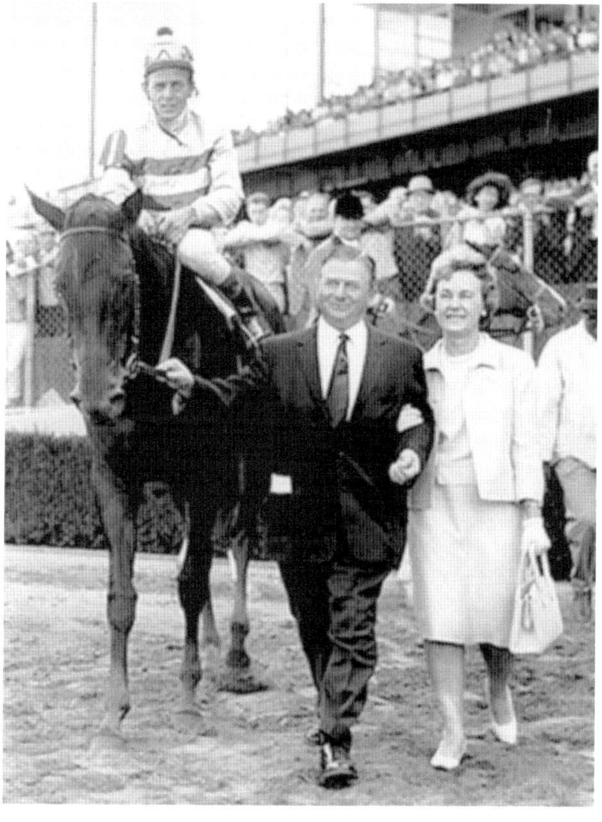

Ethel D. Jacobs and Hirsch Jacobs
The Forest Hills Gardens was home to the three-time leading Thoroughbred racehorse owner and breeder Ethel D. Jacobs (1910–2001) and her husband, Hirsch Jacobs (1904–1970), the world's foremost trainer who saddled more winners than anyone in the sport. In 1936, he saddled 177 victories and had 84 horses, which ran 632 times. One of many notable wins featured her horse Stymie, who was presented the Empire City Gold Cup at Belmont Park in 1947. Many of Ethel's horses were inducted into the US Racing Hall of Fame, and Stymie retired as the world's leading moneymaker. (Author's collection.)

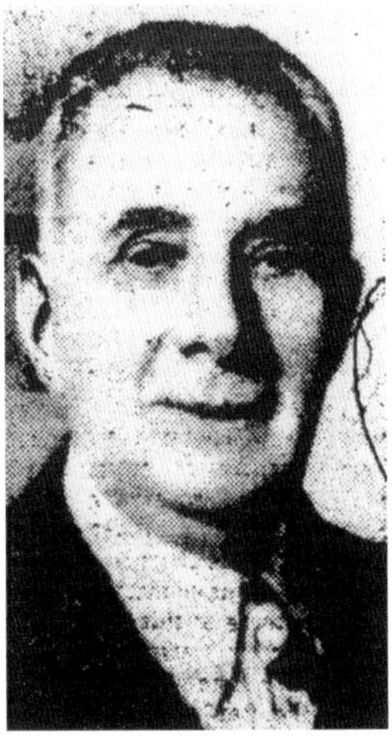

Eugene Schoen

A leading achiever of modern design was Eugene Schoen (1880–1957), who resided at 30 Olive Place in the Forest Hills Gardens. This Columbia University graduate was an architect and interior designer who designed Rockefeller Plaza interiors, several branches of the Public National Bank of New York, and his own gallery, known as the Parke-Bernet Galleries, which made a major impact on Manhattan culture. Also a furniture, rugs, and textiles designer, he was presented with the opportunity to partake in contemporary design exhibitions, and his industrial design works were featured at the Metropolitan Museum of Art. In 1931, he received the Gold Medal of the Architectural League. (Courtesy of Queens Community Board 6.)

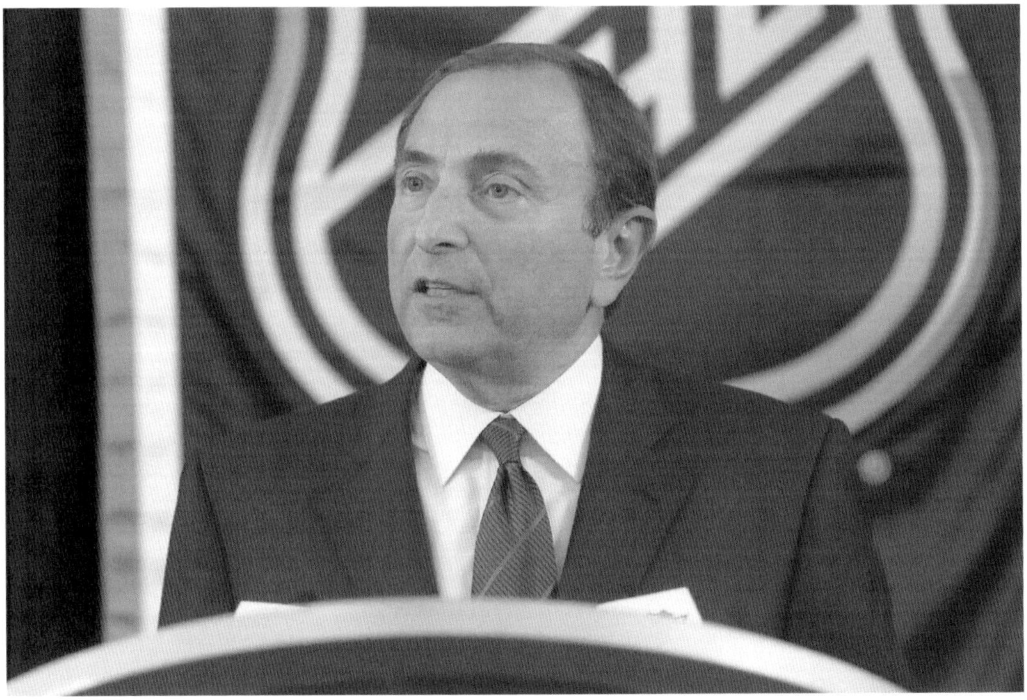

Gary Bettman

For over two decades, former Forest Hills resident Gary Bettman has served as commissioner of the National Hockey League. Reflecting upon his education at Public School 175, Public School 174, Russell Sage Junior High School, and Forest Hills High School, he stated "Those schools helped prepare me for what would lie ahead." He reminisced, "I would go to Rangers games at the old Madison Square Garden on Eighth Avenue and get in with my 'G.O.' card for 50 cents. I would go up to the balcony, eat my sandwich, do my homework, and wait for the game to start." In Forest Hills, he embraced the accessibility to the US Open at the West Side Tennis Club, and how one can get the best pizza, egg creams, deli, and outstanding knishes at Knish Nosh. (Courtesy of Getty Images–National Hockey League.)

The Hardart Family in Forest Hills

A sum of 180 Horn & Hardart Automat self-service cafeterias once dotted New York and Philadelphia, and served 800,000 patrons daily. Joseph Horn and Frank Hardart Sr. founded an American institution in 1902. Many New Yorkers retain fond memories of inserting nickels into distinctive glass compartments, opening a door, and enjoying a fresh sandwich, entrée, or pie in an Art Nouveau or Art Deco ambiance with a massive picture window admitting natural light. Fresh drip-brewed coffee emerged from a lion's or dolphin's mouth. Forest Hills offered small-scale Horn & Hardart Retail Shops at 71-63 Austin Street (pictured) and 116-63 Queens Boulevard. Frank Hardart Jr. (1884–1972), vice president of Horn & Hardart, resided at 188 Ascan Avenue and 64 Dartmouth Street in Forest Hills. (Courtesy of John W. Romas Collection of Horn & Hardart Memorabilia and Lisa Hurwitz.)

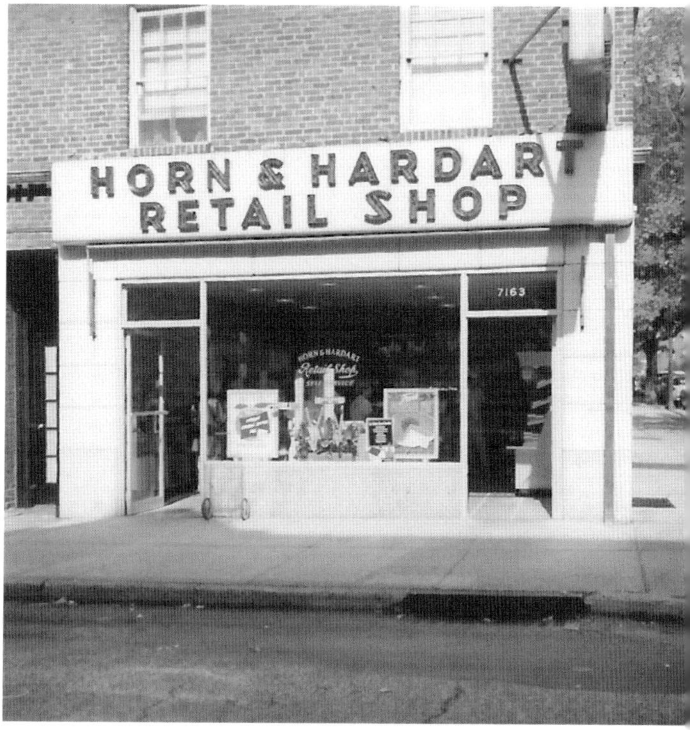

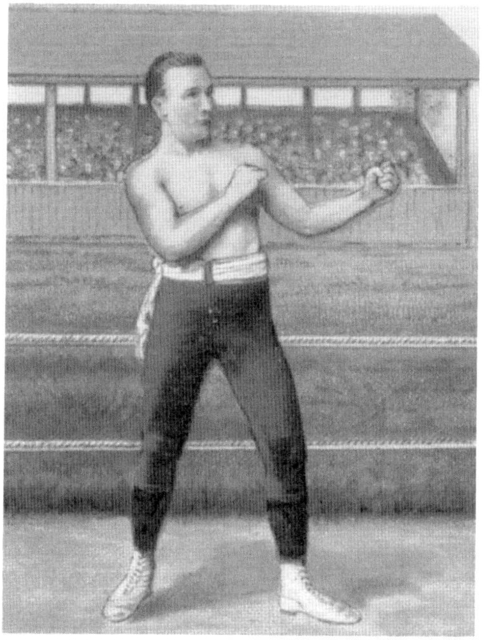

Jack McAuliffe

"The Napoleon of the Ring," Jack McAuliffe (1866–1937) was Lightweight Champion of the World from 1886 to 1893. Immigrating from Cork, Ireland, he resided at the Tilden Arms at 73-20 Austin Street. He fought his most influential battle against Jemmy Carney, which consisted of 74 rounds to a draw. At five feet, six inches, he was a two-handed fighter with "cat-quick reflexes" and straight blows, consisting of a left jab and a left-right combination. Inducted into the Ring Boxing Hall of Fame in 1954 and the International Boxing Hall of Fame in 1995, he was one of nine titleholders to retire undefeated. Jack McAuliffe is pictured here as part of the Mecca Cigarettes Champion Athlete & Prize Fighter Series in 1910. (Author's collection.)

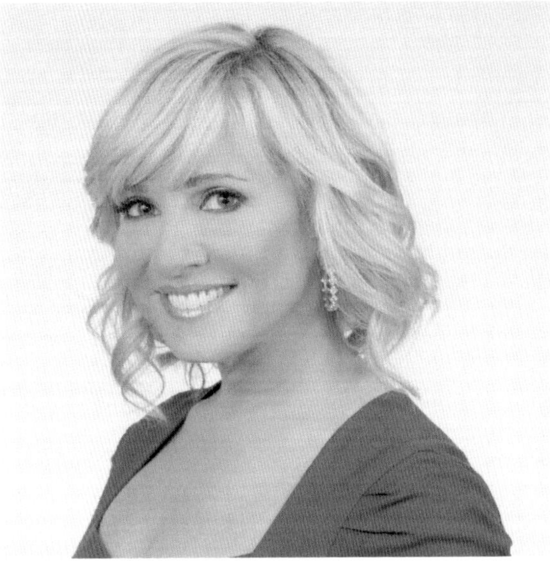

Jamie Nell Colby

Born in 1970 in Forest Hills, Jamie Nell Colby is a co-anchor of *America's News Headquarters* on the FOX News Channel. Her coverage of major national and international news stories includes Hurricane Sandy's aftermath, the Boston Marathon bombing, the Sandy Hook massacre, the inauguration of Pope Francis, and the resignation of Pope Benedict XVI. She was presented with the National Edward R. Murrow Award for her coverage of 9/11 and the Gracie Allen Award for investigative reporting. (Courtesy of Fox News Channel.)

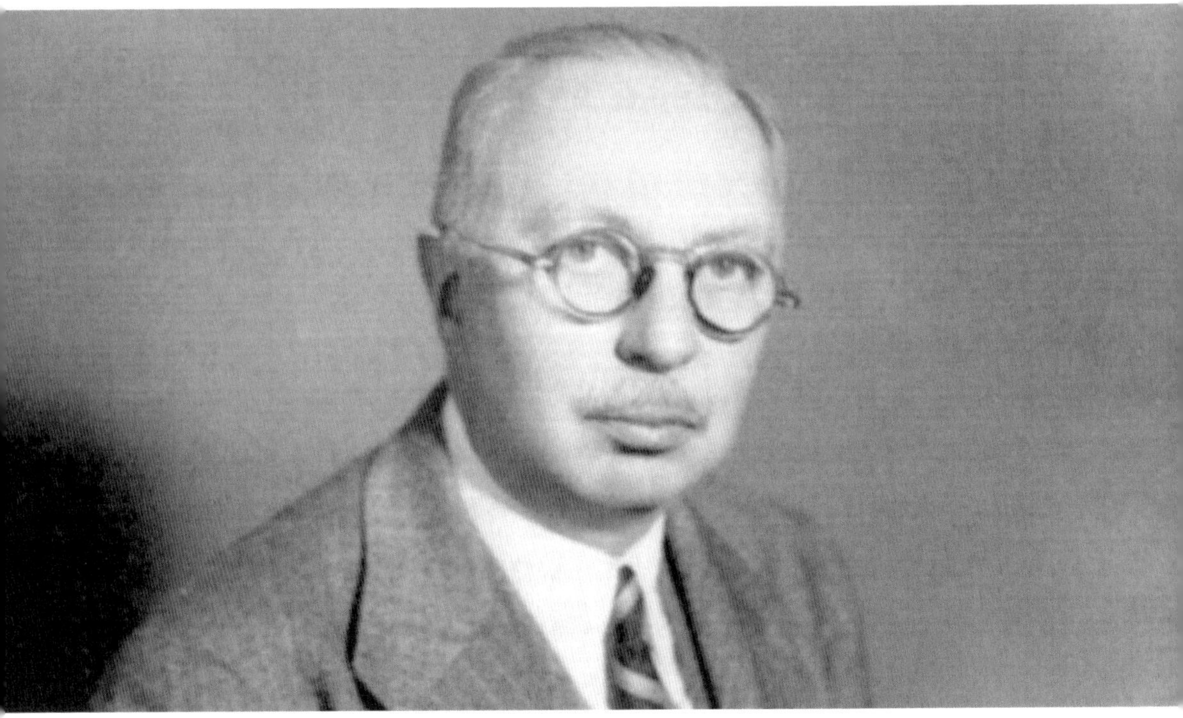

John Vincent Lawless Hogan

Pioneer engineer John Vincent Lawless Hogan (1890–1960) of 239 Greenway South in Forest Hills created the first high-fidelity radio station, W2XR, which was licensed as a 250-watt experimental station in 1934. This evolved into the 10,000-watt WQXR in New York City in 1936, which offered Classical music. He also invented single dial radio tuning. His facsimile transmission system transcribed a four-column newspaper page with illustrations at 500 words per minute, which benefited radio. Hogan was a founder and builder of the Institute of Radio Engineers (IRE), and in 1956 was awarded the IRE Medal of Honor. (Courtesy of WQXR Archives.)

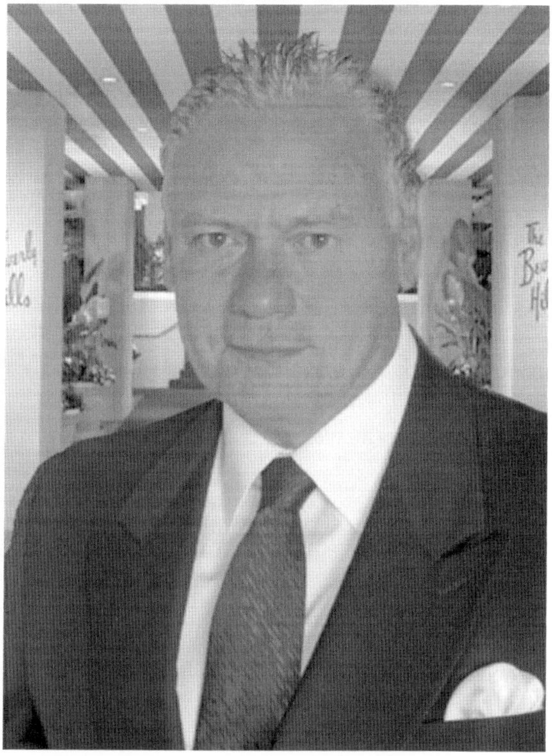

Julio Rumbaut

Two of Julio Rumbaut's proudest accomplishments are founding and presiding over Telemundo of Florida, as well as being a father to his six children. He was also cofounder and vice president of WSUA-AM and vice president of WQBA-AM and FM in Miami. He founded Rumbaut & Company, which is an internationally recognized media advisory and consulting firm.

While a senior at Forest Hills High School, he worked for *The David Frost Show* after classes. He explained, "As an immigrant from Cuba, my life was enriched by living in Forest Hills from 1961 to 1970 with other first and second-generation immigrants, many of whom had the same struggles and sought the same goals as my family." He made his home at Verona Estates at 65-35 Yellowstone Boulevard and at Walden Terrace. (Courtesy of Julio Rumbaut.)

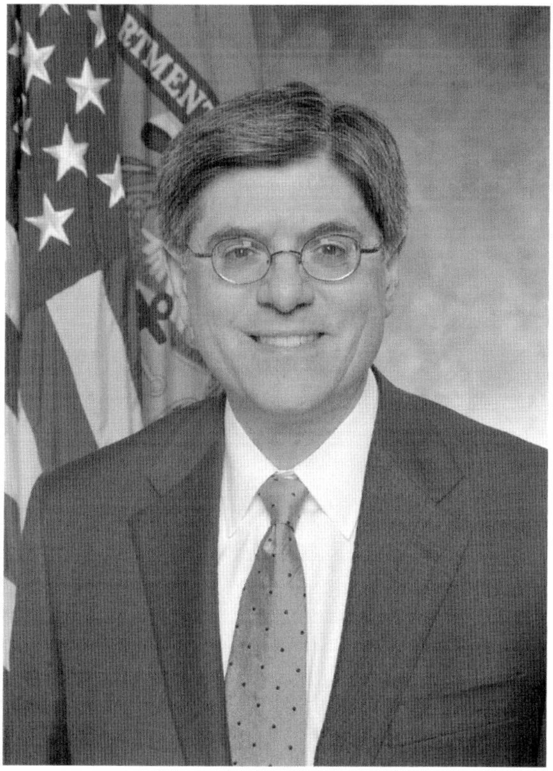

Jacob Jack Lew

Forest Hills High School graduate Jacob Jack Lew (born 1955) is a government administrator and attorney who is the 76th secretary of the treasury. From 2012 to 2013, he served as the 25th White House chief of staff under the Obama administration. From 1998 to 2001, he led the Clinton administration's budget team and served as a member of the National Security Council. He helped design Americorps, the national service program, while serving as special assistant to President Clinton from 1993 to 1994. (Courtesy of the US Treasury Department.)

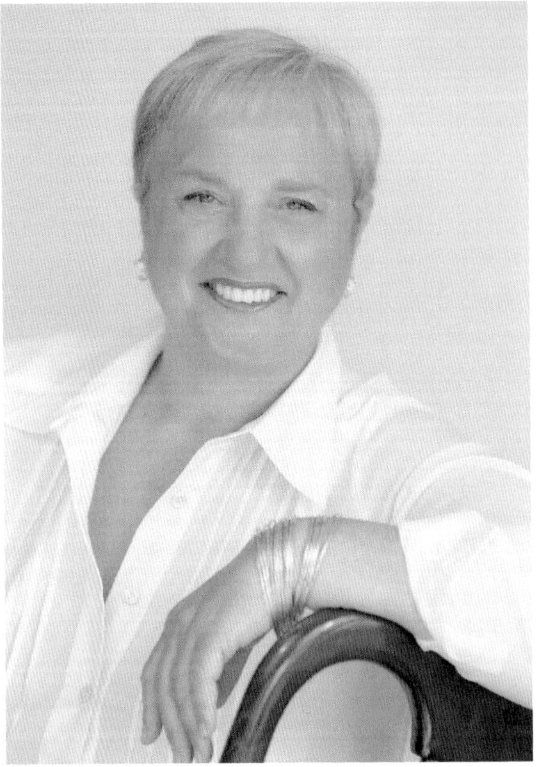

Lidia Matticchio Bastianich
From 1971 to 1981, Buonavia was a quaint and highly regarded Italian restaurant at 101-19 Queens Boulevard in Forest Hills. Lidia Matticchio Bastianich (born 1947), a native of Istria, is a self-taught chef and restaurateur. "Buonavia translates as 'on a good road,' since Queens Boulevard was a good road to be on. I love nurturing and feeding people," said Bastianich, who replanted her passion in Manhattan after undergoing two expansions. She opened Felidia (1981), Becco (1992), Esca (2000), Del Posto (2006), and Eataly (2010). She fed notables ranging from Pope Benedict XVI to Woody Allen to Meryl Streep. Also an author and television personality, she received the 2012–2013 Emmy for Outstanding Culinary Host for her PBS cooking show *Lidia's Italy.* (Courtesy of Diana DeLucia.)

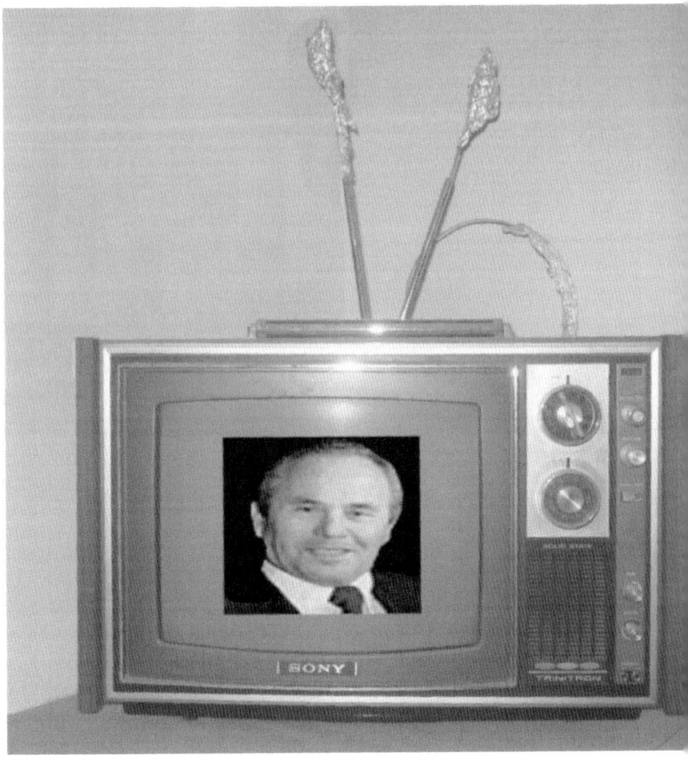

Marvin Middlemark
Self-made millionaire Marvin Middlemark (1919–1989) of the Anita Apartments in Rego Park invented the dipole antenna in 1953, better known as "rabbit ears." It boosted television reception across America, contributing to its late 1950s to 1960s boom. As a philanthropist, he donated millions to educational foundations and New York homeless shelters. As an animal enthusiast, he kept a chimpanzee on his Long Island estate and brought miniature horses and donkeys from Argentina to the United States. His smallest horse, Rembrandt, earned its name from his brand of indoor antennas. (Author's collection.)

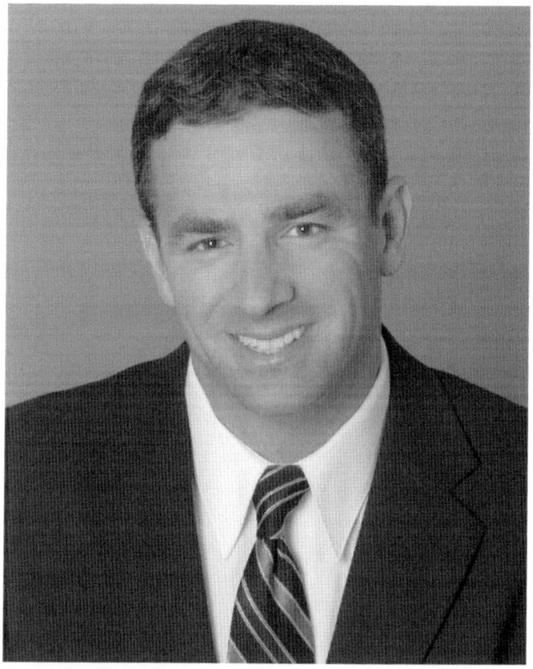

Roger Clark

Reporter Roger Clark is a staple at *NY 1 News* since 2001. Growing up in Forest Hills, he holds fond memories of Sandy's Surf Delicatessen, egg creams at John's Candy Store, and Knish Nosh, which he continues to patronize. He ushered at the Forest Hills Theatre, played in the Forest Hills Little League, and was a regular league bowler at Hollywood Lanes on Queens Boulevard and 67th Avenue. Watching news and sports, he knew he wanted to be on television or the radio. "I was always a talker and loved writing and telling stories," stated Clark. Reminiscing about his work at Alexander's Department Store, he said, "I constantly got in trouble for putting the radio on in the stockroom." He lived at 99-44 67th Road and in The Brussels at 98-01 67th Avenue. (Courtesy of *NY 1 News*.)

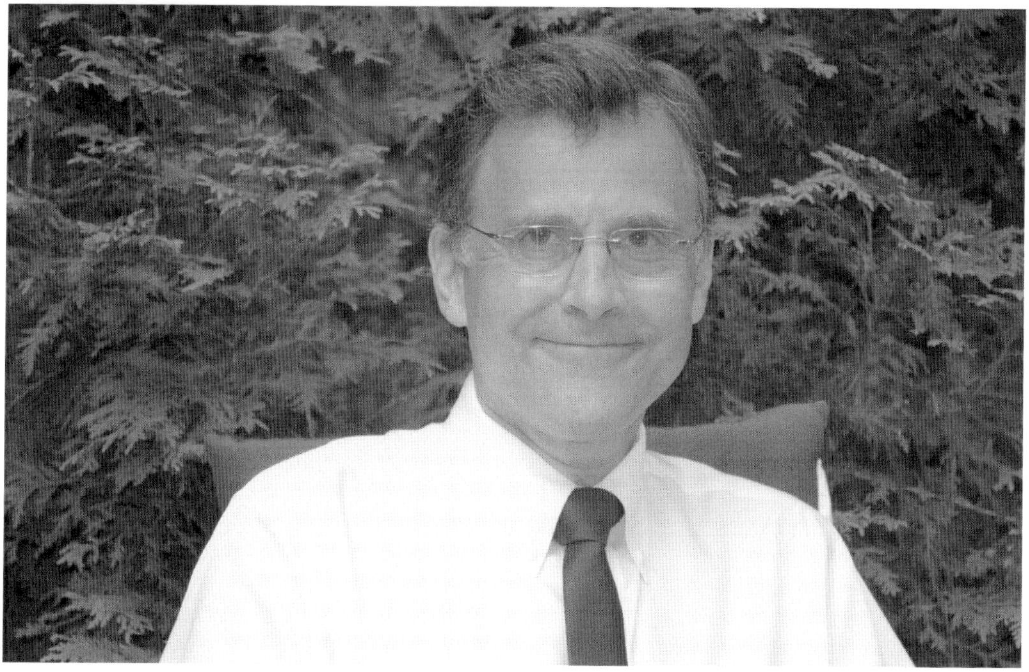

Dr. Robert Birnbaum

Success continues in the family with architect Philip Birnbaum's son, Dr. Robert J. Birnbaum. He is the founding director of the Massachusetts General Hospital Psychiatry Academy, the knowledge translation research director for the Massachusetts General Hospital Research Academy, and runs the healthcare provider education and training resources for Partners HealthCare. He is also an assistant professor of psychiatry at Harvard Medical School. (Courtesy of Dr. Robert J. Birnbaum.)

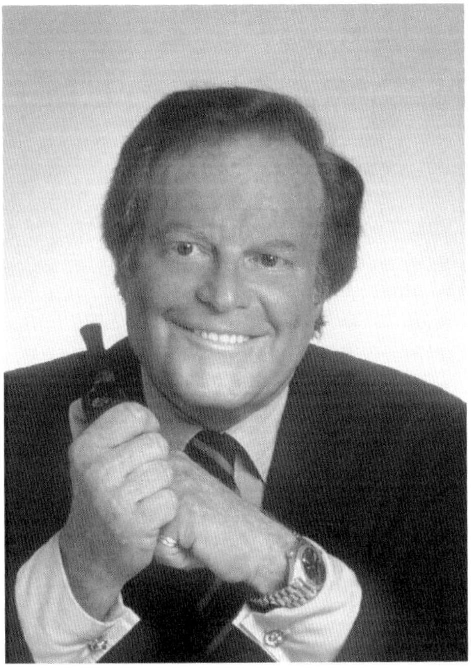

Roone Arledge

Modern American television would not quite be the same without the achievements of Roone Arledge (1931–2002). This Forest Hills native created *20/20*, *Nightline*, *ABC World News*, *Monday Night Football*, and *Primetime*. He was the president of ABC Sports between 1968 and 1986, and the president of *ABC News* between 1977 and 1998. His behind the scenes work resulted in the coverage of definitive moments such as the Olympics and the matches of Muhammad Ali. Arledge was the recipient of 37 Emmy Awards and was designated by *Life* magazine as one of the 100 Most Important Americans of the 20th Century. (Courtesy of American Broadcasting Companies Inc.)

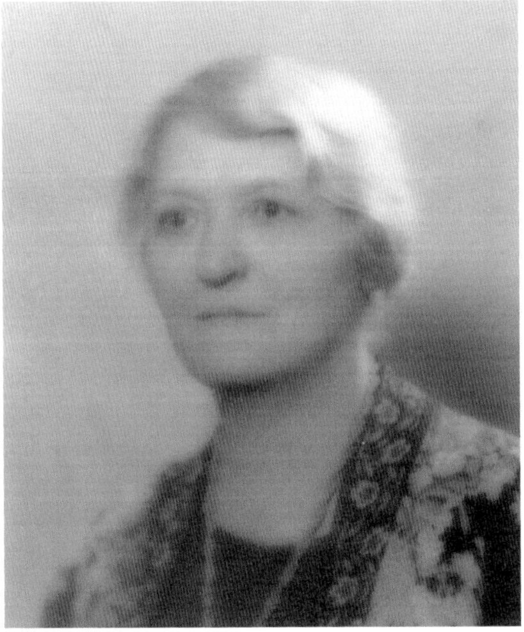

Sally Lucas Jean

Pioneer health educator Sally Lucas Jean (1878–1971) served as organizer of the Child Health Organization of America in 1918 and as advisor to the US Indian Service. As a health education consultant and extensive traveler, she developed school health educational programs from her Forest Hills home at 61 Ingram Street to parts of the United States, Asia, the West Indies, and Europe. Thousands of children were spared from ailments due to her diligence. (Courtesy of Queens Community Board 6.)

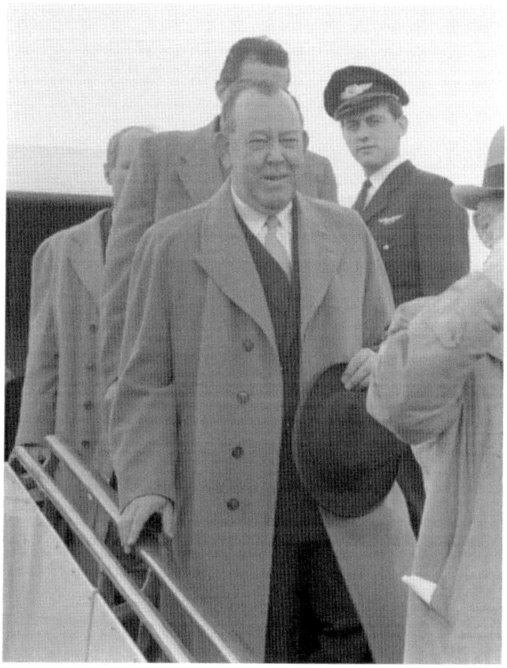

Trygve Lie

Norway native Trygve Halvdan Lie (1896–1968) was the first secretary-general of the United Nations, which he served between 1946 and 1952. Lie led the United Nations during the time of the early Cold War and the Korean War. In 1946, the United Nations financed his residency in a 14-room castle-like Forest Hills Gardens home, known as Granston Tower at 123 Greenway North, where Pres. Dwight D. Eisenhower was among his guests. Lie was a West Side Tennis Club member. (Courtesy of the Dutch National Archives.)

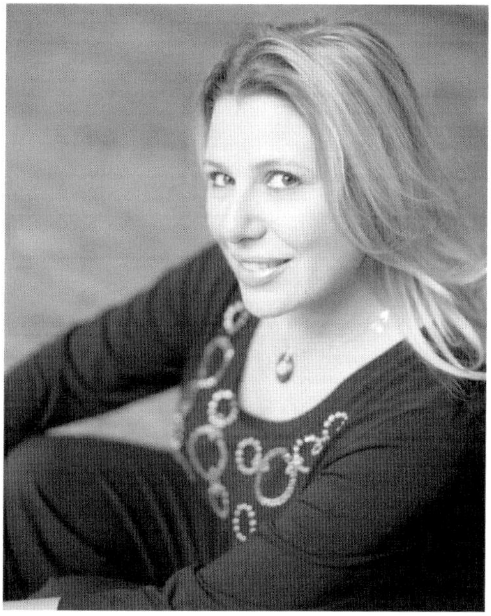

Susan Polgar

"My chess career took me to over 50 countries," said former Forest Hills resident Susan Polgar, a winner of four Women's World Championships and the sole World Chess Champion in history to win the triple crown. She is the founder of the Susan Polgar Foundation, which promotes chess and its educational, social, and competitive benefits throughout the United States for young residents, with an emphasis on females. She also directs the Susan Polgar Institute for Chess Excellence. She broke the gender barrier to qualify for the Men's World Championship Cycle in 1986 and coached a Collegiate Men's Division I team to consecutive national championships in 2011 and 2012. Her home was located at 67-76 Booth Street. (Courtesy of Susan Polgar.)

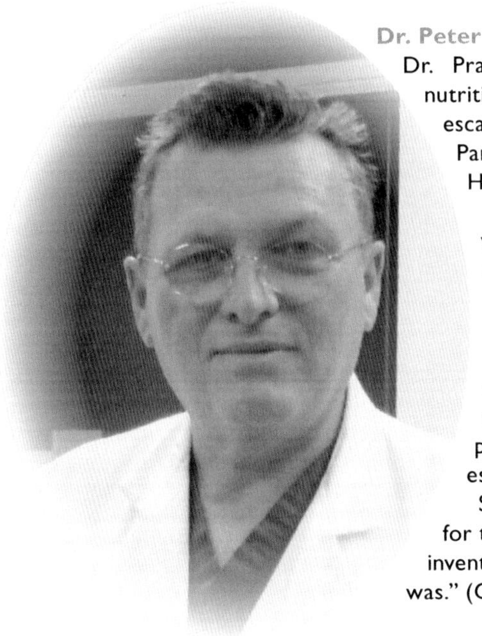

Dr. Peter Praeger

Dr. Praeger's Sensible Foods have enhanced America's nutrition since 1994. Dr. Peter Praeger (1947–2012) escaped the Hungarian Revolution in 1956, lived in Rego Park and Forest Hills, and graduated from Forest Hills High School in 1966.

As a cardiac surgeon, he was called a "miracle worker." "He operated on the sickest of patients that no other doctor would consider," stated his widow, Nurit Praeger. She expressed great pride in how he became the first to use mammary arteries instead of veins, conducted off-pump surgery (no heart-lung machine), and brought the LVAD (left-ventricular assist device) into his hospital to further save sick patients. He also engaged his passion for cooking to establish his food company.

She continued, "It was his true zest for life and zest for the lives of others, which allowed him to become the inventive, curious, compassionate, and successful man he was." (Courtesy of the Praeger family.)

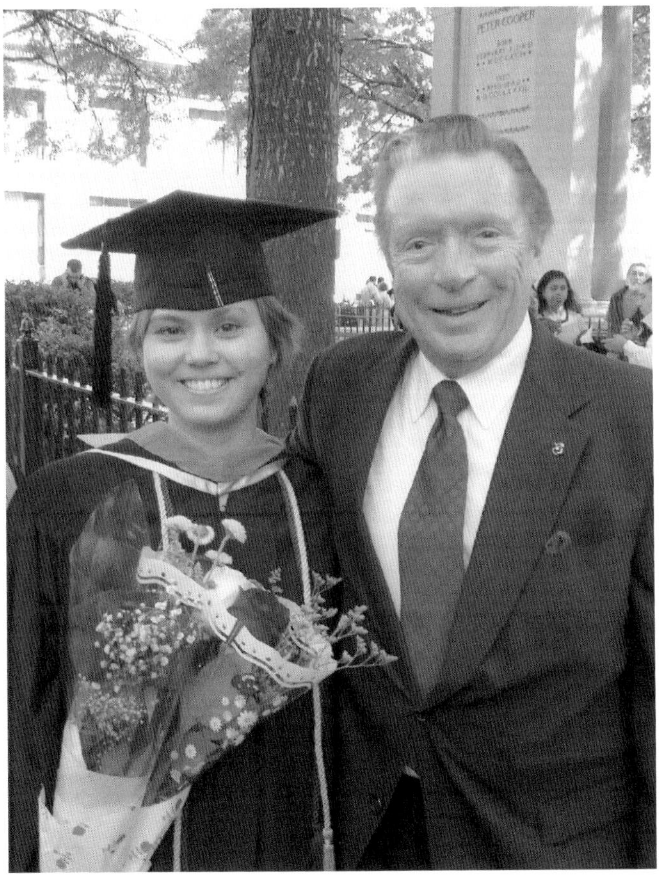

Ysrael Seinuk

Trump World Tower, the Lipstick Building, and the Condé Nast Building are a few of the many Manhattan skyscrapers that the prestigious structural engineer Ysrael Abraham Seinuk (1931–2010) of Forest Hills made possible. He was an expert at enhancing a site's structural integrity with reinforced concrete. His influence extended beyond Manhattan with Dubai's O-14 building. He was a respected 40-year professor of structural engineering at Cooper Union. He is pictured here with his student Jesicka Labud. (Courtesy of Jesicka Labud.)

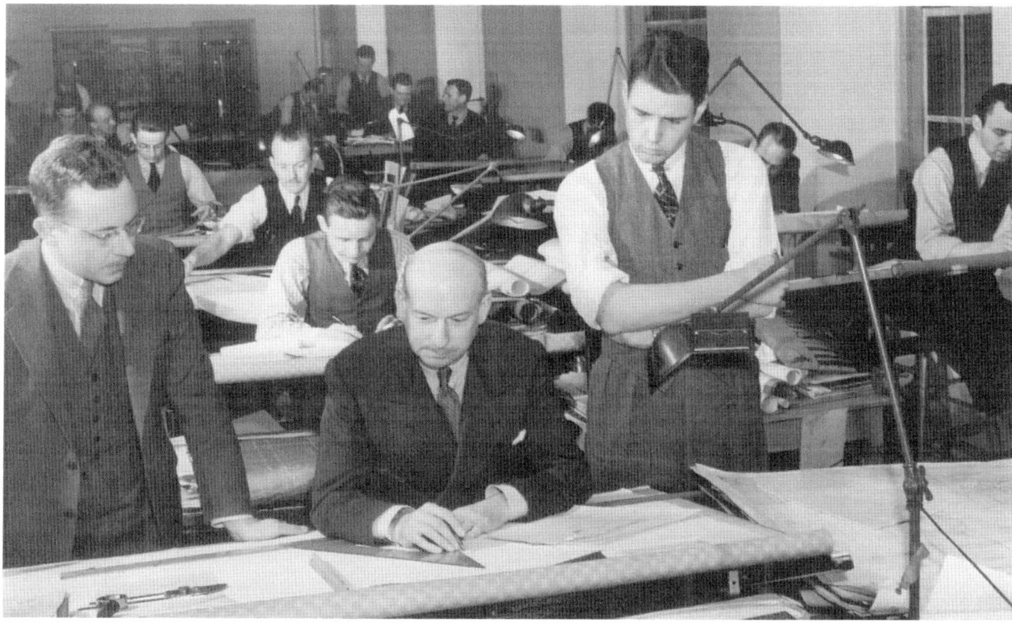

Walter Dorwin Teague

Industrial designer and illustrator Walter Dorwin Teague (1883–1960, pictured seated in front) was chairman of the Community Council of Forest Hills subcommittee, which coordinated the erection of the World War I Monument, unveiled in the Forest Hills Gardens in 1920 near his home at 83 Beechknoll Road. He made his mark on the Boeing 707 jet airliner interiors. As a member of the 1939 World's Fair design board, his work included the US Steel and Ford pavilions, and the introduction of the Art Moderne–style National Cash Register 100 model. At seven stories, it was deemed the world's largest active register, and was placed atop the NCR Building, where it tallied visitors. Among his numerous design masterpieces were the Art Deco–style Bantam Special Camera for Eastman Kodak, Steuben glassware, and the Bluebird Radio. (Courtesy of TEAGUE.)

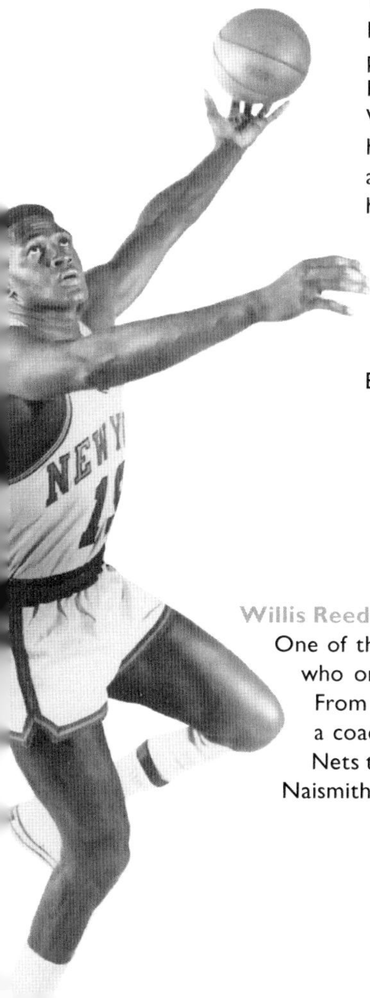

Willis Reed Jr.

One of the 50 greatest players in NBA history is Willis Reed Jr. (born 1942), who once resided at 61-35 98th Street in Park City Estates in Rego Park. From 1964 to 1974, he played with the New York Knicks, then served as a coach and as vice president of basketball operations for the New Jersey Nets to senior vice president of basketball. In 1982, he was inducted into the Naismith Memorial Basketball Hall of Fame. (Courtesy of New York Knicks.)

INDEX